How Google Tests Software

"James Whittaker has long had the pulse of the issues that are shaping testing practice. In the decade of the Cloud Transformation, this book is a must read not just for Googlers, but for all testers who want their practices to remain relevant, competitive, and meaningful."

—**Sam Guckenheimer**, Product Owner,
Visual Studio Strategy, Microsoft

"Google has consistently been an innovator in the app testing space—whether it's blending test automation with manual efforts, melding in-house and outsourced resources, or more recently, pioneering the use of in-the-wild testing to complement their in-the-lab efforts. This appetite for innovation has enabled Google to solve new problems and launch better apps.

In this book, James Whittaker provides a blueprint for Google's success in the rapidly evolving world of app testing."

—**Doron Reuveni**, CEO and Cofounder, uTest

"This book is a game changer, from daily releases to heads-up displays. James Whittaker takes a computer-science approach to testing that will be the standard for software companies in the future. The process and technical innovations we use at Google are described in a factual and entertaining style. This book is a must read for anyone involved in software development."

—**Michael Bachman**, Senior Engineering Manager
at Google Inc., AdSense/Display

"By documenting much of the magic of Google's test engineering practices, the authors have written the equivalent of the Kama Sutra for modern software testing."

—**Alberto Savoia**, Engineering Director, Google

"If you ship code in the cloud and want to build a strategy for ensuring a quality product with lots of happy customers, you must study and seriously consider the methods in this book."

—**Phil Waligora**, Salesforce.com

"James Whittaker is an inspiration and mentor to many people in the field of testing. We wouldn't have the talent or technology in this field without his contributions. I am consistently in awe of his drive, enthusiasm, and humor. He's a giant in the industry and his writing should be required reading for anyone in the IT industry."

—**Stewart Noakes**, Chairman TCL Group Ltd.,
United Kingdom

"I worked with James Whittaker during his time at Microsoft, and although I miss having him here at Microsoft, I knew he would do great things at Google. James, Jason Arbon, and Jeff Carollo have packed this book with innovative testing ideas, practical examples, and insights into the Google testing machine. Anyone with an ounce of curiosity about Google's approach to testing and quality or with the smallest desire to discover a few new ideas in testing will find value in these pages."

—**Alan Page**, Microsoft Xbox, and Author
of *How We Test Software at Microsoft*

How Google Tests Software

James Whittaker
Jason Arbon
Jeff Carollo

✦✦ Addison-Wesley

Upper Saddle River, NJ • Boston • Indianapolis • San Francisco
New York • Toronto • Montreal • London • Munich • Paris • Madrid
Capetown • Sydney • Tokyo • Singapore • Mexico City

The publisher offers excellent discounts on this book when ordered in quantity for bulk purchases or special sales, which may include electronic versions and/or custom covers and content particular to your business, training goals, marketing focus, and branding interests. For more information, please contact:

U.S. Corporate and Government Sales
(800) 382-3419
corpsales@pearsontechgroup.com

For sales outside the United States, please contact:

International Sales
international@pearson.com

Visit us on the Web: informit.com/aw

The Library of Congress cataloging-in-publication data is on file.

ISBN-13: 978-0-321-80302-3

ISBN-10: 0-321-80302-7

Text printed in the United States on recycled paper at Courier in Westford, Massachusetts.

Third Printing: December 2012

Publisher
Paul Boger

Executive Editor
Chris Guzikowski

Senior Development Editor
Chris Zahn

Managing Editor
Kristy Hart

Project Editor
Jovana San Nicolas-Shirley

Copy Editor
Ginny Bess Munroe

Indexer
Erika Millen

Proofreader
Mike Henry

Editorial Assistant
Olivia Basegio

Cover Designer
Anne Jones

Compositor
Gloria Schurick

To all testers at Google, Microsoft, and elsewhere who've made me think differently.
—James A. Whittaker

To my wife Heather and my children Luca, Mateo, Dante, and Odessa who thought I worked at Starbucks all this time.
—Jason Arbon

To Mom, Dad, Lauren, and Alex.
—Jeff Carollo

Table of Contents

Foreword by Alberto Savoia

Writing a foreword for a book you wish you had written yourself is a dubious honor; it's a bit like serving as best man for a friend who is about to spend the rest of his life with the girl *you* wanted to marry. But James Whittaker is a cunning guy. Before asking me if I'd be willing to write this preface, he exploited my weakness for Mexican food by treating me to a very nice dinner and plying me with more than a couple Dos Equis before he "popped the question." By the time this happened, I was as malleable and agreeable as the bowl of guacamole I had just finished. "*Si senor*," was pretty much all I could say. His ploy worked and here he stands with his book as his bride and I get to make the wedding speech.

As I said, he's one cunning guy.

So here we go…a preface to the book I wish I had written myself. Cue the mushy wedding music.

Does the world really need yet another software testing book, especially yet another software testing book from the prolific James Whittaker, whom I've publicly called "the Octomom[1] of test book publishing" on more than one occasion? Aren't there enough books out there describing the same old tired testing methodologies and dishing out dubious and dated advice? Well, there are enough of those books, but this book I am afraid is not one of them. That's why I wish I had written it myself. The world actually needs this particular testing book.

The Internet has dramatically changed the way most software is designed, developed, and distributed. Many of the testing best practices, embodied in any number of once popular testing books of yesteryear, are at best inefficient, possibly ineffective, and in some cases, downright counterproductive in today's environment. Things have been moving so fast in our industry that many of the software testing books written as recently as a few years ago are the equivalent of surgery books containing advice about leeches and skull drilling to rid the body of evil spirits; it would be best to recycle them into adult diapers to make sure they don't fall into the hands of the gullible.

Given the speed at which things are evolving in the software industry, I would not be too surprised if ten years from now this book will also be obsolete. But until the paradigm shifts again, *How Google Tests Software* gives you a very timely and applicable insider's view into how one of the world's most successful and fastest growing Internet companies deals with the unique challenges of software testing in the twenty-first century. James Whittaker and his coauthors have captured the very essence of how Google is successful at testing some of the most complicated and popular

---

1. Don't get the Octomom reference? Google it!

software of our times. I know this is the case because I've been there through the transition.

I first joined Google as engineering director in 2001. At the time, we had about two hundred developers and…a whopping *three* testers! My developers were already taking responsibility for testing their own code, but test-driven development and test automation tools such as JUnit were just entering the scene, so our testing was mostly *ad-hoc* and dependent on the diligence of the individual writing the code. But that was okay; we were a startup and we had to move fast and take risks or we couldn't compete with the big established players.

However, as the company grew in size and our products became more mission-critical for our users and customers (such as AdWords, one of the products I was responsible for, was quickly becoming a major source of monetizing websites), it became clear that we had to increase our focus and investment in testing. With only three testers, we had no choice but to get developers more involved in testing. Along with a few other Googlers, I introduced, taught, and promoted unit testing. We encouraged developers to make testing a priority and use tools such as JUnit to automate them. But adoption was slow and not everybody was sold on the idea of developers testing their own code. To keep the momentum going, every week at the company's Friday afternoon beer bash (appropriately named TGIF), I gave out testing awards to the developers who wrote tests. It felt a lot like an animal trainer giving treats to doggies for performing a trick, but at least it drew attention to testing. Could I be so lucky that getting developers to test would be this simple?

Unfortunately, the treats didn't work. Developers realized that in order to have adequate tests, they had to write two or three lines of unit test code for every line of code under test and that those tests required at least as much maintenance as the functional code itself and had just as much chance of being buggy. It also became clear to no one's surprise that developer-unit testing was not sufficient. We still needed integration tests, system tests, UI tests, and so on. When it came to testing, we had a lot of growing up (and substantial learning) to do, and we had to do it fast. Very fast!

Why the urgency? Well, I don't believe that any amount of testing can turn a bad idea or an ill-advised product into a success. I do believe that the wrong approach to testing can kill the chances of a good product or company or, at the very least, slow down its growth and open the door for the competition. Google was at that point. Testing had become one of the biggest barriers to continued success and coming up with the right testing strategy to keep up with our ultra-rapid growth in users, products, and employees without slowing the company down involved a lot of innovative approaches, unorthodox solutions, and unique tools. Not everything worked, of course, but in the process, we learned valuable lessons and practices that are applicable to any company that wants to grow or move at the speed of Google. We learned how to have attention to quality without derailing development or the speed at which we got things done. The resulting process, with some insights into the thinking behind them and what makes them work, is what this book is about. If you want to understand how Google met the challenges of testing in the twenty-first century on modern Internet, mobile, and client applications, then you have come to the right place. I may wish it was me who was telling the rest of the story, but James and his coauthors beat me to it and they have nailed the essence of what testing is like here at Google.

One final note on the book: James Whittaker is the guy who made this book happen. He came to Google, dug in to the culture, took on big and important projects, and shipped products such as Chrome, Chrome OS, and dozens of smaller ones. Somewhere in that time, he became the public face of Google testing. But, unlike some of his other books, much of this material is not his. He is as much a reporter on the evolution of how Google tests software as he is a contributor to it. Keep that in mind as you read it because James will probably try to take all the credit for himself!

As Google grew from 200 to over 20,000 employees, there were many people who played important roles in developing and putting into action our testing strategy. James credits many of them and they have contributed directly by writing sidebars and giving interviews that are published in this book. However, no one, not me, James, or anyone else mentioned in this book, has had as much influence as Patrick Copeland, the architect of our current organizational structure and leader of Google's Engineering Productivity team. Every tester in the company reports up through Patrick and he is the executive whose vision created what James has documented and contributed to here. If anyone can take credit for how Google tests software today, it's Patrick. I am not just saying this because he's my boss; I am saying it because he's my boss *and* he told me to say it!

Alberto Savoia is an engineering director and innovation agitator at Google. He first joined Google in 2001 when, among other things, he managed the launch of Google AdWords and played a key role in kick-starting a developer / unit testing culture in the company. He is also the author of *The Way of Testivus* and of "Beautiful Tests" in O'Reilly's *Beautiful Code*.

Note by James Whittaker: I couldn't agree more! As a scribe and journalist in this process, I owe most of the material to the organization that Patrick has created. And I am not just saying this because he gave me permission to write this book. As my boss, he made me write this book!

Foreword by Patrick Copeland

My adventure with Google started in March of 2005. If you read Alberto's foreword, you know a bit about the conditions of Google around that time. It was small but beginning to show signs of serious growing pains. It was also a time of rapid technological change as the web world was welcoming dynamic content and the cloud was becoming a viable alternative to the then dominant world of client-server.

That first week, I sat with the rest of the Nooglers topped with a tri-colored propeller hat listening to the founders discussing corporate strategy at a weekly company meeting called TGIF. I knew little about what I had gotten myself into. I was naïve enough to be excited and aware enough to be more than a little intimated. The speed and scale of Google made my previous decade of 5-year ship cycles seem like poor preparation. Worse still, I think I was the only tester wearing one of those Noogler hats. Surely there were more of us somewhere!

I joined Google when engineering was just shy of 1,000 people. The testing team had about 50 full timers and some number of temporary workers I never could get my head around. The team was called "Testing Services" and focused the majority of its energy on UI validation and jumping into projects on an as-needed basis. As you might imagine, it wasn't exactly the most glorified team at Google.

But at that time it was enough. Google's primary businesses were Search and Ads. The Google world was much smaller than it is today, and a thorough job of exploratory testing was enough to catch most quality concerns. But the world was slowly changing. Users were hitting the web in unprecedented numbers and the document-based web was giving way to the app-based web. You could feel the inevitability of growth and change where the ability to scale and get to market quickly would be the difference between relevance and…a place you did not want to be.

Inside Google, the scale and complexity issues were buckling Testing Services. What worked well with small homogenous projects was now burning out good testers as they leapt from one project that was on fire to the next. And topping all that off was Google's insistence to release quicker. Something needed to give and I had the choice between scaling this manually intensive process or changing the game completely. Testing Services needed a radical transformation to match the radical change happening to the industry and the rest of Google.

I would very much like to say that I drew upon my vast wealth of experience and conjured the perfect test organization, but the truth is that my experience had taught me little more than the *wrong way to do things*. Every test organization I ever worked as part of or led was dysfunctional in one way or the other. Stuff was always broken. The code was broken, the tests were broken, and the team was broken! I knew what it meant to be buried under quality and technical debt where every innovative idea was squashed lest it risk breaking the fragile product it depended on. If my experience taught me anything, it was how *not* to do testing.

In all my interactions up to this point, one thing about Google was clear. It respected computer science and coding skill. Ultimately, if testers were to join this club, they would have to have good computer science fundamentals and some coding prowess. First-class citizenship demanded it.

If I was going to change testing at Google, I needed to change what it meant to be a tester. I used to try to imagine the perfect team and how such a team would shoulder the quality debt and I kept coming back to the same premise: The only way a team can write quality software is when the entire team is responsible for quality. That meant product managers, developers, testers…everyone. From my perspective, the best way to do this was to have testers capable of making *testing* an actual feature of the code base. The testing feature should be equal to any feature an actual customer might see. The skill set I needed to build features was that of a developer.

Hiring testers who can code features is difficult; finding feature developers who can test is even more difficult. But the status quo was worse than either so I forged ahead. I wanted testers who could do more for their products and at the same time, I wanted to evolve the nature and ownership of the testing work, which meant asking for far larger investment from the development teams. This is the one organizational structure I had yet to see implemented in all my time in the industry and I was convinced it was right for Google, and I thought that as a company, we were ready for it.

Unfortunately, few others in the company shared my passion for such profound and fundamental change. As I began the process of socializing my equal-but-different vision for the software testing role, I eventually found it difficult to find a lunch partner! Engineers seemed threatened by the very notion that they would have to play a bigger role in testing, pointing out "that's what test is for." Among testers, the attitude was equally unsavory as many had become comfortable in their roles and the status quo had such momentum that change was becoming a very hard problem.

I kept pressing the matter mostly out of fear that Google's engineering processes would become so bogged down in technical and quality debt that I'd be back to the same five-year ship cycles I had so happily left behind in the old client-server world. Google is a company of geniuses focused on innovation and that entrepreneurial makeup is simply incompatible with long product ship cycles. This was a battle worth fighting and I convinced myself that once these geniuses understood the idea of development and testing practices for a streamlined and repeatable "technology factory," they would come around. They would see that we were not a startup anymore and with our rapidly growing user base and increasing technical debt of bugs and poorly structured code would mean the end of their coder's playground.

I toured the product teams making my case and trying to find the sweet spot for my argument. To developers, I painted a picture of continuous builds, rapid deployment, and a development process that moved quickly, leaving more time for innovation. To testers, I appealed to their desire to be full engineering partners of equal skill, equal contribution, and equal compensation.

Developers had the attitude that if we were going to hire people skilled enough to do feature development, then we should have them do feature development. Some of them were so against the idea that they filled my manager's inbox with candid advice on how to deal with my madness. Fortunately, my manager ignored those recommendations.

Testers, to my surprise, reacted similarly. They were vested in the way things were and quick to bemoan their status, but slow to do anything about it.

My manager's reaction to the complaints was telling: "This is Google, if you want something done, then do it."

And so that's what I did. I assembled a large enough cadre of like-minded folks to form interview loops and we began interviewing candidates. It was tough going. We were looking for developer skills and a tester mindset. We wanted people who could code and wanted to apply that skill to the development of tools, infrastructure, and test automation. We had to rethink recruiting and interviewing and then explain that process to the hiring committees who were entrenched and comfortable with the way things were.

The first few quarters were rough. Good candidates were often torpedoed in the vetting process. Perhaps they were too slow to solve some arcane coding problem or didn't fare well in something that someone thought was important but that had nothing to do with testing skill. I knew hiring was going to be difficult and made time each week to write hiring justification after hiring justification. These went to none other than Google co-founder Larry Page who was (and still is) the last approval in the hiring process. He approved enough of them that my team began to grow. I often wonder if every time Larry hears my name he still thinks, "Hiring testers!"

Of course, by this time, I had made enough noise trying to get buy-in that we had no choice but to perform. The entire company was watching and failure would have been disastrous. It was a lot to expect from a small test team supported by an ever-changing cast of vendors and temps. But even as we struggled to hire and I dialed back the number of temps we used, I noticed change was taking hold. The more scarce testing resources became, the more test work was left for developers to do. Many of the teams rose to the challenge. I think if technology had stayed the same as it was, this alone would have taken us nearly where we needed to be.

But technology wasn't standing still and the rules of development and testing were changing rapidly. The days of static web content were gone. Browsers were still trying to keep up. Automation around the browser was a year behind the already tardy browsers. Making testing a development problem at the same time those same developers were facing such a huge technology shift seemed a fool's errand. We lacked the ability to properly test these applications manually, much less with automation.

The pressure on the development teams was just as bad. Google began buying companies with rich and dynamic web applications. YouTube, Google Docs, and so on stretched our internal infrastructure. The problems I was facing in testing were no more daunting than the problems the development teams were facing in writing code for me to test! I was trying to solve a testing problem that simply couldn't be solved in isolation. Testing and development, when seen as separate disciplines or even as distinct problems, was wrong-headed and continuing down such a path meant we would solve neither. Fixing the test team would only get us an incremental step forward.

Progress was happening. It's a funny thing about hiring smart people: They tend to make progress! By 2007, the test discipline was better positioned. We were managing the endgame of the release cycle well. Development teams knew they could count on us as partners to production. But our existence as a late-in-the-cycle support team was confining us to the traditional QA model. Despite our ability to execute well, we were still not where I wanted us to be. I had a handle on the hiring problem and testing was moving in the right direction, but we were engaged too late in the process.

We had been making progress with a concept we called "Test Certified" (which the authors explain in some detail later in this book) where we consulted with dev teams and helped them get better code hygiene and unit testing practices established early. We built tools and coached teams on continuous integration so that products were always in a state that made them testable. There were countless small improvements and tweaks, many of them detailed in this book, that erased much of the earlier skepticism. Still, there was a lack of identity to the whole thing. Dev was still dev; test was still test. Many of the ingredients for culture change were present, but we needed a catalyst for getting them to stick.

As I looked around the organization that had grown from my idea to hire developers in a testing role, I realized that testing was only part of what we did. We had tool teams building everything from source repositories to building infrastructure to bug databases. We were test engineers, release engineers, tool developers, and consultants. What struck me was just how much the nontesting aspect of our work was impacting productivity. Our name may have been Testing Services, but our charter was so much more.

So I decided to make it official and I changed the name of the team to Engineering Productivity. With the name change also came a cultural adjustment. People began talking about productivity instead of testing and quality. Productivity is our job; testing and quality are the job of everyone involved in development. This means that developers own testing and developers own quality. The productivity team is responsible for enabling development to nail those two things.

In the beginning, the idea was mostly aspirational and our motto of "accelerating Google" may have rung hollow at first, but over time and through our actions, we delivered on these promises. Our tools enabled developers to go faster and we went from bottleneck to bottleneck clearing the clogs and solving the problems developers faced. Our tools also enabled developers to write tests and then see the result of those tests on build after build. Test cases were no longer executed in isolation on some tester's machine. Their results were posted on dashboards and accumulated over successive versions so they became part of the public record of the application's fitness for release. We didn't just demand developers get involved; we made it easy for them to do so. The difference between productivity and testing had finally become real: Google could innovate with less friction and without the accumulation of technical debt.

And the results? Well, I won't spoil the rest of the book because that's why it was written. The authors took great pains to scour their own experiences and those of other Googlers to boil our secret sauce down to a core set of practices. But we were successful in many ways—from orders of magnitude, decreases in build times, to run-it-and-forget-it test automation, to open sourcing some truly innovative testing tools. As of the writing of this preface, the Productivity Team is now about 1,200 engineers or a bit larger than all of Google Engineering in 2005 when I joined. The productivity brand is strong and our charter to accelerate Google is an accepted part of the engineering culture. The team has travelled light years from where we were on my first day sitting confused and uncertain at TGIF. The only thing that hasn't changed since that day is my tri-colored propeller hat, which sits on my desk serving as a reminder of how far we've come.

Patrick Copeland is the senior director of Engineering Productivity and the top of the testing food chain at Google. All testers in the company report up through Patrick (whose skip-level manager, incidentally, is Larry Page, Google's Co-founder and CEO). Patrick's career at Google was preceded by nearly a decade at Microsoft as a director of Test. He's a frequent public speaker and known around Google as the architect of Google's technology for rapid development, testing, and deployment of software.

Preface

Software development is hard. Testing that software is hard, too. And when you talk about development and testing at the scale of the entire web, you are talking about Google. If you are interested in how one of the biggest names in the Internet handles such large-scale testing, then you have found the right book.

Google tests and releases hundreds of millions of lines of code distributed across millions of source files daily. Billions of build actions prompt millions of automated tests to run across hundreds of thousands of browser instances daily. Operating systems are built, tested, and released within the bounds of a single calendar year. Browsers are built daily. Web applications are released at near continuous pace. In 2011, 100 features of Google+ were released over a 100-day period.

This is Google scale and Google speed—the scale of the Web itself—and this is the testing solution described in this book. We reveal how this infrastructure was conceived, implemented, and maintained. We introduce the reader to the many people who were instrumental in developing both the concepts and the implementation and we describe the infrastructure that it takes to pull it off.

But it wasn't always this way. The route Google took to get where it is today is just as interesting as the technology we use to test. Turn the clock back six years and Google was more like other companies we once worked for: Test was a discipline off the mainstream. Its practitioners were under-appreciated and over-worked. It was a largely manual process and people who were good at automating it were quickly absorbed into development where they could be more "impactful." The founding team of what Google calls "Engineering Productivity" has to overcome bias against testing and a company culture that favored heroic effort over engineering rigor. As it stands today, Google testers are paid on the same scale as developers with equivalent bonuses and promotion velocity. The fact that testers succeeded and that this culture has lived on through significant company growth (in terms of products, variety, and revenue) and structural reorganizations should be encouraging to companies following in Google's footsteps. Testing can be done right and it can be appreciated by product teams and company executives alike.

As more and more companies find their fortunes and futures on the Web, testing technology and organizational structure as described in this book might become more prevalent. If so, consider this the playbook for how to get there.

This Google testing playbook is organized according to the roles involved. In the first section, we discuss all the roles and introduce all the concepts, processes, and intricacies of the Google quality processes. This section is a must read.

The chapters can be read in any order whatsoever. We first cover the SET or software engineer in test role because this is where modern Google testing began. The SET is a technical tester and the material in that chapter is suitably technical but at a high enough level that anyone can grasp the main concepts. The SET chapter is followed by a chapter covering the other primary testing role, that of the TE or test engineer. This is a big chapter because the TE's job is broad and Google TEs cover a lot of ground during the product cycle. This is a role many traditional testers find familiar, and we imagine it will be the most widely read section of the book because it applies to the broadest practitioner audience.

The balance of the book is about test management and interviews with key Googlers who either played a part in the history of Google test or are key players on key Google products. These interviews will likely be of interest to anyone who is trying to develop Google-like testing processes or teams.

There is a final chapter that really should not be missed by any interested reader. James Whittaker gives insight into how Google testing is still evolving and he makes some predictions about where Google and the industry at large are heading test-wise. We believe many readers will find it insightful and some might even find it shocking.

A NOTE ABOUT FIGURES

Due to the complexity of the topics discussed and the graphical nature of the Internet, some figures from Chapter 3 in this book are very detailed and are intended only to provide a high-level view of concepts. Those figures are representational and not intended to be read in detail. If you prefer to view these figures on your computer, you can download them at www.informit.com/title/9780321803023.

A Word About This Book

When Patrick Copeland originally suggested that I write this book, I was hesitant to do so, and my reasons all turned out to be good ones. People would question whether I was the best Googler to write it. (They did.) Too many people would want to get involved. (This also turned out to be true.) But mostly, it was because all my prior books were written for beginners. Both the *How to Break…*series and my *Exploratory Testing* book can be told as a complete, end-to-end story. Not so with this book. Readers might well read this book in a single sitting, but it's meant as more of a reference for how Google actually performs the tasks, both small ones and big ones, that make up our practice of testing. I expect people who have tested software in a corporate environment will get more out of it than beginners because they will have a basis for comparing our Google processes to the ones they are used to. I picture experienced testers, managers, and executives picking it up, finding a topic of interest, and reading that section to see how Google performs some specific task. This is not a writing style I have often assumed!

Two heretofore unpublished co-authors have joined me in this endeavor. Both are excellent engineers and have been at Google longer than I have been. Jason Arbon's title is a test engineer, but he's an entrepreneur at heart and his impact on many of the ideas and tools that appear in the test engineer chapters of this book has been profound. Having our careers intersect has changed us both. Jeff Carollo is a tester turned developer and is categorically the best test developer I have ever met. Jeff is one of the few people I have seen succeed at "walk away automation"—which is test code written so well and so self contained that the author can create it and leave it to the team to run without intervention. These two are brilliant and we tried hard to make this book read with one voice.

There are any number of guest Googlers who have supplied material. Whenever the text and subject matter is the work of a single author, that person is identified in the heading that precedes his work. There are also a number of interviews with key Googlers who had profound impact on the way we do testing. It was the best way we could think of to include as many of the people who defined Google testing without having a book with 30 authors! Not all readers will be interested in all the interviews, but they are clearly marked in the text so they can be skipped or read individually. We thank all these contributors profusely and accept any blame if our ability to do justice to their work fell short in any way. The English language is a poor medium to describe sheer brilliance.

Happy reading, happy testing, and may you always find (and fix) the bug you are looking for.

James Whittaker
Jason Arbon
Jeff Carollo
Kirkland, Washington

Acknowledgments

We want to acknowledge every engineer at Google who has worked tirelessly to improve the quality. We also want to mention our appreciation for the open and distributed culture of Google engineering and management, which allowed us to treat our testing methodologies and practices much as we build products—with experimentation and the freedom to explore.

We'd like to specifically mention the following people who spent their energy and took risks to push testing into the cloud: Alexis O. Torres, Joe Muharksy, Danielle Drew, Richard Bustamante, Po Hu, Jim Reardon, Tejas Shah, Julie Ralph, Eriel Thomas, Joe Mikhail, and Ibrahim El Far. Also, thanks to our editors, Chris Guzikowski and Chris Zahn, who politely tolerated our engineering-speak. Thanks to interviewees who shared their views and experiences: Ankit Mehta, Joel Hynoski, Lindsay Webster, Apple Chow, Mark Striebeck, Neal Norwitz, Tracy Bialik, Russ Rufer, Ted Mao, Shelton Mar, Ashish Kumar, Sujay Sahni, Brad Green, Simon Stewart, and Hung Dang. A special thanks goes to Alberto Savoia for the inspiration to prototype and iterate quickly. Thanks to Google and the cafeteria staff and chefs for the great food and coffee. Thanks to candid feedback from Phil Waligora, Alan Page, and Michael Bachman. Ultimately, thanks to Pat Copeland for assembling and funding such an energetic and talented set of engineers who are focused on quality.

About the Authors

James Whittaker is an engineering director at Google and has been responsible for testing Chrome, maps, and Google web apps. He used to work for Microsoft and was a professor before that. James is one of the best-known names in testing the world over.

Jason Arbon is a test engineer at Google and has been responsible for testing Google Desktop, Chrome, and Chrome OS. He also served as development lead for an array of open-source test tools and personalization experiments. He worked at Microsoft prior to joining Google.

Jeff Carollo is a software engineer in test at Google and has been responsible for testing Google Voice, Toolbar, Chrome, and Chrome OS. He has consulted with dozens of internal Google development teams helping them improve initial code quality. He converted to a software engineer in 2010 and leads development of Google+ APIs. He also worked at Microsoft prior to joining Google."

CHAPTER 1
Introduction to Google Software Testing

James Whittaker

There is one question I get more than any other. Regardless of the country I am visiting or the conference I am attending, this one question never fails to surface. Even Nooglers ask it as soon as they emerge from new-employee orientation: *"How does Google test software?"*

I am not sure how many times I have answered that question or even how many different versions I have given, but the answer keeps evolving the longer time I spend at Google and the more I learn about the nuances of our various testing practices. I had it in the back of my mind that I would write a book and when Alberto, who likes to threaten to turn testing books into adult diapers to give them a reason for existence, actually suggested I write such a book, I knew it was going to happen.

Still, I waited. My first problem was that I was not the right person to write this book. There were many others who preceded me at Google and I wanted to give them a crack at writing it first. My second problem was that I as test director for Chrome and Chrome OS (a position now occupied by one of my former directs) had insights into only a slice of the Google testing solution. There was so much more to Google testing that I needed to learn.

At Google, software testing is part of a centralized organization called Engineering Productivity that spans the developer and tester tool chain, release engineering, and testing from the unit level all the way to exploratory testing. There are a great deal of shared tools and test infrastructure for web properties such as search, ads, apps, YouTube, and everything else we do on the Web. Google has solved many of the problems of speed and scale and this enables us, despite being a large company, to release software at the pace of a start-up. As Patrick Copeland pointed out in his preface to this book, much of this magic has its roots in the test team.

At Google, software testing is part of a centralized organization called Engineering Productivity.

When Chrome OS released in December 2010 and leadership was successfully passed to one of my directs, I began getting more heavily involved in other products. That was the beginning of this book, and I tested the waters by writing the first blog post,[1] "How Google Tests Software," and the rest is history. Six months later, the book was done and I wish I had not waited so long to write it. I learned more about testing at Google in the last six months than I did my entire first two years, and Nooglers are now reading this book as part of their orientation.

This isn't the only book about how a big company tests software. I was at Microsoft when Alan Page, BJ Rollison, and Ken Johnston wrote *How We Test Software at Microsoft* and lived first-hand many of the things they wrote about in that book. Microsoft was on top of the testing world. It had elevated test to a place of honor among the software engineering elite. Microsoft testers were the most sought after conference speakers. Its first director of test, Roger Sherman, attracted test-minded talent from all over the globe to Redmond, Washington. It was a golden age for software testing.

And the company wrote a big book to document it all.

I didn't get to Microsoft early enough to participate in that book, but I got a second chance. I arrived at Google when testing was on the ascent. Engineering Productivity was rocketing from a couple of hundred people to the 1,200 it has today. The growing pains Pat spoke of in his preface were in their last throes and the organization was in its fastest growth spurt ever. The Google testing blog was drawing hundreds of thousands of page views every month, and GTAC[2] had become a staple conference on the industry testing circuit. Patrick was promoted shortly after my arrival and had a dozen or so directors and engineering managers reporting to him. If you were to grant software testing a renaissance, Google was surely its epicenter.

This means the Google testing story merits a big book, too. The problem is, I don't write big books. But then, Google is known for its simple and straightforward approach to software. Perhaps this book is in line with that reputation.

How Google Tests Software contains the core information about what it means to be a Google tester and how we approach the problems of scale, complexity, and mass usage. There is information here you won't find anywhere else, but if it is not enough to satisfy your craving for how we test, there is more available on the Web. Just Google it!

There is more to this story, though, and it must be told. I am finally ready to tell it. The way Google tests software might very well become the way many companies test as more software leaves the confines of the desktop for the freedom of the Web. If you've read the Microsoft book, don't expect to find much in common with this one. Beyond the number of

---

1. http://googletesting.blogspot.com/2011/01/how-google-tests-software.html.

2. GTAC is the Google Test Automation Conference (www.GTAc.biz).

authors—both books have three—and the fact that each book documents testing practices at a large software company, the approaches to testing couldn't be more different.

> The way Google tests software might very well become the way many companies test as more software leaves the confines of the desktop for the freedom of the Web.

Patrick Copeland dealt with how the Google methodology came into being in his preface to this book and since those early days, it has continued to evolve organically as the company grew. Google is a melting pot of engineers who used to work somewhere else. Techniques proven ineffective at former employers were either abandoned or improved upon by Google's culture of innovation. As the ranks of testers swelled, new practices and ideas were tried and those that worked in practice at Google became part of Google and those proven to be baggage were jettisoned. Google testers are willing to try anything once but are quick to abandon techniques that do not prove useful.

Google is a company built on innovation and speed, releasing code the moment it is useful (when there are few users to disappoint) and iterating on features with early adopters (to maximize feedback). Testing in such an environment has to be incredibly nimble and techniques that require too much upfront planning or continuous maintenance simply won't work. At times, testing is interwoven with development to the point that the two practices are indistinguishable from each other, and at other times, it is so completely independent that developers aren't even aware it is going on.

> At times, testing is interwoven with development to the point that the two practices are indistinguishable from each other, and at other times, it is so completely independent that developers aren't even aware it is going on.

Throughout Google's growth, this fast pace has slowed only a little. We can nearly produce an operating system within the boundaries of a single calendar year; we release client applications such as Chrome every few weeks; and web applications change daily—all this despite the fact that our start-up credentials have long ago expired. In this environment, it is almost easier to describe what testing is not—dogmatic, process-heavy, labor-intensive, and time-consuming—than what it is, although this book is an attempt to do exactly that. One thing is for sure: Testing must not create friction that slows down innovation and development. At least it will not do it twice.

Google's success at testing cannot be written off as owing to a small or simple software portfolio. The size and complexity of Google's software testing problem are as large as any company's out there. From client operating systems, to web apps, to mobile, to enterprise, to commerce and social,

Google operates in pretty much every industry vertical. Our software is big; it's complex; it has hundreds of millions of users; it's a target for hackers; much of our source code is open to external scrutiny; lots of it is legacy; we face regulatory reviews; our code runs in hundreds of countries and in many different languages, and on top of this, users expect software from Google to be simple to use and to "just work." What Google testers accomplish on a daily basis cannot be credited to working on easy problems. Google testers face nearly every testing challenge that exists every single day.

Whether Google has it right (probably not) is up for debate, but one thing is certain: The approach to testing at Google is different from any other company I know, and with the inexorable movement of software away from the desktop and toward the cloud, it seems possible that Google-like practices will become increasingly common across the industry. It is my and my co-authors' hope that this book sheds enough light on the Google formula to create a debate over just how the industry should be facing the important task of producing reliable software that the world can rely on. Google's approach might have its shortcomings, but we're willing to publish it and open it to the scrutiny of the international testing community so that it can continue to improve and evolve.

Google's approach is more than a little counterintuitive: We have fewer dedicated testers in our entire company than many of our competitors have on a single product team. Google Test is no million-man army. We are small and elite Special Forces that have to depend on superior tactics and advanced weaponry to stand a fighting chance at success. As with military Special Forces, it is this scarcity of resources that forms the base of our secret sauce. The absence of plenty forces us to get good at prioritizing, or as Larry Page puts it: "Scarcity brings clarity." From features to test techniques, we've learned to create high impact, low-drag activities in our pursuit of quality. Scarcity also makes testing resources highly valued, and thus, well regarded, keeping smart people actively and energetically involved in the discipline. The first piece of advice I give people when they ask for the keys to our success: Don't hire too many testers.

> The first piece of advice I give people when they ask for the keys to our success: Don't hire too many testers.

How does Google get by with such small ranks of test folks? If I had to put it simply, I would say that at Google, the burden of quality is on the shoulders of those writing the code. Quality is never "some tester's" problem. Everyone who writes code at Google is a tester, and quality is literally the problem of this collective (see Figure 1.1). Talking about dev to test ratios at Google is like talking about air quality on the surface of the sun. It's not a concept that even makes sense. If you are an engineer, you are a tester. If you are an engineer with the word test in your title, then you are an enabler of good testing for those other engineers who do not.

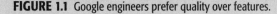

FIGURE 1.1 Google engineers prefer quality over features.

The fact that we produce world-class software is evidence that our particular formula deserves some study. Perhaps there are parts of it that will work in other organizations. Certainly there are parts of it that can be improved. What follows is a summary of our formula. In later chapters, we dig into specifics and show details of just how we put together a test practice in a developer-centric culture.

Quality ≠ Test

"Quality cannot be tested in" is so cliché it has to be true. From automobiles to software, if it isn't built right in the first place, then it is never going to *be* right. Ask any car company that has ever had to do a mass recall how expensive it is to bolt on quality after the fact. Get it right from the beginning or you've created a permanent mess.

However, this is neither as simple nor as accurate as it sounds. Although it is true that quality cannot be tested in, it is equally evident that without testing, it is impossible to develop anything of quality. How does one decide if what you built is high quality without testing it?

The simple solution to this conundrum is to stop treating development and test as separate disciplines. Testing and development go hand in hand. Code a little and test what you built. Then code some more and test some more. Test isn't a separate practice; it's part and parcel of the development process itself. Quality is not equal to test. Quality is achieved by putting development and testing into a blender and mixing them until one is indistinguishable from the other.

> Quality is not equal to test. Quality is achieved by putting development and testing into a blender and mixing them until one is indistinguishable from the other.

At Google, this is exactly our goal: to merge development and testing so that you cannot do one without the other. Build a little and then test it. Build some more and test some more. The key here is *who* is doing the testing. Because the number of actual dedicated testers at Google is so disproportionately low, the only possible answer has to be the developer. Who better to do all that testing than the people doing the actual coding? Who better to find the bug than the person who wrote it? Who is more incentivized to avoid writing the bug in the first place? The reason Google can get by with so few dedicated testers is because developers own quality. If a product breaks in the field, the first point of escalation is the developer who created the problem, not the tester who didn't catch it.

This means that quality is more an act of prevention than it is detection. Quality is a development issue, not a testing issue. To the extent that we are able to embed testing practice inside development, we have created a process that is hyper-incremental where mistakes can be rolled back if any one increment turns out to be too buggy. We've not only prevented a lot of customer issues, we have greatly reduced the number of dedicated testers necessary to ensure the absence of recall-class bugs. At Google, testing is aimed at determining how well this prevention method works.

Manifestations of this blending of development and testing are inseparable from the Google development mindset, from code review notes asking "where are your tests?" to posters in the bathrooms reminding developers about best-testing practices.[3] Testing must be an unavoidable aspect of development, and the marriage of development and testing is where quality is achieved.

> Testing must be an unavoidable aspect of development, and the marriage of development and testing is where quality is achieved.

Roles

In order for the "you build it, you break it" motto to be real (and kept real over time), there are roles beyond the traditional feature developer that are necessary. Specifically, engineering roles that enable developers to do testing efficiently and effectively have to exist. At Google, we have created

---

3. http://googletesting.blogspot.com/2007/01/introducing-testing-on-toilet.html.

roles in which some engineers are responsible for making other engineers more productive and more quality-minded. These engineers often identify themselves as *testers*, but their actual mission is one of productivity. Testers are there to make developers more productive and a large part of that productivity is avoiding re-work because of sloppy development. Quality is thus a large part of that productivity. We are going to spend significant time talking about each of these roles in detail in subsequent chapters; therefore, a summary suffices for now.

The **software engineer** (SWE) is the traditional developer role. SWEs write functional code that ships to users. They create design documentation, choose data structures and overall architecture, and they spend the vast majority of their time writing and reviewing code. SWEs write a lot of test code, including test-driven design (TDD), unit tests, and, as we explain later in this chapter, participate in the construction of small, medium, and large tests. SWEs own quality for everything they touch whether they wrote it, fixed it, or modified it. That's right, if a SWE has to modify a function and that modification breaks an existing test or requires a new one, they must author that test. SWEs spend close to 100 percent of their time writing code.

The **software engineer in test** (SET) is also a developer role, except his focus is on testability and general test infrastructure. SETs review designs and look closely at code quality and risk. They refactor code to make it more testable and write unit testing frameworks and automation. They are a partner in the SWE codebase, but are more concerned with increasing quality and test coverage than adding new features or increasing performance. SETs also spend close to 100 percent of their time writing code, but they do so in service of quality rather than coding features a customer might use.

SETs are partners in the SWE codebase, but are more concerned with increasing quality and test coverage than adding new features or increasing performance. SETs write code that allows SWEs to test their features.

The **test engineer** (TE) is related to the SET role, but it has a different focus. It is a role that puts testing on behalf of the user first and developers second. Some Google TEs spend a good deal of their time writing code in the form of automation scripts and code that drives usage scenarios and even mimics the user. They also organize the testing work of SWEs and SETs, interpret test results, and drive test execution, particularly in the late stages of a project as the push toward release intensifies. TEs are product experts, quality advisers, and analyzers of risk. Many of them write a lot of code; many of them write only a little.

> **Note**
> The TE role puts testing on behalf of the user first. TEs organize the overall quality practices, interpret test results, drive test execution, and build end-to-end test automation.

From a quality standpoint, SWEs own features and the quality of those features in isolation. They are responsible for fault-tolerant designs, failure recovery, TDD, unit tests, and working with the SET to write tests that exercise the code for their features.

SETs are developers who provide testing features. A framework that can isolate newly developed code by simulating an actual working environment (a process involving such things as stubs, mocks, and fakes, which are all described later) and submit queues for managing code check-ins. In other words, SETs write code that enables SWEs to test their features. Much of the actual testing is performed by the SWEs. SETs are there to ensure that features are testable and that the SWEs are actively involved in writing test cases.

Clearly, an SET's primary focus is on the developer. Individual feature quality is the target and enabling developers to easily test the code they write is the primary focus of the SET. User-focused testing is the job of the Google TE. Assuming that the SWEs and SETs performed module- and feature-level testing adequately, the next task is to understand how well this collection of executable code and data works together to satisfy the needs of the user. TEs act as double-checks on the diligence of the developers. Any obvious bugs are an indication that early cycle developer testing was inadequate or sloppy. When such bugs are rare, TEs can turn to the primary task of ensuring that the software runs common user scenarios, meets performance expectations, is secure, internationalized, accessible, and so on. TEs perform a lot of testing and manage coordination among other TEs, contract testers, crowd sourced testers, dogfooders,[4] beta users, and early adopters. They communicate among all parties the risks inherent in the basic design, feature complexity, and failure avoidance methods. After TEs get engaged, there is no end to their mission.

Organizational Structure

In most organizations I have worked with, developers and testers exist as part of the same product team. Organizationally, developers and testers

---

4. The term *dogfood* is used by most software companies in the U.S. to denote internal adoption of software that is not yet released. The phrase "eating your own dogfood" is meant to convey the idea that if you make a product to sell to someone else, you should be willing to use it yourself to find out if it is any good.

report to the same product team manager. One product, one team, and everyone involved is always on the same page.

Unfortunately, I have never actually seen it work that way. Senior managers tend to come from program management or development and not testing ranks. In the push to ship, priorities often favor getting features complete and other fit-and-finish tasks over core quality. As a single team, the tendency is for testing to be subservient to development. Clearly, this is evident in the industry's history of buggy products and premature releases. Service Pack 1 anyone?

> ## Note
>
> As a single team, senior managers tend to come from program management or development and not testing ranks. In the push to ship, priorities often favor getting features complete and other fit-and-finish tasks over core quality. The tendency for such organizational structures is for testing to be subservient to development.

Google's reporting structure is divided into what we call Focus Areas or FAs. There is an FA for Client (Chrome, Google Toolbar, and so on), Geo (Maps, Google Earth, and so on), Ads, Apps, Mobile, and so on. All SWEs report to a director or VP of a FA.

SETs and TEs break this mold. Test exists in a separate and horizontal (across the product FAs) Focus Area called Engineering Productivity. Testers are essentially on loan to the product teams and are free to raise quality concerns and ask questions about functional areas that are missing tests or that exhibit unacceptable bug rates. Because we don't report to the product teams, we can't simply be told to get with the program. Our priorities are our own and they never waiver from reliability, security, and so on unless we decide something else takes precedence. If a development team wants us to take any shortcuts related to testing, these must be negotiated in advance and we can always decide to say no.

This structure also helps to keep the number of testers low. A product team cannot arbitrarily lower the technical bar for testing talent or hire more testers than they need simply to dump menial work on them. Menial work around any specific feature is the job of the developer who owns the feature and it cannot be pawned off on some hapless tester. Testers are assigned by Engineering Productivity leads who act strategically based on the priority, complexity, and needs of the product team in comparison to other product teams. Obviously, we can get it wrong, and we sometimes do, but in general, this creates a balance of resources against actual and not perceived need.

> **Note**
>
> Testers are assigned to product teams by Engineering Productivity leads who act strategically based on the priority, complexity, and needs of the product team in comparison to other product teams. This creates a balance of resources against actual and not perceived need. As a central resource, good ideas and practices tend to get adopted companywide.

The on-loan status of testers also facilitates movement of SETs and TEs from project to project, which not only keeps them fresh and engaged, but also ensures that good ideas move rapidly around the company. A test technique or tool that works for a tester on a Geo product is likely to be used again when that tester moves to Chrome. There's no faster way of moving innovations in test than moving the actual innovators.

It is generally accepted that 18 months on a product is enough for a tester and that after that time, he or she can (but doesn't have to) leave without repercussion to another team. One can imagine the downside of losing such expertise, but this is balanced by a company full of generalist testers with a wide variety of product and technology familiarity. Google is a company full of testers who understand client, web, browser, and mobile technologies, and who can program effectively in multiple languages and on a variety of platforms. And because Google's products and services are more tightly integrated than ever before, testers can move around the company and have relevant expertise no matter where they go.

Crawl, Walk, Run

One of the key ways Google achieves good results with fewer testers than many companies is that we rarely attempt to ship a large set of features at once. In fact, the exact opposite is the goal: Build the core of a product and release it the moment it is useful to as large a crowd as feasible, and then get their feedback and iterate. This is what we did with Gmail, a product that kept its beta tag for four years. That tag was our warning to users that it was still being perfected. We removed the beta tag only when we reached our goal of 99.99 percent uptime for a real user's email data. We did it again with Android producing the G1, a useful and well-reviewed product that then became much better and more fully featured with the Nexus line of phones that followed it. It's important to note here that when customers are paying for early versions, they have to be functional enough to make them worth their while. Just because it is an early version doesn't mean it has to be a poor product.

> **Note**
>
> Google often builds the "minimum useful product" as an initial version and then quickly iterates successive versions allowing for internal and user feedback and careful consideration of quality with every small step. Products proceed through canary, development, testing, beta, and release channels before making it to users.

It's not as cowboy a process as it might sound at first glance. In fact, in order to make it to what we call the beta channel release, a product must go through a number of other channels and prove its worth. For Chrome, a product I spent my first two years at Google working on, multiple channels were used depending on our confidence in the product's quality and the extent of feedback we were looking for. The sequence looks something like this:

- **Canary Channel**: This is used for daily builds we suspect aren't fit for release. Like a canary in a coalmine, if a daily build fails to survive, then it is a sign our process has gotten chaotic and we need to re-examine our work. Canary Channel builds are only for the ultra-tolerant user running experiments and certainly not for someone depending on the application to get real work done. In general, only engineers (developer and testers) and managers working on the product pull builds from the canary channel.

> **Note**
>
> The Android team goes one step further, and has its core development team's phone continually running on the nearly daily build. The thought is that they will be unlikely to check in bad code it if impacts the ability to call home.

- **Dev Channel:** This is what developers use for their day-to-day work. These are generally weekly builds that have sustained successful usage and passed some set of tests (we discuss this in subsequent chapters). All engineers on a product are *required* to pick up the Dev Channel build and use it for real work and for sustained testing. If a Dev Channel build isn't suitable for real work, then back to the Canary channel it goes. This is not a happy situation and causes a great deal of re-evaluation by the engineering team.

- **Test Channel:** This is essentially the best build of the month in terms of the one that passes the most sustained testing and the one engineers trust the most for their work. The Test Channel build can be picked up by internal dogfood users and represents a candidate Beta Channel build given good sustained performance. At some point, a Test Channel build becomes stable enough to be used internally companywide and sometimes given to external collaborators and partners who would benefit from an early look at the product.

- **Beta Channel** or **Release Channel:** These builds are stable Test Channel builds that have survived internal usage and pass every quality bar the team sets. These are the first builds to get external exposure.

This crawl, walk, run approach gives us the chance to run tests and experiment on our applications early and obtain feedback from real human beings in addition to all the automation we run in each of these channels every day.

Types of Tests

Instead of distinguishing between code, integration, and system testing, Google uses the language of *small*, *medium*, and *large* tests (not to be confused with t-shirt sizing language of estimation among the agile community), emphasizing scope over form. Small tests cover small amounts of code and so on. Each of the three engineering roles can execute any of these types of tests and they can be performed as automated or manual tests. Practically speaking, the smaller the test, the more likely it is to be automated.

> Instead of distinguishing between code, integration, and system testing, Google uses the language of *small*, *medium*, and *large* tests, emphasizing scope over form.

Small tests are mostly (but not always) automated and exercise the code within a single function or module. The focus is on typical functional issues, data corruption, error conditions, and off-by-one mistakes. Small tests are of short duration, usually running in seconds or less. They are most likely written by a SWE, less often by an SET, and hardly ever by TEs. Small tests generally require mocks and faked environments to run. (Mocks and fakes are stubs—substitutes for actual functions—that act as placeholders for dependencies that might not exist, are too buggy to be reliable, or too difficult to emulate error conditions. They are explained in greater detail in later chapters.) TEs rarely write small tests but might run them when they are trying to diagnose a particular failure. The question a small test attempts to answer is, *"Does this code do what it is supposed to do?"*

Medium tests are usually automated and involve two or more interacting features. The focus is on testing the interaction between features that call each other or interact directly; we call these *nearest neighbor functions*. SETs drive the development of these tests early in the product cycle as individual features are completed and SWEs are heavily involved in writing, debugging, and maintaining the actual tests. If a medium test fails or breaks, the developer takes care of it autonomously. Later in the development cycle, TEs can execute medium tests either manually (in the event the test is difficult or prohibitively expensive to automate) or with automation. The question a medium test attempts to answer is, *"Does a set of near neighbor functions interoperate with each other the way they are supposed to?"*

Large tests cover three or more (usually more) features and represent real user scenarios, use real user data sources, and can take hours or even longer to run. There is some concern with overall integration of the features, but large tests tend to be more results-driven, checking that the software satisfies user needs. All three roles are involved in writing large tests and everything from automation to exploratory testing can be the vehicle to accomplish them. The question a large test attempts to answer is, *"Does the product operate the way a user would expect and produce the desired results?"* End-to-end scenarios that operate on the complete product or service are large tests.

> ### Note
> **Small tests** cover a single unit of code in a completely faked environment. **Medium tests** cover multiple and interacting units of code in a faked or real environment. **Large tests** cover any number of units of code in the actual production environment with real and not faked resources.

The actual language of small, medium, and large isn't important. Call them whatever you want as long as the terms have meaning that everyone agrees with.[5] The important thing is that Google testers share a common language to talk about what is getting tested and how those tests are scoped. When some enterprising testers begin talking about a fourth class they dubbed *enormous tests,* every other tester in the company could imagine a systemwide test covering every feature and that runs for a very long time. No additional explanation is necessary.[6]

The primary driver of what gets tested and how much is a very dynamic process and varies from product to product. Google prefers to release often and leans toward getting a product out to users quickly so we can get feedback and iterate. Google tries hard to develop only products that users will find compelling and to get new features out to users as early

---

5. The original purpose of using small, medium, and large was to standardize terms that so many testers brought in from other employers where smoke tests, BVTs, integrations tests, and so on had multiple and conflicting meanings. Those terms had so much baggage that it was felt that new ones were needed.

6. Indeed, the concept of an enormous test is formalized and Google's automation infrastructure uses these designations of small, medium, and so on to determine the execution sequence during automated runs. This is described in more detail in the chapter on SETs later in this book.

as possible so they might benefit from them. Plus, we avoid over-investing in features no user wants because we learn this early. This requires that we involve users and external developers early in the process so we have a good handle on whether what we are delivering hits the mark.

Finally, the mix between automated and manual testing definitely favors the former for all three sizes of tests. If it can be automated and the problem doesn't require human cleverness and intuition, then it should be automated. Only those problems, in any of the previous categories, that specifically require human judgment, such as the beauty of a user interface or whether exposing some piece of data constitutes a privacy concern, should remain in the realm of manual testing.

> The mix between automated and manual testing definitely favors the former for all three sizes of tests. If it can be automated and the problem doesn't require human cleverness and intuition, then it should be automated.

Having said that, it is important to note that Google performs a great deal of manual testing, both scripted and exploratory, but even this testing is done under the watchful eye of automation. Recording technology converts manual tests to automated tests, with point-and-click validation of content and positioning, to be re-executed build after build to ensure minimal regressions, and to keep manual testers always focusing on new issues. We also automate the submission of bug reports and the routing of manual testing tasks.[7] For example, if an automated test breaks, the system determines the last code change that is the most likely culprit, sends email to its authors, and files a bug automatically. The ongoing effort to automate to within the "last inch of the human mind" is currently the design spec for the next generation of test-engineering tools Google builds.

---

7. Google's recording technology and automation-assisted manual testing are described in detail in subsequent chapters on the TE role.

CHAPTER 2
The Software Engineer in Test

Imagine for a moment the perfect development process. It would begin with test. Before even a single line of code is written, a developer would ponder what it will take to test it. He will write tests for boundary cases, for data values too large and too small, for values that would push loops beyond their limits, and for a myriad of other concerns. Some of these tests will be part of the functions she writes, self-testing code or unit tests. For these types of tests, the person who writes the code and understands it best is the one who is most qualified to test it.

Other tests require knowledge outside the actual codebase and must rely on external infrastructure. For example, a test that retrieves data from a remote data store (a database server or the cloud) either requires that database to exist or requires a simulated version of it be available for testing. Over the years, the industry has used any number of terms to describe such scaffolding including *test harnesses*, *test infrastructure*, *mocks*, and *fakes*. In a perfect development process, such scaffolding would be available for every interface a developer would ever encounter so that any aspect of any function you would ever want to write could be tested any time you wanted to test it (remember, we are imagining a perfect world!).

This is the first place where a perfect development process requires a tester. There is a different kind of thinking involved in writing feature code and writing test code. It becomes necessary to distinguish between a feature developer and a test developer. For feature code, the mindset is *creating* and considering users, use cases, and workflow. For test code, the mindset is about *breaking* and writing code that will draw out cases that disrupt the user and his workflow. Because we are in the fairytale land of the perfect development process, we might as well employ separate developers: one who writes features and one who enables them to be broken.

> There is a different kind of thinking involved in writing feature code and writing test code.

Our utopian development process requires any number of feature developers and test developers collaborating to build a complicated product. True utopia should even allow for one developer per feature and any number of test developers buzzing around working on a central test infrastructure and assisting feature developers with their specific unit-testing issues that might otherwise distract them from the construction process that requires most of their concentration.

As feature developers write functional code and test developers write test code, a third concern rears its head: that of the user. Clearly in our perfect utopian testing world, this task should fall on a third class of engineer with the feature developers and test developers gainfully occupied elsewhere. Let's call this newcomer a user developer. User-oriented tasks like use cases, user stories, user scenarios, exploratory testing, and so on are the order of business here. User developers concern themselves with how the features tie together and form an integrated whole. They work on system-wide issues and generally take the view of the user when asking whether the sum of the parts is actually something useful to a real community of end users.

This is our idea of software development utopia, three classes of developers collaborating on usable, reliable perfection—each of them specialized to handle something important and each of them interoperating and collaborating as equals.

Who wouldn't want to work for a company that implemented software this way? You can certainly sign us up!

Unfortunately, none of us work for that company. Google, like all the other companies before it, has done its best to measure up and perhaps because of our position at the end of the queue of those who tried, we've learned from the mistakes of our forebears. Google has also benefitted from being at the inflection point of software moving from massive client-side binaries with multi-year release cycles to cloud-based services that are released every few weeks, days, or hours.[1] This confluence of happy circumstances has endowed us with some similarities to the utopian software development process.

Google SWEs are feature developers, responsible for building components that ship to customers. They write feature code and unit test code for those features.

Google SETs are test developers, responsible for assisting SWEs with the unit test portion of their work and also in writing larger test frameworks to assist SWEs in writing small and medium tests to assess broader quality concerns.

Google TEs are user developers, responsible for taking the users' perspectives in all things that have to do with quality. From a development

---

[1] It is interesting to note that even with client software, Google attempts to make updating frequent and reliable with the development of an "auto update" feature, a necessary feature for any client application.

perspective, they create automation for user scenarios and from a product perspective, they assess the overall coverage and effectiveness of the ensemble of testing activity performed by the other engineering roles. It is not utopia, but it is our best attempt at achieving it in a practical way where real-world concerns have a way of disrupting best intentions in the most unforeseen and unforgiving way.

> **Note**
>
> Google SWEs are feature developers. Google SETs are test developers. Google TEs are user developers.

In this book, we are concerned primarily with the activity of the SET and TE roles and include the activity of the SWE as a subset of both of these roles because the SWE is heavily involved but usually under the direction of an engineer who actually has the word test in his or her title.

The Life of an SET

In the early days of any company, testers generally don't exist.[2] Neither do PMs, planners, release engineers, system administrators, or any other role. Every employee performs all of these roles as one. We often like to imagine Larry and Sergey puzzling over user scenarios and unit tests in those early days! But as Google grew, the SET was the first role that combined the engineering flavor of a developer with the quality-minded role of a tester.[3]

Development and Test Workflow

Before we dig into the workflow specific to SETs, it is helpful to understand the overall development context in which SETs work. SETs and SWEs form a tight partnership in the development of a new product or service and there is a great deal of overlap in their actual work. This is by design because Google believes it is important that testing is owned by the entire engineering team and not just those with the word test in their job title.

Shipping code is the primary shared artifact between engineers on a team. It is the organization of this code, its development, care, and feeding that becomes the focus of everyday effort. Most code at Google shares a single repository and common tool chain. These tools and repository feed

---

[2] "The Life of" is a tip of the hat to a series of Google internal courses on how Search and Ads work. Google has courses for Nooglers (new Google employees) called Life of a Query that details the dynamics of how a search query is implemented and Life of a Dollar to show how Ads work.

[3] Patrick Copeland covers the dawn of the SET in his preface to this book.

Google's build and release process. All Google engineers, regardless of their role, become intimately familiar with this environment to the point that performing any tasks associated with checking in new code, submitting and executing tests, launching a build, and so on can be done without conscious thought by anyone on the team (assuming that person's role demands it).

Shipping code is the primary shared artifact between engineers on a team. It is the organization of this code, its development, care, and feeding that becomes the focus of everyday effort.

This single repository makes a great deal of sense as engineers moving from project to project have little to relearn and so called "20 percent contributors"[4] can be productive from their first day on a project. It also means that any source code is available to any engineer who needs to see it. Web app developers can see any browser code they need to make their job easier without asking permission. They can view code written by more experienced engineers and see how others performed similar tasks. They can pick up code for reuse at the module or even the control structure or data structure level of detail. Google is one company and has one easily searchable (of course!) source repository.

This openness of the codebase, the harmony of the engineering toolset, and companywide sharing of resources has enabled the development of a rich set of shared code libraries and services. This shared code works reliably on Google's production infrastructure, speeding projects to completion and ensuring few failures due to underlying shared libraries.

This openness of the codebase, the harmony of the engineering toolset, and companywide sharing of resources has enabled the development of a rich set of shared code libraries and services.

---

[4] "Twenty percent time" is what Googlers call *side projects*. It's more than a concept; it is an official structure that allows any Googler to take a day a week and work on something besides his day job. The idea is that you spend four days a week earning your salary and a day a week to experiment and innovate. It is entirely optional and some former Googlers have claimed the idea is a myth. In our experience, the concept is real and all three of us have been involved in 20 percent projects. In fact, many of the tools outlined in this book are the result of 20 percent efforts that eventually turned into real, funded products. But many Googlers choose to simply work on another product in their 20 percent time, and thus, the concept of a 20 percent contributor is something many products, particularly the new cool ones, enjoy.

Code associated with the shared infrastructure has a special type of treatment by engineers, and those working on it follow a set of unwritten but common practices that speak to the importance of the code and the care that engineers take when modifying it.

- All engineers must reuse existing libraries, unless they have very good reason not to based on a project-specific need.

- All shared code is written first and foremost to be easily located and readable. It must be stored in the shared portion of the repository so it can be easily located. Because it is shared among various engineers, it must be easy to understand. All code is treated as though others will need to read or modify it in the future.

- Shared code must be as reusable and as self-contained as possible. Engineers get a lot of credit for writing a service that is picked up by multiple teams. Reuse is rewarded far more than complexity or cleverness.

- Dependencies must be surfaced and impossible to overlook. If a project depends on shared code, it should be difficult or impossible to modify that shared code without engineers on dependent projects being made aware of the changes.

- If an engineer comes up with a better way of doing something, he is tasked with refactoring all existing libraries and assisting dependent projects to migrate to the new libraries. Again, such benevolent community work is the subject of any number of available reward mechanisms.[5]

- Google takes code reviews seriously, and, especially with common code, developers must have all their code reviewed by someone with a "readability" in the relevant programming language. A committee grants readabilities after a developer establishes a good track record for writing clean code which adheres to style guidelines. Readabilities exist for C++, Java, Python, and JavaScript: Google's four primary languages.

- Code in the shared repository has a higher bar for testing (we discuss this more later).

Platform dependencies are dealt with by minimizing them. Every engineer has a desktop OS as identical as possible to Google's production system. Linux distributions are carefully managed to keep dependencies at a minimum so that a developer doing local testing on his own machine will likely achieve the same results as if he were testing on the production system. From desktop to data center, the variations between CPU and

---

[5] The most common of which is Google's often touted "peer bonus" benefit. Any engineer whose work is positively impacted by another engineer can serve a peer bonus as a thank you. Managers additionally have access to other bonus structures. The idea is that impactful community work be positively reinforced so it keeps happening! Of course, there is also the informal practice of *quid pro quo*.

operating system are minimal.[6] If a bug occurs on a tester's machine, chances are it will reproduce on a developer's machine and in production.

All code that deals with platform dependencies is pushed into libraries at the lowest level of the stack. The same team that manages the Linux distributions also manages these platform libraries. Finally, for each programming language Google uses, there is exactly one compiler, which is well maintained and constantly tested against the one Linux distribution. None of this is magic, but the work involved in limiting the impact of multiple environments saves a great deal of testing downstream and reduces hard-to-debug environmental issues that distract from the development of new functionality. Keep it simple, keep it safe.

Note

Keeping it simple and uniform is a specific goal of the Google platform: a common Linux distribution for engineering workstations and production deployment machines; a centrally managed set of common, core libraries; a common source, build, and test infrastructure; a single compiler for each core programming language; language independent, common build specification; and a culture that respects and rewards the maintenance of these shared resources.

The single platform, single repository theme continues with a unified build system, which simplifies working within the shared repository. A build specification language that is independent of a project's specific programming language directs the build system. Whether a team uses C++, Python, or Java, they share the same "build files."

A build is achieved by specifying a build target (which is either a library, binary, or test set) composed of some number of source files. Here's the overall flow:

1. Write a class or set of functions for a service in one or more source files and make sure all the code compiles.

2. Identify a library build target for this new service.

3. Write a unit test that imports the library, mocks out its nontrivial dependencies, and executes the most interesting code paths with the most interesting inputs.

4. Create a test build target for the unit test.

5. Build and run the test target, making necessary changes until all the tests pass cleanly.

---

[6] The only local test labs Google maintains outside this common infrastructure are for Android and Chrome OS where various flavors of hardware must be kept on hand to exercise a new build.

6. Run all required static analysis tools that check for style guide compliance and a suite of common problems.

7. Send the resulting code out for code review (more details about the code review follow), make appropriate changes, and rerun all the unit tests.

The output of all this effort is a pair of build targets: the library build target representing the new service we wish to ship and a test build target that tests the service. Note that many developers at Google perform test-driven development, which means step 3 precedes steps 1 and 2.

Larger services are constructed by continuing to write code and link together progressively larger library build targets until the entire service is complete. At this point, a binary build target is created from the main source file that links against the service library. Now you have a Google product that consists of a well-tested standalone binary, a readable, reusable service library with a suite of supporting libraries that can be used to create other services, and a suite of unit tests that cover all the interesting aspects of each of these build targets.

A typical Google product is a composition of many services and the goal is to have a 1:1 ratio between a SWE and a service on any given product team. This means that each service can be constructed, built, and tested in parallel and then integrated together in a final build target once they are all ready. To enable dependent services to be built in parallel, the interfaces that each service exposes are agreed on early in the project. That way, developers take dependencies on agreed-upon interfaces rather than the specific libraries that implement them. Fake implementations of these interfaces are created early to unblock developers from writing their service-level tests.

SETs are involved in much of the test target builds and identify places where small tests need to be written. But it is in the integration of multiple build targets into a larger application build target where their work steps up and larger integration tests are necessary. On an individual library build target, mostly small tests (written by the SWE who owns that functionality with support from any SET on the project) are run. SETs get involved and write medium and large tests as the build target gets larger.

As the build target increases in size, small tests written against integrated functionality become part of the regression suite. They are always expected to pass and when they fail, bugs are raised against the tests and are treated no differently than bugs in features. Test is part of the functionality, and buggy tests are functional bugs and must be fixed. This ensures that new functionality does not break existing functionality and that any code modifications do not break any tests.

In all of this activity, the SETs are centrally involved. They assist developers in deciding what unit tests to write. They write many of the mocks and fakes. They write medium and large integration tests. It is this set of tasks the SET performs that we turn to now.

Who Are These SETs Anyway?

SETs are the engineers involved in enabling testing at all levels of the Google development process we just described. SETs are Software Engineers in Test. First and foremost, SETs are *software engineers* and the role is touted as a 100 percent coding role in our recruiting literature and internal job promotion ladders. It's an interesting hybrid approach to testing that enables us to get testers involved early in a way that's not about touchy-feely "quality models" and "test plans" but as active participants in designing and creating the codebase. It creates an equal footing between feature developers and test developers that is productive and lends credibility to all types of testing, including manual and exploratory testing that occurs later in the process and is performed by a different set of engineers.

Note

Test is just another feature of the application, and SETs are the owner of the testing feature.

SETs sit side by side with feature developers (literally, it is the goal to have SWEs and SETs co-located). It is fair to characterize test as just another feature of the application and SETs as the owner of the testing feature. SETs also participate in reviewing code written by SWEs and vice versa.

When SETs are interviewed, the "coding bar" is nearly identical to the SWE role with the added requirement that SETs know how to test the code they create. In other words, both SWEs and SETs answer coding questions. SETs are expected to nail a set of testing questions as well.

As you might imagine it is a difficult role to fill and it is entirely possible that the relatively low numbers of Google SETs isn't because Google has created a magic formula for productivity, but more of a result of adapting our engineering practice around the reality that the SET skill set is hard to find. However, one of the nice side effects of the similarity of the SWE and SET roles is that both communities make excellent recruiting grounds for the other and conversions between the roles are something that Google tries its best to facilitate. Imagine a company full of developers who can test and testers who can code. We aren't there yet and probably never will be, but there is a cross section of these communities, SWE-leaning SETs, and SET-leaning SWEs, who are some of our best engineers and make up some of our most effective product teams.

The Early Phase of a Project

There is no set rule at Google for when SETs engage in a project, as there are no set rules for establishing when projects become "real." A common scenario for new project creation is that some informal 20 percent effort takes a life of its own as an actual Google-branded product. Gmail and Chrome OS are both projects that started out as ideas that were not formally sanctioned by Google but overtime grew into shipping products with teams of developers and testers working on them. In fact, our friend Alberto Savoia (see his preface to this book) is fond of saying that "quality is not important until the software is important."

There is a lot of innovation going on within loose-knit teams doing 20 percent work. Some of this work will end up nowhere, some will find its way into a larger project as a feature, and some may grow into an official Google product. None of them get testing resources as some inalienable right of their existence. Stacking a project potentially doomed to failure with a bunch of testers so they can build testing infrastructure is a waste of resources. If a project ends up being cancelled, what did that testing infrastructure accomplish?

Focusing on quality before a product concept is fully baked and determined to be feasible is an exercise in misplaced priorities. Many of the early prototypes that we have seen come from Google 20 percent efforts end up being redesigned to the point that little of the original code even exists by the time a version is ready for dogfood or beta. Clearly testing in this experimental context is a fool's errand.

Of course, there is risk in the opposite direction too. If a product goes too long without testing involvement, it can be difficult to undo a series of design decisions that reduce testability to the point that automation is too hard and resulting test tools too brittle. There may be some rework that has to be done in the name of higher quality down the road. Such quality "debt" can slow products down for years.

Google doesn't make specific attempts to get testers involved early in the lifecycle. In fact, SETs involved early are often there with their developer hat on as opposed to their testing hat. This is not an intentional omission, nor is it a statement that early quality involvement is not important. It is more an artifact of Google's informal and innovation-driven project creation process. Google rarely creates projects as a big bang event where months of planning (which would include quality and test) are followed by a large development effort. Google projects are born much less formally.

Chrome OS serves as a case in point. It was a product all three authors of this book worked on for over a year. But before we joined formally, a few developers built a prototype, and much of it was scripts and fakes that allowed the concept of a browser-only app model to be demonstrated to Google brass for formal project approval. In this early prototyping phase, the concentration was on experimentation and proving that the concept was actually viable. A great deal of time testing or even designing for testability would have been moot given the project was still unofficial and all of the demonstration scripts would eventually be replaced by real C++ code. When the scripts fulfilled the demonstration purpose and the product was approved, the development director sought us out to provide testing resources.

This is a different kind of culture that exists at Google. No project gets testing resources as some right of its existence. The onus is on the development teams to solicit help from testers and convince them that their project is exciting and full of potential. As the Chrome OS development directors explained their project, progress, and ship schedule, we were able to place certain demands concerning SWE involvement in testing, expected unit testing coverage levels, and how the duties of the release process were going to be shared. We may not have been involved at project inception, but once the project became real, we had vast influence over how it was to be executed.

No project gets testing resources as some right of its existence. The onus is on the development teams to solicit help from testers and convince them that their project is exciting and full of potential.

Team Structure

SWEs often get caught up in the code they are writing and generally that code is a single feature or perhaps even smaller in scope than that. SWEs tend to make decisions optimized for this local and narrow view of a product. A good SET must take the exact opposite approach and assume not only a broad view of the entire product and consider all of its features but also understand that over a product's lifetime, *many* SWEs will come and go and the product will outlive the people who created it.

A product like Gmail or Chrome is destined to live for many versions and will consume hundreds of developers' individual work. If a SWE joins a product team working on version 3 and that product is well documented, testable, and has working stable test automation and processes that make it clear how to add new code into this mix, then that is a sign that the early SETs did their job correctly.

With all of the features added, versions launched, patches made, and good intentioned rewrites and renames that happen during the life of a project, it can be hard to identify when or if a project ever truly comes to an end. Every software project has a definite beginning, though. We refine our goals during that early phase. We plan. We try things out. We even attempt to document what we think we are going to do. We try to ensure that the decisions made early on are the right decisions for the long-term viability of the product.

The amount of planning, experimentation, and documentation we produce before we begin to implement a new software project is proportional to the strength of our convictions in the long-term viability and success of that project. We don't want to begin with little in the way of planning only to find out later that planning would have been worthwhile. We also don't want to spend weeks in the early phase only to discover at its conclusion that the world around us has either changed or is not what it was originally thought to be. For these reasons, some structure around documentation and process during this early phase is wise. However, it is ultimately up to the engineers who create these projects to decide what and how much is enough.

Google product teams start with a tech lead and one or more founding members of various engineering roles. At Google, tech lead or TL is an informal title granted to the engineer or engineers responsible for setting the technical direction, coordinating activities, and acting as the main engineering representative of the project to other teams. He knows the answer to any question about the project or can point to someone who does. A project's tech lead is usually a SWE or an engineer of another discipline working in a SWE capacity.

The tech lead and founding members of a project begin their work by drafting the project's first design doc (described in the next section). As the document matures, it is leveraged as evidence of the need for additional engineers of various specializations. Many tech leads request an SET early on, despite their relative scarcity.

Design Docs

Every project at Google has a primary design doc. It is a living document, which means that it evolves alongside the project it describes. In its earliest form, a design doc describes the project's objective, background, proposed team members, and proposed designs. During the early phase, the team works together to fill in the remaining relevant sections of the primary design doc. For sufficiently large projects, this might involve creating and linking to smaller design docs that describe the major subsystems. By the end of the early design phase, the project's collection of design documents should be able to serve as a roadmap of all future work to be done. At this point, design docs might undergo one or more reviews by other tech leads in a project's domain. Once a project's design docs have received sufficient review, the early phase of the project draws to a close and the implementation phase officially begins.

As SETs, we are fortunate to join a project during its early phase. There is significant high-impact work to be done here. If we play our cards right, we can simplify the life of everyone on the project while accelerating the work of all those around us. Indeed, SETs have the one major advantage of being the engineer on the team *with the broadest view of the product*. A good SET can put this breadth of expertise to work for the more laser-focused developers and have impact far beyond the code they write. Generally broad patterns of code reuse and component interaction design are identified by SETs and not SWEs. The remainder of this section focuses on the high-value work an SET can do during the early phase of a project.

Note

A SET's role in the design phase is to simplify the life of everyone on the project while accelerating the work of all those around him.

There is no substitute for an additional pair of eyes on a body of work. As SWEs fill in the various sections of their design docs, they should be diligent about getting peer feedback prior to sending their document to a wider audience for official review. A good SET is eager to review such documents and proactively volunteers his time to review documents written by the team and adds quality or reliability sections as necessary. Here are several reasons why:

- An SET needs to be familiar with the design of the system she tests (reading all of the design docs is part of this) so being a reviewer accomplishes both SET and SWE needs.

- Suggestions made early on are much more likely to make it into the document and into the codebase, increasing an SET's overall impact.

- By being the first person to review all design documents (and thus seeing all their iterations), an SET's knowledge of the project as a whole will rival that of the tech lead's knowledge.

- It is a great chance to establish a working relationship with each of the engineers whose code and tests the SET will be working with when development begins.

Reviewing design documents should be done with purpose and not just be a general breeze through, as though you are reading a newspaper. A good SET is purposeful during his review. Here are some things we recommend:

- **Completeness:** Identify parts of the document that are incomplete or that require special knowledge not generally available on the team, particularly to new members of the team. Encourage the document's author to write more details or link to other documentation that fill in these gaps.

- **Correctness:** Look for grammar, spelling, and punctuation mistakes; this is sloppy work that does not bode well for the code they will write later. Don't set a precedent for sloppiness.

- **Consistency:** Ensure that wording matches diagrams. Ensure that the document does not contradict claims made in other documents.

- **Design:** Consider the design proposed by the document. Is it achievable given the resources available? What infrastructure does it propose to build upon? (Read the documentation of that infrastructure and learn its pitfalls.) Does the proposed design make use of that infrastructure in a supported way? Is the design too complex? Is it possible to simplify? Is it too simple? What more does the design need to address?

- **Interfaces and protocols:** Does the document clearly identify the protocols it will use? Does it completely describe the interfaces and protocols that the product will expose? Do these interfaces and protocols accomplish what they are meant to accomplish? Are they standard across other Google products? Can you encourage the developer to go one step further and define his protocol buffers? (We discuss more about protocol buffers later.)

- **Testing:** How testable is the system or set of systems described by the document? Are new testing hooks required? If so, ensure those get added to the documentation. Can the design of the system be tweaked to make testing easier or use pre-existing test infrastructure? Estimate what must be done to test the system and work with the developer to have this information added to the design document.

Note
Reviewing design documents is purposeful and not like reading a newspaper. There are specific goals to pursue.

When an SET discusses this review with the SWE who created the design document, a serious conversation about the amount of work required to test it and the way in which that work is shared among the roles happens. This is a great time to document the goals of developer unit testing along with the best practices team members will follow when delivering a well tested product. When this discussion happens in a collaborative way, you know you are off to a good start.

Interfaces and Protocols

Documenting interfaces and protocols at Google is easy for developers as it involves writing code! Google's protocol buffer language[7] is a language-neutral, platform-neutral, extensible mechanism for serializing structured data—think XML, but smaller, faster, and easier. A developer defines how data is to be structured after it is in the protocol buffer language, and then uses generated source code to read and write the structured data from and to a variety of data streams in a variety of languages (Java, C++, or Python). Protocol buffer source is often the first code written for a new project. It is not uncommon to have design docs refer to protocol buffers as the specification of how things will work once the full system is implemented.

An SET reviews protocol buffer code thoroughly, because he will soon implement most of the interfaces and protocols described by that protocol buffer code. That's right, it is an SET who typically implements most of the

---

[7] Google's protocol buffers are open sourced; see http://code.google.com/apis/protocolbuffers/.

interfaces and protocols in the system first, because the need for integration testing often arises before it is possible to construct all subsystems on which the entire system depends. To enable integration testing early on, the SET provides mocks and fakes of the necessary dependencies of each component. Such integration tests have to be written eventually, and they're more valuable when they're available as the code is still being developed. Further, the mocks and fakes would be required for integration testing at any stage, as it is much easier to inject failures and establish error conditions through mocks than it is to do so within a system's production dependencies.

> To enable integration testing early on, the SET provides mocks and fakes of the necessary dependencies of each component.

Automation Planning

A SET's time is limited and spread thinly and it is a good idea to create a plan for automating testing of the system as early as possible and to be practical about it. Designs that seek to automate everything end-to-end all in one master test suite are generally a mistake. Certainly no SWE is impressed by such an all-encompassing endeavor and an SET is unlikely to get much assistance. If an SET is going to get help from SWEs, his automation plan must be sensible and impactful. The larger an automation effort is, the harder it is to maintain and the more brittle it becomes as the system evolves. It's the smaller, more special purpose automation that creates useful infrastructure and that attracts the most SWEs to write tests.

Overinvesting in end-to-end automation often ties you to a product's specific design and isn't particularly useful until the entire product is built and in stable form. By then, it's often too late to make design changes in the product, so whatever you learn in testing at that point is moot. Time that the SET could have invested in improving quality was instead spent on maintaining a brittle end-to-end test suite.

> Overinvesting in end-to-end automation often ties you to a product's specific design.

At Google, SETs take the following approach.

We first isolate the interfaces that we think are prone to errors and create mocks and fakes (as described in the previous section) so that we can control the interactions at those interfaces and ensure good test coverage.

The next step is to build a lightweight automation framework that allows the mocked system to be built and executed. That way, any SWE who writes code that uses one of the mocked interfaces can do a private build and run the test automation before they check their code changes into the main codebase, ensuring only well tested code gets into the codebase in the first place. This is one key area where automation excels: keeping bad code out of the ecosystem and ensuring the main codebase stays clean.

In addition to the automation (mocks, fakes, and frameworks) to be delivered by the SET, the plan should include how to surface information about build quality to all concerned parties. Google SETs include such reporting mechanisms and dashboards that collect test results and show progress as part of the test plan. In this way, an SET increases the chances of creating high-quality code by making the whole process easy and transparent.

Testability

SWEs and SETs work closely on product development. SWEs write the production code and tests for that code. SETs support this work by writing test frameworks that enable SWEs to write tests. SETs also take a share of maintenance work. Quality is a shared responsibility between these roles.

A SET's first job is testability. They act as consultants recommending program structure and coding style that lends itself to better unit testing and in writing frameworks to enable developers to test for themselves. We discuss frameworks later; first, let's talk about the coding process at Google.

To make SETs true partners in the ownership of the source code, Google centers its development process around code reviews. There is far more fanfare about reviewing code than there is about writing it.

Reviewing code is a fundamental aspect of being a developer and it is an activity that has full tool support and an encompassing culture around it that has borrowed somewhat from the open source community's concept of "committer" where only people who have proven to be reliable developers can actually commit code to the source tree.

> Google centers its development process around code reviews. There is far more fanfare about reviewing code than there is about writing it.

At Google everyone is a committer, but we use a concept called *readability* to distinguish between proven committers and new developers. Here's how the whole process works:

Code is written and packaged as a unit that we call a *change list*, or CL for short. A CL is written and then submitted for review in a tool known internally as Mondrian (named after the Dutch painter whose work inspired abstract art). Mondrian then routes the code to qualified SWEs or SETs for review and eventual signoff.[8]

CLs can be blocks of new code, changes to existing code, bug fixes, and so on. They range from a few lines to a few hundred lines with larger CLs almost always broken into smaller CLs at the behest of reviewers. SWEs and SETs who are new to Google will eventually be awarded with a *readability* designation by their peers for writing consistently good CLs. Readabilities are language specific and given for C++, Java, Python, and JavaScript, the primary languages Google uses. They are credentials that designate an experienced, trustworthy developer and help ensure the entire codebase has the look and feel of having been written by a single developer.[9]

There are a number of automated checks that occur before a CL is routed to a reviewer. These *pre-submit rules* cover simple things such as adherence to the Google coding style guide and more involved things such as ensuring that every existing test associated with the CL has been executed (the rule is that all tests must pass). The tests for a CL are almost always included in the CL itself—test code lives side by side with the functional code. After these checks are made, Mondrian notifies the reviewer via email with links to the appropriate CLs. The reviewer then completes the review and makes recommendations that are then handled by the SWE. The process is repeated until both the reviewers are happy and the pre-submit automation runs clean.

A submit queue's primary goal in life is to keep the build "green," meaning all tests pass. It is the last line of defense between a project's continuous build system and the version control system. By building code and running tests in a clean environment, the submit queue catches environmental failures that might not be caught by a developer running tests on an individual workstation, but that might ultimately break the continuous build or, worse, make its way into the version control system in a broken state.

A submit queue also enables members of large teams to collaborate on the main branch of the source tree. This further eliminates the need to have scheduled code freezes while branch integrations and test passes take place. In this way, a submit queue enables developers on large teams to work as efficiently and independently as developers on small teams. The only real downside is that it makes the SET's job harder because it increases the rate at which developers can write and submit code!

---

[8] An open-source version of Mondrian hosted on App Engine is publicly available at http://code.google.com/p/rietveld/.

[9] Google's *C++ Style Guide* is publicly available at http://google-styleguide.googlecode.com/svn/trunk/cppguide.xml.

How Submit Queues and Continuous Builds Came Into Being

by Jeff Carollo

In the beginning, Google was small. Having a policy of writing and running unit tests before checking in changes seemed good enough. Every now and then, a test would break and people would spend time figuring out why and then fix the problem.

The company grew. To realize the economies of scale, high-quality libraries and infrastructure were written, maintained, and shared by all developers. These core libraries grew in number, size, and complexity over time. Unit tests were not enough; integration testing was now required for code that had significant interactions with other libraries and infrastructure. At some point, Google realized that many test failures were introduced by dependencies on other components. As tests were not being run until someone on a project wanted to check in a change to that project, these integration failures could exist for days before being noticed.

Along came the "Unit Test Dashboard." This system treated every top-level directory in the companywide source tree as a "project." This system also allowed anyone to define their own "project," which associated a set of build and test targets with a set of maintainers. The system would run all tests for each project every day. The pass and fail rate for each test and project was recorded and reported through the dashboard. Failing tests would generate emails to the maintainers of a project every day, so tests did not stay broken for long. Still, things broke.

Teams wanted to be even more proactive about catching the breaking changes. Running every test every 24 hours was not enough. Individual teams began to write Continuous Build scripts, which would run on dedicated machines and continuously build and run the unit and integration tests of their team. Realizing that such a system could be made generic enough to support any team, Chris Lopez and Jay Corbett sat down together and wrote the "Chris/Jay Continuous Build," which allowed any project to deploy its own Continuous Build system by simply registering a machine, filling in a configuration file, and running a script. This practice became popular quite rapidly, and soon most projects at Google had a Chris/Jay Continuous Build. Failing tests would generate emails to the person or persons most likely to be the cause of those tests failing within minutes of those changes being checked in! Additionally, the Chris/Jay Continuous Build would identify "Golden Change Lists," checkpoints in the version control system at which all tests for a particular project built and passed. This enabled developers to sync their view of the source tree to a version not affected by recent check-ins and build breakages (quite useful for selecting a stable build for release purposes).

Teams still wanted to be more proactive about catching breaking changes. As the size and complexity of teams and projects grew, so too did the cost of having a broken build. Submit Queues were built out of necessity as protectors of Continuous Build systems. Early implementations required all CLs to wait in line to be tested and approved by the system serially before those changes could be submitted (hence, the "queue" suffix). When lots of long-running tests were necessary, a several-hour backlog between a CL being sent to the queue and that CL actually being submitted into version control was common. Subsequent implementations allowed all pending CLs to run in parallel with one another, but isolated from each other's changes. While this "improvement" did introduce race conditions, those races were rare, and they would be caught by the Continuous Build eventually. The time saved in being able to submit within minutes of entering the submit queue greatly outweighed the cost of having to resolve the occasional Continuous Build failure. Most large projects at Google adopted the use of Submit Queues. Most of these large projects also rotated team members into a position of "build cop," whose job it was to respond quickly to any issues uncovered in the project's Submit Queue and Continuous Build.

This set of systems (the Unit Test Dashboard, the Chris/Jay Continuous Build, and Submit Queues) had a long life at Google (several years). They offered tremendous benefit to teams in exchange for a small amount of set-up time and varying amounts of ongoing maintenance. At some point, it became both feasible and practical to implement all of these systems in an integrated way as shared infrastructure for all teams. The Test Automation Program, or TAP, did just that. As of this writing, TAP has taken the place of each of these systems and is in use by nearly all projects at Google outside of Chromium and Android (which are open source and utilize separate source trees and build environments from the server side of Google).

The benefits of having most teams on the same set of tools and infrastructure cannot be overstated. With a single, simple command, an engineer is able to build and run all binaries and tests that might be affected by a CL in parallel in the cloud, have code coverage collected, have all results stored and analyzed in the cloud, and have those results visualized at a new permanent web location. The output of that command to the terminal is "PASS" or "FAIL" along with a hyperlink to the details. If a developer chooses to run his tests this way, the results of that test pass, including the code coverage information, are stored in the cloud and made visible to code reviewers through the internal Google code review tool.

SET Workflow: An Example

Now let's put all this together in an example. Warning: this section is going to get technical and go into a bunch of low-level details. If you are interested only in the big picture, feel free to skip to the next section.

Imagine a simple web application that allows users to submit URLs to Google that would then be added to Google's index. The HTML form accepts two fields: url and comment, and it generates an HTTP GET request to Google's servers resembling the following:

```
GET /addurl?url=http://www.foo.com&comment=Foo+comment HTTP/1.1
```

The server-side of this example web application is broken into at least two parts: the AddUrlFrontend (which accepts the raw HTTP request, parses it, and validates it) and the `AddUrlService` backend. This backend service accepts requests from the `AddUrlFrontend`, checks them for errors, and further interacts with persistent storage backends such as Google's Bigtable[10] or the Google File System.[11]

The SWE writing this service begins by creating a directory for this project:

```
$ mkdir depot/addurl/
```

He or she then defines the protocol of the `AddUrlService` using the Google Protocol Buffer[12] description language as follows:

```
File: depot/addurl/addurl.proto
message AddUrlRequest {
  required string url = 1;   // The URL entered by the user.
  optional string comment = 2;   // Comments made by the user.
}

message AddUrlReply {
  // Error code, if an error occurred.
  optional int32 error_code = 1;
  // Error message, if an error occurred.
  optional string error_details = 2;
}

service AddUrlService {
  // Accepts a URL for submission to the index.
  rpc AddUrl(AddUrlRequest) returns (AddUrlReply) {
    option deadline = 10.0;
  }
}
```

The addurl.proto file defines three important items: the `AddUrlRequest` and `AddUrlReply` messages and the `AddUrlService` Remote Procedure Call (RPC) service.

We can tell by inspecting the definition of the `AddUrlRequest` message that a `url` field must be supplied by the caller and that a `comment` field can be optionally supplied.

We can similarly see by inspecting the definition of the `AddUrlReply` message that both the `error_code` and `error_details` fields can optionally be supplied by the service in its replies. We can safely assume that these fields are left empty in the common case where a URL is accepted successfully, minimizing the amount of data transferred. This is the convention at Google: Make the common case fast.

Inspection of the `AddUrlService` reveals that there is a single service method, `AddUrl`, that accepts an `AddUrlRequest` and returns an `AddUrlReply`. By default, calls to the `AddUrl` method time out after an elapsed time of 10 seconds, if the client did not receive a response in that time. Implementations of the `AddUrlService` interface might involve any

---

[10] http://labs.google.com/papers/bigtable.html.

[11] http://labs.google.com/papers/gfs.html.

[12] http://code.google.com/apis/protocolbuffers/docs/overview.html.

number of persistent storage backends, but that is of no concern to clients of this interface, so those details are not present in the addurl.proto file.

The '= 1' notation on message fields has no bearing on the values of those fields. The notation exists to allow the protocol to evolve over time. For example, in the future, someone might want to add a uri field to the AddUrlRequest message in addition to the fields that were already there. To do this, they can make the following change:

```
message AddUrlRequest {
  required string url = 1;   // The URL entered by the user.
  optional string comment = 2;   // Comments made by the user.
  optional string uri = 3;   // The URI entered by the user.
}
```

But that would be silly. Someone is more likely to want to rename the url field to uri. If they keep the number and type the same, then they maintain compatibility between the old and new versions:

```
message AddUrlRequest {
  required string uri = 1;   // The URI entered by the user.
  optional string comment = 2;   // Comments made by the user.
}
```

Having written addurl.proto, our developer proceeds to create a proto_library build rule, which generates C++ source files that define the items from addurl.proto and that compile into a static addurl C++ library. (With additional options, source for Java and Python language bindings are also possible.)

```
File: depot/addurl/BUILD
proto_library(name="addurl",
              srcs=["addurl.proto"])
```

The developer invokes the build system and fixes any issues uncovered by the build system in addurl.proto and in its build definitions in the BUILD file. The build system invokes the Protocol Buffer compiler, generating source code files addurl.pb.h and addurl.pb.cc, as well as generating a static addurl library that can be linked against.

The AddUrlFrontend can now be written by creating a class declaration of AddUrlFrontend in a new file, addurl_frontend.h. This code is largely boilerplate.

```
File: depot/addurl/addurl_frontend.h
#ifndef ADDURL_ADDURL_FRONTEND_H_
#define ADDURL_ADDURL_FRONTEND_H_

// Forward-declaration of dependencies.
class AddUrlService;
class HTTPRequest;
class HTTPReply;

// Frontend for the AddUrl system.
// Accepts HTTP requests from web clients,
// and forwards well-formed requests to the backend.
class AddUrlFrontend {
 public:
  // Constructor which enables injection of an
  // AddUrlService dependency.
```

```
  explicit AddUrlFrontend(AddUrlService* add_url_service);
  ~AddUrlFrontend();

  // Method invoked by our HTTP server when a request arrives
  // for the /addurl resource.
  void HandleAddUrlFrontendRequest(const HTTPRequest* http_request,
                                   HTTPReply* http_reply);

 private:
  AddUrlService* add_url_service_;

  // Declare copy constructor and operator= private to prohibit
  // unintentional copying of instances of this class.
  AddUrlFrontend(const AddUrlFrontend&);
  AddUrlFrontend& operator=(const AddUrlFrontend& rhs);
};

#endif  // ADDURL_ADDURL_FRONTEND_H_
```

Continuing on to the definitions of the `AddUrlFrontend` class, the developer now creates addurl_frontend.cc. This is where the logic of the `AddUrlFrontend` class is coded. For the sake of brevity, portions of this file have been omitted.

```
File: depot/addurl/addurl_frontend.cc
#include "addurl/addurl_frontend.h"

#include "addurl/addurl.pb.h"
#include "path/to/httpqueryparams.h"

// Functions used by HandleAddUrlFrontendRequest() below, but
// whose definitions are omitted for brevity.
void ExtractHttpQueryParams(const HTTPRequest* http_request,
                            HTTPQueryParams* query_params);
void WriteHttp200Reply(HTTPReply* reply);
void WriteHttpReplyWithErrorDetails(
    HTTPReply* http_reply, const AddUrlReply& add_url_reply);

// AddUrlFrontend constructor that injects the AddUrlService
// dependency.
AddUrlFrontend::AddUrlFrontend(AddUrlService* add_url_service)
    : add_url_service_(add_url_service) {
}

// AddUrlFrontend destructor - there's nothing to do here.
AddUrlFrontend::~AddUrlFrontend() {
}

// HandleAddUrlFrontendRequest:
// Handles requests to /addurl by parsing the request,
// dispatching a backend request to an AddUrlService backend,
// and transforming the backend reply into an appropriate
// HTTP reply.
//
// Args:
//   http_request - The raw HTTP request received by the server.
//   http_reply - The raw HTTP reply to send in response.
void AddUrlFrontend::HandleAddUrlFrontendRequest(
    const HTTPRequest* http_request, HTTPReply* http_reply) {
  // Extract the query parameters from the raw HTTP request.
  HTTPQueryParams query_params;
  ExtractHttpQueryParams(http_request, &query_params);

  // Get the 'url' and 'comment' query components.
  // Default each to an empty string if they were not present
  // in http_request.
  string url =
```

```
      query_params.GetQueryComponentDefault("url", "");
  string comment =
      query_params.GetQueryComponentDefault("comment", "");

  // Prepare the request to the AddUrlService backend.
  AddUrlRequest add_url_request;
  AddUrlReply add_url_reply;
  add_url_request.set_url(url);
  if (!comment.empty()) {
    add_url_request.set_comment(comment);
  }

  // Issue the request to the AddUrlService backend.
  RPC rpc;
  add_url_service_->AddUrl(
      &rpc, &add_url_request, &add_url_reply);

  // Block until the reply is received from the
  // AddUrlService backend.
  rpc.Wait();

  // Handle errors, if any:
  if (add_url_reply.has_error_code()) {
    WriteHttpReplyWithErrorDetails(http_reply, add_url_reply);
  } else {
    // No errors. Send HTTP 200 OK response to client.
    WriteHttp200Reply(http_reply);
  }
}
```

HandleAddUrlFrontendRequest is a busy member function. This is the nature of many web handlers. The developer can choose to simplify this function by extracting some of its functionality into helper functions. However, such refactoring before the build is stable, unit tests are in place, and unit tests are passing is unusual.

At this point, the developer modifies the existing build specification for the addurl project, adding an entry for the addurl_frontend library. This creates a static C++ library for AddUrlFrontend when built.

```
File: /depot/addurl/BUILD
# From before:
proto_library(name="addurl",
              srcs=["addurl.proto"])

# New:
cc_library(name="addurl_frontend",
           srcs=["addurl_frontend.cc"],
           deps=[
               "path/to/httpqueryparams",
               "other_http_server_stuff",
               ":addurl", # Link against the addurl library above.
           ])
```

The developer starts his build tools again, fixing compiler and linker errors in addurl_frontend.h and addurl_frontend.cc until everything builds and links cleanly without warnings or errors. At this point, it's time to write unit tests for AddUrlFrontend. These are written in a new file, addurl_frontend_test.cc. This test defines a fake of the AddUrlService backend and leverages the AddUrlFrontend constructor to inject this fake at test time. In this way, the developer is able to inject expectations and errors into the workflow of AddUrlFrontend without modification of the AddUrlFrontend code itself.

```
File: depot/addurl/addurl_frontend_test.cc
#include "addurl/addurl.pb.h"
#include "addurl/addurl_frontend.h"

// See http://code.google.com/p/googletest/
#include "path/to/googletest.h"

// Defines a fake AddUrlService, which will be injected by
// the AddUrlFrontendTest test fixture into AddUrlFrontend
// instances under test.
class FakeAddUrlService : public AddUrlService {
 public:
  FakeAddUrlService()
      : has_request_expectations_(false),
        error_code_(0) {
  }

  // Allows tests to set expectations on requests.
  void set_expected_url(const string& url) {
    expected_url_ = url;
    has_request_expectations_ = true;
  }
  void set_expected_comment(const string& comment) {
    expected_comment_ = comment;
    has_request_expectations_ = true;
  }

  // Allows for injection of errors by tests.
  void set_error_code(int error_code) {
    error_code_ = error_code;
  }
  void set_error_details(const string& error_details) {
    error_details_ = error_details;
  }

  // Overrides of the AddUrlService::AddUrl method generated from
  // service definition in addurl.proto by the Protocol Buffer
  // compiler.
  virtual void AddUrl(RPC* rpc,
                      const AddUrlRequest* request,
                      AddUrlReply* reply) {
    // Enforce expectations on request (if present).
    if (has_request_expectations_) {
      EXPECT_EQ(expected_url_, request->url());
      EXPECT_EQ(expected_comment_, request->comment());
    }

    // Inject errors specified in the set_* methods above if present.
    if (error_code_ != 0 || !error_details_.empty()) {
      reply->set_error_code(error_code_);
      reply->set_error_details(error_details_);
    }
  }

 private:
  // Expected request information.
  // Clients set using set_expected_* methods.
  string expected_url_;
  string expected_comment_;
  bool has_request_expectations_;

  // Injected error information.
  // Clients set using set_* methods above.
  int error_code_;
  string error_details_;
};

// The test fixture for AddUrlFrontend. It is code shared by the
// TEST_F test definitions below. For every test using this
```

```
// fixture, the fixture will create a FakeAddUrlService, an
// AddUrlFrontend, and inject the FakeAddUrlService into that
// AddUrlFrontend. Tests will have access to both of these
// objects at runtime.
class AddurlFrontendTest : public ::testing::Test {
 protected:
  // Runs before every test method is executed.
  virtual void SetUp() {
    // Create a FakeAddUrlService for injection.
    fake_add_url_service_.reset(new FakeAddUrlService);

    // Create an AddUrlFrontend and inject our FakeAddUrlService
    // into it.
    add_url_frontend_.reset(
        new AddUrlFrontend(fake_add_url_service_.get()));
  }

  scoped_ptr<FakeAddUrlService> fake_add_url_service_;
  scoped_ptr<AddUrlFrontend> add_url_frontend_;
};

// Test that AddurlFrontendTest::SetUp works.
TEST_F(AddurlFrontendTest, FixtureTest) {
  // AddurlFrontendTest::SetUp was invoked by this point.
}

// Test that AddUrlFrontend parses URLs correctly from its
// query parameters.
TEST_F(AddurlFrontendTest, ParsesUrlCorrectly) {
  HTTPRequest http_request;
  HTTPReply http_reply;

  // Configure the request to go to the /addurl resource and
  // to contain a 'url' query parameter.
  http_request.set_text(
      "GET /addurl?url=http://www.foo.com HTTP/1.1\r\n\r\n");

  // Tell the FakeAddUrlService to expect to receive a URL
  // of 'http://www.foo.com'.
  fake_add_url_service_->set_expected_url("http://www.foo.com");

  // Send the request to AddUrlFrontend, which should dispatch
  // a request to the FakeAddUrlService.
  add_url_frontend_->HandleAddUrlFrontendRequest(
      &http_request, &http_reply);

  // Validate the response.
  EXPECT_STREQ("200 OK", http_reply.text());
}

// Test that AddUrlFrontend parses comments correctly from its
// query parameters.
TEST_F(AddurlFrontendTest, ParsesCommentCorrectly) {
  HTTPRequest http_request;
  HTTPReply http_reply;

  // Configure the request to go to the /addurl resource and
  // to contain a 'url' query parameter and to also contain
  // a 'comment' query parameter that contains the
  // url-encoded query string 'Test comment'.
  http_request.set_text("GET /addurl?url=http://www.foo.com"
                  "&comment=Test+comment HTTP/1.1\r\n\r\n");

  // Tell the FakeAddUrlService to expect to receive a URL
  // of 'http://www.foo.com' again.
  fake_add_url_service_->set_expected_url("http://www.foo.com");

  // Tell the FakeAddUrlService to also expect to receive a
  // comment of 'Test comment' this time.
  fake_add_url_service_->set_expected_comment("Test comment");
```

```
    // Send the request to AddUrlFrontend, which should dispatch
    // a request to the FakeAddUrlService.
    add_url_frontend ->HandleAddUrlFrontendRequest(
        &http_request, &http_reply);

    // Validate that the response received is a '200 OK' response.
    EXPECT_STREQ("200 OK", http_reply.text());
}

// Test that AddUrlFrontend sends proper error information when
// the AddUrlService encounters a client error.
TEST_F(AddurlFrontendTest, HandlesBackendClientErrors) {
    HTTPRequest http_request;
    HTTPReply http_reply;

    // Configure the request to go to the /addurl resource.
    http_request.set_text("GET /addurl HTTP/1.1\r\n\r\n");

    // Configure the FakeAddUrlService to inject a client error with
    // error_code 400 and error_details of 'Client Error'.
    fake_add_url_service ->set_error_code(400);
    fake_add_url_service ->set_error_details("Client Error");

    // Send the request to AddUrlFrontend, which should dispatch
    // a request to the FakeAddUrlService.
    add_url_frontend ->HandleAddUrlFrontendRequest(
        &http_request, &http_reply);

    // Validate that the response contained a 400 client error.
    EXPECT_STREQ("400\r\nError Details: Client Error",
                 http_reply.text());
}
```

The developer would likely write many more tests than this, but this is enough to demonstrate the common patterns of defining a fake, injecting that fake into a system under test, and using that fake in tests to inject errors and validation logic into the workflow of a system under test. One notable test missing here is one that would mimic a network timeout between the `AddUrlFrontend` and the `FakeAddUrlService` backend. Such a test would reveal that our developer forgot to check for and handle the condition where a timeout occurred.

Agile testing veterans will point out that everything done by `FakeAddUrlService` was simple enough that a mock could have been used instead. These veterans would be correct. We implement these features via a fake purely for illustrative purposes.

Anyhow, our developer now wants to run these tests. To do so, he must first update his build definitions to include a new test rule that defines the `addurl_frontend_test` test binary.

```
File: depot/addurl/BUILD
# From before:
proto_library(name="addurl",
              srcs=["addurl.proto"])

# Also from before:
cc_library(name="addurl_frontend",
           srcs=["addurl_frontend.cc"],
           deps=[
               "path/to/httpqueryparams",
               "other_http_server_stuff",
               ":addurl", # Depends on the proto_library above.
           ])
```

```
# New:
cc_test(name="addurl_frontend_test",
        size="small", # See section on Test Sizes.
        srcs=["addurl_frontend_test.cc"],
        deps=[
            ":addurl_frontend", # Depends on library above.
            "path/to/googletest_main"])
```

Once again, the developer uses his build tools to compile and run the addurl_frontend_test binary, fixing any compiler and linker errors uncovered by the build tools and this time also fixing the tests, test fixtures, fakes, and/or AddUrlFrontend itself based on any test failures that occur. This process starts immediately after defining the previous FixtureTest, and is repeated as the remaining test cases are added one at a time. When all of the tests are in place and passing, the developer creates a CL that contains all of these files, fixes any small issues caught by presubmit checks, sends that CL out for review, and then moves on to the next task (likely writing a real AddUrlService backend) while waiting for review feedback.

```
$ create_cl BUILD \
            addurl.proto \
            addurl_frontend.h \
            addurl_frontend.cc \
            addurl_frontend_test.cc

$ mail_cl -m reviewer@google.com
```

When review feedback arrives, the developer makes the appropriate changes (or works with the reviewer to agree on an alternative), potentially undergoes additional review, and then submits the CL to the version control system. From this point on, whenever someone makes changes to any of the code in these files, Google's test automation systems know to run the addurl_frontend_test to verify that those changes did not break the existing tests. Additionally, anyone seeking to modify addurl_frontend.cc has addurl_frontend_test as a safety net to run while making their modifications.

Test Execution

Test automation goes beyond writing individual test programs. If we consider what it takes to be useful, we have to include compiling test programs, executing them, and analyzing, storing, and reporting the results of each execution as part of the automated testing challenge. Test automation is in effect an entire software development effort in its own right.

Having to worry about all these issues distracts engineers from concentrating on writing the right automation and making it useful for their projects. Test code is only useful in the context of being executable in a way that accelerates development and doesn't slow it down. Thus, it has to be integrated into the actual development process in a way that makes it part of development and not separate from it. Functional code never exists in a vacuum. Neither should test code.

Thus, a common infrastructure that performs the compilation, execution, analysis, storage, and reporting of tests has evolved, reducing the problem back to where we want it to be: Google engineers writing individual test programs and submitting them to this common infrastructure to handle the execution details and ensuring that the test code gets the same treatment as functional code.

After an SET writes a new test program, he creates a build specification of that test for the Google build infrastructure. A test build specification includes the name of the test, the source files from which it is built, its dependencies on any libraries or data, and finally a test size. Every test must specify its size as either small, medium, large, or enormous. After the code and build specifications for a test are in place, Google's build tools and test execution infrastructure take care of the rest. From that moment forward, a single command initiates a build, runs the automation, and provides views for the results of that test.

Google's test execution infrastructure places constraints on how tests are written. These constraints and how we manage them are described in the following section.

Test Size Definitions

As Google grew and new employees were hired, a confusing nomenclature of types of tests persisted: Unit tests, code-based tests, white box tests, integration tests, system tests, and end-to-end tests all add different levels of granularity, as shown in Figure 2.1. Early on, it was decided enough is enough, so we created a standard set of names.

FIGURE 2.1 Google employs many different types of test execution.

Small tests verify the behavior of a single unit of code generally isolated from its environment. Examples include a single class or a small group of related functions. Small tests should have no external dependencies. Outside of Google, small tests are commonly known as "unit tests."

Small tests have the narrowest scope of any of the test categories and focus on a function operating in isolation, as depicted in Figure 2.2. This limited scope enables small tests to provide comprehensive coverage of low-level code in a way that larger tests cannot.

Within small tests, external services such as file systems, networks, and databases *must* be mocked or faked. Where appropriate, mocking of internal services within the same module as the class under test is also encouraged to further reduce any external dependencies.

Isolated scope and absence of external dependencies mean that small tests can be run quickly; therefore, they are executed frequently, leading to quicker discovery of bugs. The general idea is that as developers execute these tests and as they modify functional code, they also maintain the small tests for that code. Isolation can also enable shorter build and execution times for tests.

FIGURE 2.2   Illustration of the scope of a small test where often only a single function is involved.

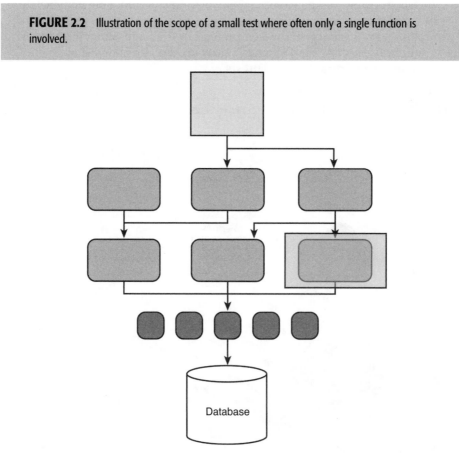

Medium tests validate the interaction of one or more application modules, as depicted in Figure 2.3. Larger scopes and longer running times differentiate medium tests from small tests. Whereas small tests might attempt to exercise all of a single function's code, medium tests are aimed at testing interaction across a limited subset of modules. Outside of Google, medium tests are often called "integration tests."

The longer running times of medium tests require test execution infrastructure to manage them and they often do not execute as frequently as smaller tests. Medium tests are generally organized and executed by SETs.

Note

Small tests verify the behavior of a single unit of code. Medium tests validate the interaction of one or more units of code. Large tests verify that the system works as a whole.

Mocking external services for medium tests is encouraged but not required, unless performance considerations mandate mocking. Lightweight fakes, such as in-memory databases, can be used to improve performance where true mocking might not be immediately practical.

FIGURE 2.3 Medium tests include multiple modules and can include external data sources.

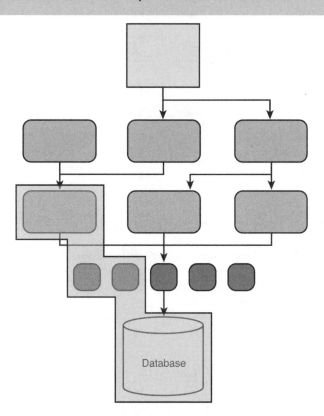

Large and *enormous tests* are commonly referred to as "system tests" or "end-to-end tests" outside of Google. Large tests operate on a high level and verify that the application as a whole works. These tests are expected to exercise any or all application subsystems from the UI down to backend data storage, as shown in Figure 2.4, and might make use of external resources such as databases, file systems, and network services.

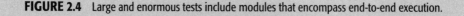

FIGURE 2.4   Large and enormous tests include modules that encompass end-to-end execution.

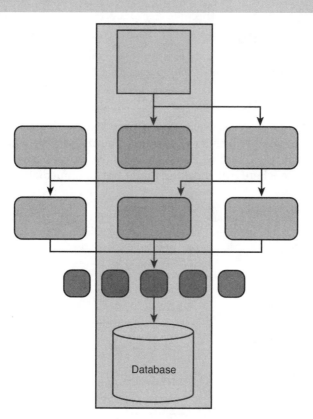

Database

Use of Test Sizes in Shared Infrastructure

Automation of test execution can be a difficult service to provide in a universal way. For a large engineering organization to share common test execution infrastructure, that infrastructure must support execution of a variety of testing jobs.

Some common jobs that share Google test execution infrastructure are

- A developer compiles and runs a small test and would like to get the results immediately.

- A developer would like to run all the small tests for a project and get the results quickly.

- A developer would like to compile and run only the tests in a project that are impacted by a pending change and get the results immediately.

- An engineer would like to collect code coverage for a project and view the results.

- A team would like to run all small tests for a project for every CL submitted and distribute the results for review within the team.

- A team would like to run all tests for a project after a CL is committed to the version control system.

- A team would like to collect code coverage results weekly and track progress over time.

There might be times when all of the previous jobs are submitted to Google's test execution system simultaneously. Some of these tests might hog resources, bogging down shared machines for hours at a time. Others might take only milliseconds to run and could be run in parallel with hundreds of other tests on a single shared machine. When each test is labeled as small, medium, or large, it makes it easier to schedule the jobs because the scheduler has an idea of how long a job will take to run, thus it can optimize the job queue to good effect.

Google's test execution system uses test sizes to distinguish fast jobs from slower ones. Test sizes guarantee an upper bound on each test's execution time, as described in Table 2.1. Test sizes also imply the potential resource needs of a test, as described in Table 2.2. Google's test execution system cancels execution and reports a failure for any test that exceeds the time or resource requirements associated with its test size. This forces engineers to provide appropriate test size labels. Accurate test sizing enables Google's test execution system to make smart scheduling decisions.

TABLE 2.1   Goals and Limits of Test Execution Time by Test Size

	Small Tests	**Medium Tests**	**Large Tests**	**Enormous Tests**
Time Goals (per method)	Execute in less than 100 ms	Execute in less than 1 sec	Execute as quickly as possible	Execute as quickly as possible
Time Limits Enforced	Kill small test targets after 1 minute	Kill medium test targets after 5 minutes	Kill large test targets after 15 minutes	Kill enormous test targets after 1 hour

TABLE 2.2   Resource Usage by Test Size

Resource	Large	Medium	Small
Network Services (Opens a Socket)	Yes	localhost only	Mocked
Database	Yes	Yes	Mocked
File System Access	Yes	Yes	Mocked
Access to User-Facing Systems	Yes	Discouraged	Mocked
Invoke Syscalls	Yes	Discouraged	No
Multiple Threads	Yes	Yes	Discouraged
Sleep Statements	Yes	Yes	No
System Properties	Yes	Yes	No

Benefits of Test Sizes

Each test size offers its own set of benefits. Figure 2.5 summarizes these benefits. The benefits and weaknesses of each test size are listed for comparison.

FIGURE 2.5   Limitations of various test sizes.

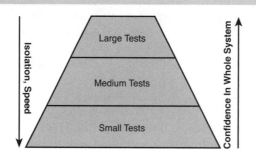

Large Tests

The benefits and weaknesses of large tests include the following:

- Test what is ultimately most important: how the application works. Account for the behavior of external subsystems.

- They can be nondeterministic because of dependencies on external systems.

- Broad scope means that when tests fail, the cause might be difficult to find.

- The data setup for testing scenarios can be time-consuming.

- A high level of operation often makes it impractical to exercise specific corner cases. That's what small tests are for.

Medium Tests

The benefits and weaknesses of medium tests include the following:

- With looser mocking requirements and runtime limitations, provide development groups a stepping stone they can use to move from large tests toward small tests.
- They run relatively fast, so developers can run them frequently.
- They run in a standard developer environment, so developers can run them easily.
- Account for the behavior of external subsystems.
- They can be nondeterministic because of dependencies on external systems.
- They are not as fast as small tests.

Small Tests

The benefits and weaknesses of small tests include the following:

- Lead to cleaner code because methods must be relatively small and tightly focused to be easily tested; mocking requirements lead to well-defined interfaces between subsystems.
- Because they run quickly, they can catch bugs early and provide immediate feedback when code changes are made.
- They run reliably in all environments.
- They have a tighter scope, which allows for easier testing of edge cases and error conditions, such as null pointers.
- They have focused scope, which makes isolation of errors very easy.
- Don't exercise integration between modules. That's what the other test categories do.
- Mocking subsystems can sometimes be challenging.
- Mock or fake environments can get out of sync with reality.

Small tests lead to code quality, good exception handling, and good error reporting, whereas larger tests lead to overall product quality and data validation. No single test size in isolation can solve all of a project's testing needs. For this reason, projects at Google are encouraged to maintain a healthy mixture of test sizes among their various test suites. It is considered just as wrong to perform all automation through a large end-to-end testing framework as it is to provide only small unit tests for a project.

Note
Small tests lead to code quality. Medium and large tests lead to product quality.

Code coverage is a great tool for measuring whether a project's tests have a healthy mixture of small, medium, and large tests. A project can create a coverage report running only its small tests and another report running only its medium and large tests. Each report should show an acceptable amount of coverage for the project in isolation. If medium and large tests produce only 20 percent code coverage in isolation, while small tests provide nearly 100 percent coverage, the project is likely lacking in evidence that the system works end-to-end. If the numbers were reversed, it would likely be hard to maintain or extend the project without spending a lot of time debugging. Google engineers are able to create and view these coverage reports on-the-fly using the same tools they use to build and run their tests by specifying an additional command-line flag. Coverage reports are stored in the cloud and can be viewed internally in any web browser by any engineer.

Google spans many types of projects, many with very different testing needs so the exact ratios of small-to-medium-to-large tests are left up to the teams—this is not prescribed. The general rule of thumb is to start with a rule of 70/20/10: 70 percent of tests should be small, 20 percent medium, and 10 percent large. If projects are user-facing, have a high degree of integration, or complex user interfaces, they should have more medium and large tests. Infrastructure or data-focused projects such as indexing or crawling have a very large number of small tests and far fewer medium or large tests.

Another internal tool we use for monitoring test coverage is Harvester. Harvester is a visualization tool that tracks all of a project's CLs and graphs things such as the ratio of test code to new code in individual CLs; the sizes of changes; frequency of changes over time and by date; changes by developer, and others. Its purpose is to give a general sense of how a project'stesting changes over time.

Test Runtime Requirements

Whatever a test's size, Google's test execution system requires the following behavior. It is, after all, a shared environment:

- Each test must be independent from other tests so that tests can be executed in any order.
- Tests must not have any persistent side effects. They must leave their environment exactly in the state when it started.

These requirements are simple enough to understand, but they can be tricky to abide by. Even if the test itself does its best to comply, the software under test might offend through the saving of data files or setting environment and configuration information. Fortunately, Google's test execution environment provides a number of features to make compliance straightforward.

For the independence requirement, engineers can specify a flag when they execute their tests to randomize the order of test execution. This feature eventually catches order-related dependencies. However, "any order" means that concurrency is also a possibility. The test execution system might choose to execute two tests on the same machine. If those two tests each require exclusive access to system resources, one of them might fail. For example:

- Two tests want to bind to the same port number to exclusively receive network traffic.

- Two tests want to create a directory at the same path.

- One test wants to create and populate a database table while another test wants to drop that same table.

These sorts of collisions can cause failures not only for the offending test, but also for other tests running on the test execution system, even if those other tests play by the rules. The system has a way of catching these tests and notifying the owners of the test. By setting a flag, a test can be marked to run exclusively on a specific machine. However, exclusivity is only a temporary fix. Most often, tests or the software being tested must be rewritten to drop dependencies on singular resources. The following remedies solve these problems:

- Have each test request an unused port number from the test execution system, and have the software under test dynamically bind to that port number.

- Have each test create all directories and files under a temporary unique directory that is created for and assigned to it by the test execution system just prior to test execution and injected into the process's environment.

- Have each test start its own database instance in a private, isolated environment based on directories and ports assigned to them by the test execution system.

The maintainers of Google's test execution system went so far as to document their test execution environment fairly exhaustively. Their document is known as Google's "Test Encyclopedia" and is the final answer on what resources are available to tests at runtime. The "Test Encyclopedia" reads like an IEEE RFC, using well-defined meanings of "must" and "shall." It explains in detail the roles and responsibilities of tests, test executors, host systems, libc runtimes, file systems, and so on.

Most Google engineers have likely not found the need to read the "Test Encyclopedia" and instead learn from others or by trial and error as their tests fail to run properly, or through feedback during code reviews. Unbeknownst to them, it is the details expressed in that document that allowed a single shared test execution environment to serve the test execution needs of every Google project. Nor are those engineers aware that the "Test Encyclopedia" is the main reason that the behaviors of tests running in the shared execution environment exactly match the behaviors of tests running on their personal workstations. The gory details of great platforms are invisible to those who use them. Everything just works!

Testing at the Speed and Scale of Google
by Pooja Gupta, Mark Ivey, and John Penix

Continuous integration systems play a crucial role in keeping software working while it is being developed. The basic steps most continuous integration systems follow are:

1. Get the latest copy of the code.

2. Run all tests.

3. Report results.

4. Repeat 1–3.

This works great while the codebase is small; code flux is reasonable and tests are fast. As a codebase grows over time, the efficiency of such a system decreases. As more code is added, each clean run takes much longer and more changes get crammed into a single run. If something breaks, finding and backing out the bad change is a tedious and error-prone task for development teams.

Software development at Google happens quickly and at scale. The Google codebase receives over 20 changes per minute and 50 percent of the files change every month! Each product is developed and released from "head" relying on automated tests verifying the product behavior. Release frequency varies from multiple times per day to once every few weeks, depending on the product team.

With such a huge, fast-moving codebase, it is possible for teams to get stuck spending a lot of time just keeping their build "green." A continuous integration system should help by providing the *exact* change at which a test started failing, instead of a range of suspect changes or doing a lengthy binary search for the offending change. To find the exact change that broke a test, we can run every test at every change, but that would be very expensive.

To solve this problem, we built a continuous integration system (see Figure 2.6) that uses dependency analysis to determine all the tests a change transitively affects and then runs only those tests for every change. The system is built on top of Google's cloud computing infrastructure, enabling many builds to be executed concurrently and allowing the system to run affected tests as soon as a change is submitted.

Here is an example where our system can provide faster and more precise feedback than a traditional continuous build. In this scenario, there are two tests and three changes that affect these tests. The gmail_server_tests are broken by the second change; however, a typical continuous integration system will only be able to tell that either change #2 or change #3 caused this test to fail. By using concurrent builds, we can launch tests without waiting for the current build-test cycle to finish. Dependency analysis limits the number of tests executed for each change, so that in this example, the total number of test executions is the same as before.

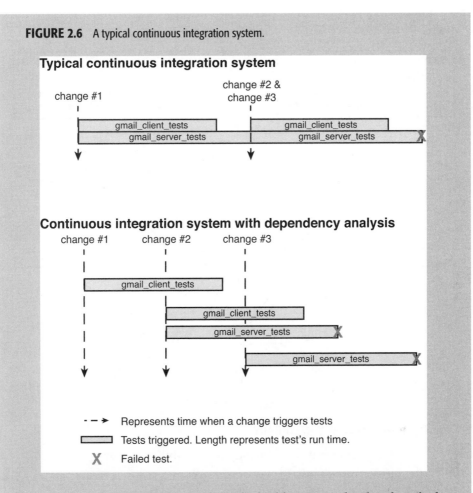

FIGURE 2.6 A typical continuous integration system.

Our system uses dependencies from the build system rules that describe how code is compiled and data files are assembled to build applications and tests. These build rules have clearly defined inputs and outputs that chain together to precisely describe what needs to happen during a build. Our system maintains an in-memory graph of these build dependencies (see Figure 2.7) and keeps it up to date with each change that gets checked in. This allows us to determine all tests that depend (directly or indirectly) on the code modified by a change, and hence, need to be re-run to know the current state of the build. Let's walk through an example.

FIGURE 2.7   Example of build dependencies.

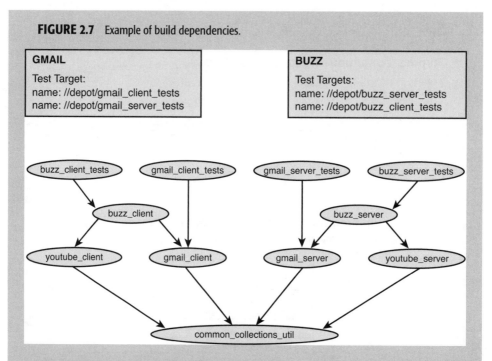

We see how two isolated code changes, at different depths of the dependency tree, are analyzed to determine affected tests, that is the minimal set of tests that needs to be run to ensure that both Gmail and Buzz projects are "green."

CASE 1: CHANGE IN COMMON LIBRARY

For first scenario, consider a change that modifies files in common_collections_util, as shown in Figure 2.8.

FIGURE 2.8   Change in common_collections_util.h.

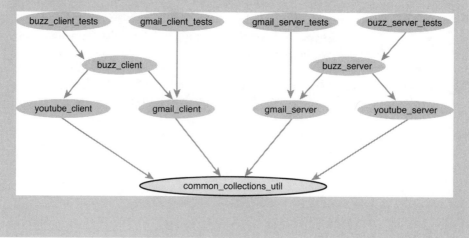

When this change is submitted, we follow the dependency edges back up the graph, eventually finding all tests that depend on it. When the search is complete (after a fraction of a second), we have all the tests that need to be run and can determine the projects that need to have their statuses updated based on results from these tests (see Figure 2.9).

FIGURE 2.9 Tests affected by change.

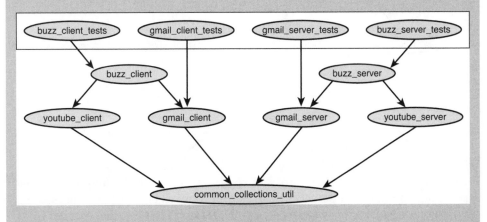

CASE 2: CHANGE IN A DEPENDENT PROJECT

For the second scenario, we look at a change that modifies files in youtube_client (see Figure 2.10).

FIGURE 2.10 Change in youtube_client.

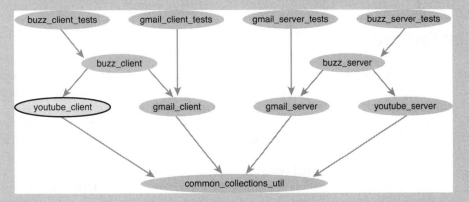

We perform the same analysis to conclude that only the buzz_client_tests are affected and the status of Buzz project needs to be updated (see Figure 2.11).

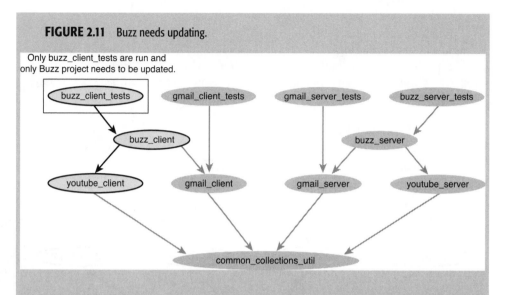

FIGURE 2.11   Buzz needs updating.

This example illustrates how we optimize the number of tests run per change without sacrificing the accuracy of end results for a project. Running fewer tests per change allows us to run all *affected* tests for every change that gets checked in, making it easier for a developer to detect and deal with an offending change.

Use of smart tools and cloud computing infrastructure in the continuous integration system makes it fast and reliable. While we are constantly working on making improvements to this system, thousands of Google projects are already using it to launch and iterate quickly, making faster user-visible progress.

Test Certified

Patrick Copeland's preface to this book underscores the difficulty in getting developers to participate in testing. Hiring highly technical testers was only step one. We still needed to get developers involved. One of the key ways we did this was by a program called Test Certified. In retrospect, the program was instrumental in getting the developer-testing culture ingrained at Google.

Test Certified started out as a contest. Can we get developers to take testing seriously if we make it a prestigious matter? If developers follow certain practices and achieve specific results, can we say they are "certified" and create a badge system (see Figure 2.12) that provides some bragging rights?

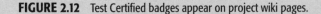

FIGURE 2.12 Test Certified badges appear on project wiki pages.

Well, that's Test Certified: a system of testing challenges that if a team completes earns the team a "certified" designation. Level 0 is the starting level for all teams. After a team shows a mastery of basic code hygiene practices, it reaches level 1 and then progresses through the levels, which end at 5 to match some external models such as capability maturity model.[13]

Summary of Test Certified Levels

Level 1

Set up test coverage bundles.

Set up a continuous build.

Classify your tests as Small, Medium, and Large.

Identify nondeterministic tests.

Create a smoke test suite.

Level 2

No releases with red tests.

Require a smoke test suite to pass before a submit.

Incremental coverage by all tests >= 50%.

Incremental coverage by small tests >= 10%.

At least one feature tested by an integration test.

Level 3

Require tests for all nontrivial changes.

Incremental coverage by small tests >= 50%.

New significant features are tested by integration tests.

---

[13] http://www.sei.cmu.edu/cmmi/start/faq/related-faq.cfm.

Level 4

Automate running of smoke tests before submitting new code.

Smoke tests should take less than 30 minutes to run.

No nondeterministic tests.

Total test coverage should be at least 40%.

Test coverage from small tests alone should be at least 25%.

All significant features are tested by integration tests.

Level 5

Add a test for each nontrivial bug fix.

Actively use available analysis tools.

Total test coverage should be at least 60%.

Test coverage from small tests alone should be at least 40%.

The program was piloted slowly with a few teams of testing-minded developers who were keen to improve their practices. After the kinks were worked out of the program, a big contest to get certified was held as a companywide push and adoption was brisk.

It wasn't as hard a sell as one might think. The benefit to development teams was substantial:

- They got lots of attention from good testers who signed up to be Test Certified Mentors. In a culture where testing resources were scarce, signing up for this program got a product team far more testers than it ordinarily would have merited.

- They received guidance from experts and learned how to write better small tests.

- They understood which teams were doing a better job of testing and thus who to learn from.

- They were able to brag to the other teams that they were higher on the Test Certified scale!

After the companywide push, most teams were climbing the ladder and they were all aware of it. Development Directors with teams moving up the ladder were given good review feedback from Engineering Productivity leads and teams who scoffed at it did so at their own peril. Again, in a company where testing resources are hard to come by, what team would want to alienate Engineering Productivity? Still it wasn't all flowers and puppies. But we'll let the people who ran the program tell the whole story.

An Interview with the Founders of the Test Certified Program

The authors sat down with four Googlers who were instrumental in starting the Test Certified program. Mark Striebeck is a development manager for Gmail. Neal Norwitz is an SWE working on tools for developer velocity, Tracy Bialik and Russ Rufer are SETs who as nonmanagers are among the highest-leveled SETs in the company; both are staff-level engineers.

HGTS: What are the origins of the Test Certified program? What problems did the original TC team try to solve? Are those the same problems that the program tries to solve today?

Tracy: We wanted to change Google's developer culture to include testing as part of every feature developer's responsibility. They shared their positive experiences with testing and encouraged teams to write tests. Some teams were interested, but didn't know how to start. Others would put "improve testing" on their team objectives and key results (OKRs),[14] which isn't always actionable. It was like putting "lose weight" on your New Year's resolutions. That's a fine, lofty goal, but if that's all you say, don't be surprised if it never happens.

Test Certified provided small, clear, actionable steps that teams could take. The first level is getting the basics in place: setting up automation for running tests and gathering test coverage, noting any nondeterministic tests, and making a smoke test suite (if the full test suite was long-running). Each level becomes more difficult, requiring more test maturity. Level 2 targets policies and getting started on improving incremental coverage. Level 3 focuses on testing newly written code. Level 4 focuses on testing of legacy code, which typically requires at least some refactoring for testability. Level 5 demands better overall coverage, writing tests for all bug fixes and using available static and dynamic analysis tools.

Now, all Googlers know that testing is a feature developer's responsibility. So that problem has been solved. But we still have the problem of teams needing to take action to improve their testing maturity and capability, so Test Certified continues to serve that need.

HGTS: What was the early feedback the Test Certified team received from the SWEs?

Neal: That it's too hard. They thought our goals were too lofty and many teams were struggling with the basics. We needed to make the levels correspond to work that could be accomplished in their spare time. Also there were issues around Google's tools at the time and some of the things we were asking for

---

[14] OKRs are objectives and key results that individuals, teams, and even the company as a whole write each quarter and assess their progress against. Basically, they are the things an individual or team intends to accomplish.

were just too advanced. It was really hard for folks to get started, so we had to think about providing them with some softballs to start the process and convince them they were making progress.

Mark: Yes, we had to make several iterations downward. We tried to meet them halfway by being more realistic and making the runway toward eventual take-off a lot longer. We didn't mind increasing the runway but we still wanted escape velocity at some point. That's how we ended up with the first step being "set up a continuous build, have some green builds, know your coverage." It was a freebie, but it established some discipline and helped them get from 0 to 1 and put them in a position to want more.

HGTS: Who was eager to adopt?

Neal: It started with most of the people in the Testing Grouplet. This grouplet was meeting regularly and was comprised of the people who were the most enthusiastic about testing. We then branched out to other folks we knew. I think there were a ton of eager folks and that was a nice surprise. We generated more enthusiasm with ToTT[15] and other activities that made testing look more fun or sexy: fixits,[16] VP mass emails, posters, talks at TGIF, and so on.

Mark: As soon as we reached out to other teams (and we had a bunch of teams who were interested), they realized that this will a) require some serious work, and b) that they don't have the expertise. That made the beginning really frustrating.

HGTS: Who was reluctant to adopt?

Neal: Most projects. As I mentioned, it was perceived as too hard. We needed to scale back our initial ambitions. There were pretty much two sets of projects: those with no tests and those with really crappy tests. We needed to make it seem so simple that they could do many of the required testing tasks in an afternoon (and they really could with our help).

Mark: Also, this was still the time when the value of testing and test automation wasn't fully appreciated at Google. Not like it is today, not by a long shot. By far, most teams had the attitude that these are cute ideas, but that they had more important things to do (a.k.a. writing production code).

HGTS: What hurdles did the team have to overcome to get its initial set of adopters?

Neal: Inertia. Bad tests. No tests. Time. Testing was seen as someone else's problem, be it another developer or a testing team. Who's got time to test when you are writing all that code?

---

[15] ToTT is Testing on the Toilet, which has been mentioned before in this book and appears often on the Google Testing blog at googletesting.blogspot.com.

[16] "Fixits" are another Google cultural event that bring people together to "fix" something that is deemed broken. A team might have a fixit to reduce bug debt. They might have one for security testing. They might have one to increase the usage of #include in C code or for refactoring. Fixits have been known to leap the technical divide and can be applied to improving the food in a café or making meetings run smoother. Any event that brings people together to solve a common problem is a fixit.

Mark: Finding teams that were: a) interested enough, b) didn't have too much of a legacy codebase problem, and c) had someone on the team who would be the testing champion (and who knew enough about testing). These were the three hurdles and we jumped them one at a time, team by team.

HGTS: What pushed the Test Certified program into the mainstream? Was growth viral or linear?

Russ: First there was a pilot that included teams that were especially friendly to testing and teams that the initial Test Certified instigators had close contacts with. We chose our early adopters well, basically the ones who had the best chance of succeeding.

At the point when we announced the "global launch" of Test Certified in mid-2007, there were 15 pilot teams at various rungs of the ladder. Just before the launch, we plastered the walls of every building in Mountain View, New York, and a few other offices with "TC Mystery" posters. Each poster had images representing several of the pilot teams, based on internal project names like Rubix, Bounty, Mondrian, and Red Tape. The only text on the posters said, "The future is now" and "This is big, don't be left behind" with a link. We got a ton of hits on the link from puzzle-loving Googlers who wanted to see what the mystery was or simply to confirm their guesses. We also leveraged ToTT to advertise the new program and direct those readers to places they could get more information. It was a blitz of information.

That information included why Test Certified was important for teams and what kind of help they could get. It stressed that teams got a Test Certified Mentor and an "in" to a larger community of test expertise. We also offered teams two gifts for participation. First, a glowing build-status orb to show the team when tests on their (often new) continuous build passed (green) or failed (red). The second gift was a nifty Star Wars Potato Head kit. The so-called Darth Tater kit included three progressively larger units, and we awarded these to teams as they climbed higher on the Test Certified ladder. Teams displaying their orbs and potato heads helped build more curiosity and word of mouth about the program.

Testing Grouplet members were the early mentors and spokesmen for the project. As more teams joined, they often had enthusiastic engineers who helped create a buzz around Test Certified and acted as mentors for other teams.

As we each tried to convince more teams to join the program, we shared the best arguments with one another. Some teams joined because you could convince them the ladder steps and mentor availability would help their team improve this important area. Some teams felt they could improve either way, but were convinced the "official" levels would help them get credit for the work they were doing. Other teams were already very mature in their testing approach, but could be convinced to join as a signal to the rest of the company that they felt proper testing was important.

Several months in, with somewhere around 50 teams, a few enterprising members of our Test Engineering organization signed up to be Test Certified Mentors, which was the beginning of a stronger partnership between engineers from product teams and engineers from Engineering Productivity.

It was all very viral, very grass roots with a lot of one-on-one conversations. We went specifically to sell some teams. Other teams came to us.

About a year in, with over 100 Test Certified teams, it felt like new adoption was slowing. Bella Kazwell, who led this volunteer effort at the time, master-minded the Test Certified Challenge. A point system was developed that included activities like writing new tests, signing new teams into Test Certified, and teams improving testing practices or gaining TC levels. There were individual awards, and sites across the globe were also pitted against one another to earn the highest score. Volunteers were energized, and in turn this energized more teams across the company, re-accelerating adoption and attracting more volunteer mentors.

Teams in Test Certified had always used the ladder rungs and criteria as crisp, measurable team goals. By late 2008, there were areas in which some managers began to use these to evaluate teams under their purview, and where Engineering Productivity used a team's progress against the TC ladder to gauge how serious they were about improving testing, and so how valuable it would be to invest time from the limited pool of test experts with a given team. In certain limited areas, it became a management expectation or launch criteria for teams to reach a level on the ladder.

Today, in 2011, new volunteer mentors continue to join, and new teams continue to sign up, and TC has presence across the company.

HGTS: What changes did the Test Certified program undergo in its first couple of years? Did ladder requirements change? Did the mentoring system change? What adjustments were successful in improving the experience for participants?

Tracy: The biggest change was the number of levels and some of the ladder requirements. We originally had four levels. Going from level 0 to level 1 was deliberately easy. Many teams were finding it difficult to move from level 1 to level 2, especially teams with legacy code that wasn't testable. These teams became discouraged and were inclined to give up on Test Certified. We added a new level between 1 and 2 that was an easier step to take. We debated calling the new level 1.5, but decided to insert the new level as 2 and renumber the higher levels.

We also found that some of the requirements were too prescriptive, suggesting a ratio of small to medium to large tests that didn't apply to all teams. When we added the new level, we also updated the criteria to include some "incremental coverage" numbers and remove the test size ratios.

The mentoring system is still in place, but we now have many teams who "self-mentor." Because the culture of testing is more pervasive now, we have many teams who don't need much advice; they just want to track their progress. For those teams, we don't assign a mentor, but do provide a mailing list for answering their questions and for another pair of eyes to validate their level transitions.

Russ: It's also worth noting that from the beginning, we knew the Test Certified criteria had to be reasonably applied. Testing isn't a cookie cutter activity and, occasionally, teams don't fit the mold we had in mind when selecting the criteria, or a typical tool for tracking test coverage or some other metric won't work properly for a team. Each criterion had a rationale behind it, and we've been open at various points to customizing the criteria for teams that meet the spirit of that prescribed rationale.

HGTS: What does a team stand to gain from participating in the Test Certified program today? What are the costs associated with participating?

Tracy: Bragging rights. Clear steps. Outside help. A cool glowing orb. But the real gain for teams is improved testing.

The costs are minimal, beyond the team focusing on improving their testing maturity. We have a custom tool that allows mentors to track the team's progress, checking off as each step is achieved. The data is displayed on a page that includes all teams by level, with the ability to click through and see details about a specific team.

HGTS: Are there any steps on the ladder that seem to give teams more trouble than others?

Tracy: The most difficult step is "require tests for all nontrivial changes." For a greenfield project written in a testable way, this is easy. For a legacy project that wasn't originally written with testing in mind, this can be tough. This might require writing a big end-to-end test and trying to force the system through particular code paths to exercise the behavior and then figuring out how to witness the result in an automated way. The better, but sometimes longer-term approach is refactoring the code to be more testable. Some teams with code that wasn't written with testability in mind also find it challenging to provide enough of their test coverage, specifically from small, narrowly focused unit tests versus larger tests covering clusters of classes, or end-to-end tests.

HGTS: Efforts at Google tend to last weeks or quarters, but Test Certified has been around for nearly five years and shows no signs of stopping soon. What contributed to Test Certified passing the test of time? What challenges does Test Certified face going forward?

Russ: It has staying power because it's not just an activity some individuals took part in; it's a cultural change at the company. Together with the Testing Grouplet, ToTT, supporting mailing lists, tech talks, and contributions to job ladders and coding style documents, regular testing has become an expectation of all engineers across the company. Whether a team participates in Test Certified or not, it is expected to have a well considered automated testing strategy, either on its own or in partnership with a smaller population of engineers who act as testing experts.

It continues because it's proven to work. We have very few areas left with even a small fraction of testing done manually, or thrown over the wall. To that end, Test Certified has done its job and this is likely to be its legacy even if the "official" grass-roots program was to end some day.

HGTS: What tips would you give to engineers at other companies who are considering starting similar efforts in their organizations?

Tracy: Start with teams that are already friendly to testing. Grow a kernel of teams that gain value from your program. Don't be shy about evangelizing and asking others to do so as well. The mentoring aspect was a big part of Test Certified's success. When you ask a team to try something new or to improve, it's going to be a lot smoother if they have a contact point into the larger community to ask for help. An engineer or a team might be embarrassed to ask what might be a stupid question on a mailing list, but they'll feel a lot more comfortable asking that question of a single, trusted TC mentor.

Also find ways to make it fun. Come up with a better name that doesn't include "certified," as that can evoke pointy-haired bureaucrats. Or, do what we did, go with a pointy-haired name like "certified" and use it as a foil to constantly remind your larger community that it's a bad name because you're not "that kind of program." Define steps small enough that teams can see and show their progress. Don't get bogged down trying to create the perfect system with a perfect set of measurements. Nothing will ever be perfect for everyone. Agreeing on something reasonable and moving forward is important when the alternative is being paralyzed. Be flexible where it makes sense to be, but hold the line where you shouldn't bend.

This concludes the chapter on the life of an SET. The remainder of the material is optional reading about how Google interviews SETs and an interview with Googler Ted Mao who talks about some of the tools Google SETs use.

Interviewing SETs

Successful SETs are good at everything: strong enough programmers to write feature code, strong enough testers to test about anything, and able to manage their own work and tools. Good SETs see both the forest and the trees—they can look at a small function prototype or API and imagine all the ways the underlying code can be used and how it can be broken.

All code at Google is in a single source tree, which means that any code can be used by anyone at anytime—so it better be solid. SETs not only find the bugs that the feature developers missed, but they also look to make sure it is obvious to other engineers how to leverage that code or component, and worry about future-proofing the functionality. Google moves fast, so the code must be clean, consistent, and work long after the original developer has stopped thinking about it.

How do we interview for this skill set and mentality? It's not easy, but we've found hundreds of engineers who fit the bill. We look for a hybrid: a developer with a strong interest and aptitude in testing. A common and effective way to spot great SETs is to give them the same programming questions as we do for all developers and look for how they approach quality and testing. SETs have twice the opportunity to give a wrong answer in an interview!

Simple questions often identify the best SETs. Too much time wasted on tricky coding problems or insisting on functional correctness takes away from time you should use to understand how the candidate thinks about coding and quality. There will be a SWE or SET on an interview loop who poses algorithm problems; the better SET interviewers focus on how the candidate *thinks* about the solution, not so much the elegance of the solution itself.

Note

SET interviewers focus on how the candidate *thinks* about the solution, not so much the elegance of the solution itself.

Here's an example. Pretend it is your first day on the job and you are asked to implement the function `acount(void* s);` that returns a count of the number of As in a string.

A candidate who dives directly into writing the code is sending a strong message: There is only one thing to do and I am doing it. That one thing is code. The life of an SET does not follow such a serialized view of the world. We want to hear questions.

What is this function used for? Why are we building it? Does the function prototype even look correct? We look for signs the candidate is worried about correctness and how to validate the right behaviors. A problem deserves to be treated with more respect! Candidates who mindlessly jump into coding problems will do the same with testing problems. If we pose a problem to add test variations to modules, we don't want them to start listing tests until we tell them to stop; we want the best tests first.

An SET's time is limited. We want candidates to take a step back and find the most efficient way to solve the problem, and the previous function definition can use some improvement. A good SET looks at a poorly defined API and turns it into something beautiful while testing it.

Decent candidates spend a few minutes understanding the specification by asking questions and making statements such as:

- What is the encoding of the incoming string: ASCII, UTF-8, or another?

- The function name is weak, should it be CamelCased, more descriptive, or are there other standard naming practices to be followed here?

- What is the return type? (Maybe the interviewer forgot, so I'll add an int to the front of the function prototype.)

- That void* is dangerous. We should give it an appropriate type, such as char*, so we can benefit from compile-time type checking.

- What counts as an A? Should it count lowercase As, too?

- Doesn't this function already exist in a standard library? (For the purpose of the interview, pretend you are the first one implementing this functionality.)

Better candidates will do even more:

- **Think about scale:** Maybe the return type should be a 64-bit integer because Google often deals with large amounts of data.

- **Think about re-use:** Why does this function count only As? It is probably a good idea to parameterize this so that an arbitrary character can be counted instead of having a different function defined for each one.

- **Think about safety:** Are these pointers coming from trusted sources?

The best candidates will:

- **Think about scale:**

    - Is this function to be run as part of a MapReduce[17] on sharded[18] data? Maybe that's the most useful form of calling this function. Are there issues to worry about in this scenario? Consider the performance and correctness implications of running this function on every document on the entire Internet.

    - If this subroutine is called for every Google query and would be called only with safe pointers because the wrapper does this validation already; maybe avoiding a null check will save hundreds of millions of CPU cycles a day and reduce user-visible latency by some small amount. At least understand the possible implications of full textbook parameter validation.

- **Think about optimizations based on invariants:**

    - Can we assume the data coming in is already sorted? If so, we might be able to exit quickly after we find the first B.

    - What is the texture of the input data? Is it most often all As, is it most often a mix of all characters, or is it only As and spaces? If so, there may be optimizations in our comparison operations. When dealing with large data, even small, sublinear changes can be significant for actual compute latencies when the code executes.

- **Think about safety:**

    - On many systems, and if this is a security-sensitive section of code, consider testing for more than just nonnull pointers; 1 is an invalid pointer value on some systems.

    - Add a length parameter to help ensure the code doesn't walk off the end of the string. Check the length parameter's value for sanity. Null-terminated character strings are a hacker's best friend.

---

[17] MapReduce is a form of distributed computing where the computation is broken into smaller pieces, categorized by key (mapped), and then rolled up (reduced) by key. See http://en.wikipedia.org/wiki/MapReduce.

[18] Sharding is a form of database partitioning. Horizontal partitioning is a database design principle whereby rows of a database table are held separately, rather than splitting by columns. See http://en.wikipedia.org/wiki/Shard_(database_architecture).

- If there is a possibility the buffer can be modified by some other thread while this function executes, there may be thread safety issues.

- Should we be doing this check in a try/catch? Or, if the calling code isn't expecting exceptions, we should probably return error codes to the caller. If there are error codes, are those codes well defined and documented? This shows thinking about the context of the larger code-base and runtime, and this kind of thinking can avoid errors of confusion or omission down the road.

Ultimately, the best candidates come up with a new angle for these questions. All angles are interesting to consider, if they are considered intelligently.

Note

A good SET candidate should not have to be told to test the code she writes. It should be an automatic part of her thinking.

The key in all this questioning of the spec and the inputs is that any engineer who has passed an introductory programming course can produce basic functional code for this question. These questions and thinking from the candidates differentiate the best candidates from the decent ones. We do make sure that the candidate feels comfortable enough socially and cultur-ally to ask questions, and if not, we prod them a bit to ask, making sure their straight-to-the-code behavior isn't just because they are in an inter-view situation. Googlers should question most everything without being annoying and by still getting the problem solved.

It would be boring to walk through the myriad of possible correct implementations and all the common mistakes as this isn't a programming or interviewing book. But, let's show a simple and obvious implementation for discussion's sake. Note: Candidates can usually use the language they are most comfortable with such as Java or Python, though that usually elic-its some questions to ensure they understand things such as garbage collec-tion, type–safety, compilation, and runtime concerns.

```
int64 Acount(const char* s) {
  if (!s) return 0;
  int64 count = 0;
  while (*s++) {
    if (*s == 'a') count++;
  }
  return count;
}
```

Candidates should be able to walk through their code, showing the evolution of pointer and counter values as the code executes with test inputs.

In general, decent SET candidates will do the following:

- Have little trouble with the basics of coding this solution. When doing so, they do not have trouble rewriting or fumbling over basic syntax issues or mixing up syntax or keywords from different languages.

- Show no sign of misunderstanding pointers or allocating anything unnecessarily.

- Perform some input validation upfront to avoid pesky crashes from dereferencing null pointers and such, or have a good explanation of why they are not doing such parameter validation when asked.

- Understand the runtime or Big O[19] of their code. Anything other than linear here shows some creativity, but can be concerning.

- If there are minor issues in the code, they can correct them when pointed out.

- Produce code that is clear and easily readable by others. If they are using bitwise operators or put everything on one line, this is not a good sign, even if the code functionally works.

- Walk through their code with a single test input of A or null.

Better candidates will do even more.

- Consider int64 for counters and return type for future compatibility and avoiding overflow when someone inevitably uses this function to count As in an insanely long string.

- Write code to shard/distribute the counting computation. Some candidates unfamiliar with MapReduce can come up with some simple variants on their own to decrease latency with parallel computation for large strings.

- Write in assumptions and invariants in notes or comments in the code.

- Walk through their code with many different inputs and fix every bug that they find. SET candidates who don't spot and fix bugs are a warning sign.

- Test their function before being asked. Testing should be something they don't have to be told to do.

- Continue trying to optimize the solution until asked to stop. No one can be sure that their code is perfect after just a few minutes of coding and applying a few test inputs. Some tenacity over correctness should be evident.

Now, we want to see if the candidate can test his own code. Convoluted or tricky test code is likely the worst test code in the world and definitely worse than no code. When tests fail at Google, it needs to be clear what the

---

[19] Big O notation describes how long it takes some function to execute based on the size of the input data. See http://en.wikipedia.org/wiki/Big_O_notation.

test is doing. If not, engineers might disable, mark as flaky, or ignore the failures—it happens, and it's the fault of the SETs and SWEs who wrote and reviewed the code for letting this bad test code into the tree.

SETs should be able to approach testing in a black box manner, operating under the assumption that someone else implemented the function, or in a white box manner, knowing which test cases might be irrelevant given the specifics of their implementation.

In general, decent candidates will do the following:

- Are methodical and systematic. Supplying test data according to some identifiable characteristic (such as string size) and not just random strings.

- Focus on generating interesting test data. Consider how to run large tests and where to get real-world test data.

- Better candidates:

  - Want to spin up concurrent threads executing this function to look for cross talk, deadlock, and memory leaks.

  - Build long running tests, such as spin up tests in a `while(true)` loop, and ensure they continue to work over the long haul.

  - Remain interested in coming up with test cases and interesting approaches to test data generation, validation, and execution.

Example of a Great Candidate *by Jason Arbon*

One recent candidate (who has since proven to be amazing on the job) was asked how he would do boundary testing for a version of this API with 64-bit integers. He realized quickly that it wouldn't be physically possible because of time and space constraints, but for the sake of completeness and curiosity when thinking about this level of scale, thought about how to host at least very large amounts of data for such a test and considered using Google's index of the Web as input data.

How did he validate the answer? He suggested using a parallel implementation and making sure the two produced the same result. He also thought of a statistical sampling approach: What is the expected frequency of A in web pages, and because we know the number of pages indexed, the number computed should be close. This is a Google-like way to think about testing. Even if we don't build these monster tests, thinking about these large solutions usually leads to more interesting or efficient solutions for normal-scale work.

Another thing we interview for is "Googliness," or culture fit. Is the SET candidate technically curious during the interview? When presented with some new ideas, can the candidate incorporate these into her solution? How does she handle ambiguity? Is she familiar with academic approaches to quality such as theorem proving? Does she understand measures of quality or automation in other fields such as civil or aerospace engineering?

Is she defensive about bugs you might find in her implementation? Does she think big? Candidates don't have to be all of these things, but the more, the merrier! And, finally, would we like to work with this person on a daily basis?

It is important to note that if someone interviewing for an SET position isn't that strong of a coder, it does not mean that she will not be a successful TE. Some of the best TEs we've ever hired originally interviewed for the SET position.

An interesting note about SET hiring at Google is that we often lose great candidates because they run into a nontesting SWE or an overly focused TE on their interview loop. We want this diversity in the folks interviewing SET candidates, because they will work together on the job, and SETs are really hybrids, but this can sometimes result in unfavorable interview scores. We want to make sure the bad scores come from interviewers who truly appreciate all aspects of what it takes to be a great SET.

As Pat Copeland says in his forward, there has been and still is a lot of diversity of opinion on SET hiring. Should an SET just be doing feature work if he is good at coding? SWEs are also hard to hire. Should they just be focusing on pure testing problems if they are that good at testing? The truth, as it often is, lies somewhere in the middle.

Getting good SET hires is a lot of trouble but it's worth it. A single rock star SET can make a huge impact on a team.

An Interview with Tool Developer Ted Mao

Ted Mao is a developer at Google but he's a developer who has been exclusively focused on building test tools. Specifically, he's building test tools for web applications that scale to handle everything Google builds internally. As such, he's a well-known person in SET circles because an SET without good tools will find it hard to be effective. Ted is probably more familiar with the common web test infrastructure at Google than anyone in the company.

HGTS: When did you start at Google, and what excited you about working here?

Ted: I joined Google in June 2004. Back then, I only had experience working at large companies like IBM and Microsoft, and Google was the hot startup to work for and they were attracting a lot of talented engineers. Google was attempting to solve many interesting, challenging problems, and I wanted to work on these problems alongside some of the best engineers in the world.

HGTS: You are the inventor of Buganizer,[20] Google's bug database. What were the core things you were trying to accomplish with Buganizer versus the older BugDB?

---

[20] The open-source version of Buganizer is called Issue Tracker and is available through the Chromium project at http://code.google.com/chromium/issues/list.

Ted: BugsDB was impeding our development process rather than supporting it. To be honest, it was wasting a lot of valuable engineering time and this was a tax paid by every team that used it. The issues manifested themselves in many ways, including UI latency, awkward workflows, and the practice of using "special" strings in unstructured text fields. In the process of designing Buganizer, we made sure that our data model and UI reflected our users' actual development processes and that the system would be amenable to future extension both in the core product and through integrations.

HGTS: Well you nailed Buganizer. It's truly the best bug database any of us have ever used. How did you start working on web-testing automation, did you see the need or were you asked to solve a problem with test execution?

Ted: While working on Buganizer, AdWords, and other products at Google, I consistently found that the web-testing infrastructure we had available was insufficient for my needs. It was never quite as fast, scalable, robust, or useful as I needed it to be. When the tools team announced that they were looking for someone to lead an effort in this area, I jumped on the opportunity to solve this problem. This effort became known as the Matrix project and I was the tech lead for it.

HGTS: How many test executions and teams does Matrix support today?

Ted: It really depends on how you measure test executions and teams. For example, one metric we use is what we call a "browser session"—every new browser session for a particular browser is guaranteed to start in the same state, and thus, a test running in the browser will behave deterministically insomuch as the test, browser, and operating system are deterministic. Matrix is used by practically every web frontend team at Google and provisions more than a million new browser sessions per day.

HGTS: How many people worked on these two projects: Buganizer and Matrix?

Ted: During their peak development periods, Buganizer had about five engineers and Matrix had four engineers. It's always somewhat sad for me to think of what we might have been able to accomplish with a larger, more sustained development team, but I think we did a great job given what we had to work with.

HGTS: What were the toughest technical challenges you faced while building these tools?

Ted: I think that the toughest and often the most interesting challenges for me have always come at design time—understanding a problem space, weighing different solutions and their tradeoffs, and then making good decisions. Implementation is usually straightforward from that point. These types of decisions have to be made throughout the life of a project, and together with implementation, they can make or break the product.

HGTS: What general advice would you give to other software engineers in the world who are working on testing tools?

Ted: Focus on your users, understand their needs, and solve their problems. Don't forget about "invisible" features like usability and speed. Engineers are uniquely capable of solving their own problems—enable them to leverage your tools in ways you didn't foresee.

HGTS: What do you see as the next big or interesting problem to be solved in the test tools and infrastructure space?

Ted: One problem I've been thinking about lately is how our tools are getting more complex and powerful, but consequently, harder to understand and use. For example, with our current web-testing infrastructure at Google, an engineer can execute one command to run thousands of web tests, in parallel, against multiple browsers. On one hand, it's great that we're abstracting away the details of how it all works—where those tests are actually running, where the browsers are coming from, how the test environment is configured, and so on. However, if the test fails and the engineer has to debug it, those details can be essential. We already have a few initiatives in this area, but there's a lot more we could and should be doing.

An Interview with Web Driver Creator Simon Stewart

> *Simon Stewart is the creator of WebDriver and browser automation guru at Google. WebDriver is an open source web application testing tool popular inside and outside of Google and historically one of the hottest topics at GTAC, the Google Test Automation Conference. The authors sat down with him recently and got his thoughts on web app test automation and the future of WebDriver.*

HGTS: I don't think many people understand the distinction between Selenium and WebDriver, can you clear it up?

Simon: Selenium was a project started by Jason Huggins while he was at ThoughtWorks. Jason was writing a web application and was targeting IE which at the time was 90+ percent of the market. But he kept getting bug reports from users who had adopted FireFox and he had this problem where he would fix a bug for FF and break the app for IE. For him, Selenium was developed as a way to rev his app and then test to make sure it worked on both browsers.

I was building what became WebDriver a year or so later, but before Selenium was really stable, and was focused on more general web app testing. Not surprisingly, the two of us took different approaches to our implementations. Selenium was built on JavaScript running inside the browser, WebDriver was integrated into the browser itself using automation APIs. Each approach had its advantages and disadvantages. For example, Selenium supported new browsers, like Chrome, almost instantly, but couldn't do file uploads or handle user interaction very well because it was JavaScript and limited to what was possible in the JS sandbox. Since WebDriver was built into the browser, it could sidestep these limitations, but adding new browsers was very painful. Once both of us started working for Google, we decided to integrate the two.

HGTS: But I still hear people talking about both. Are they still two separate projects?

Simon: Selenium is the name we use for the umbrella project for all browser automation tools. WebDriver happens to be one of those tools. The official name is "Selenium WebDriver."

HGTS: So how did Google get involved?

Simon: Google hired some former ThoughtWorkers when Google opened the London office a few years back and those guys invited me to come give a tech talk on WebDriver. That talk didn't inspire a lot of confidence on my part, some guy in the front row fell sound asleep and I had to compete with his snores for the audience. As luck would have it, the recording of the talk failed and there was enough interest that I was invited back to give a snore-free presentation at GTAC. I joined Google shortly thereafter. Now I know where the bodies are buried!

HGTS: Yes, indeed, skeletons in every closet. Seriously though we've seen you talk before, it is hard to imagine anyone falling asleep on you. Was this anyone we know?

Simon: No. He's long gone from Google. Let's just assume he had a late night beforehand!

HGTS: Let that be a lesson to readers. Falling asleep on Simon Stewart is bad for your career! Now once you joined Google was WebDriver your full time job?

Simon: No, it was my 20 percent project. My day job was working as a product SET but I still managed to move WebDriver forward and at this time some outside contributors were really doing good work. In the early stage of an open source project people pick it up because they need it and there are no other alternatives. It's built-in incentive to contribute. Now many of the WebDriver users are told by others to use it and they approach it more as a consumer than as a contributor. But in the early days the grass roots WebDriver community really moved the tool forward.

HGTS: Well we all know how the story turns out. WebDriver is very popular within Google. How did it start? Was there one project that piloted it? Any false starts?

Simon: It began with Wave, a social networking product built in our Sydney office that has since gone away. The Wave engineers tried to use Selenium for their test infrastructure but it couldn't cope. Wave was too complicated. The engineers were diligent enough to track WebDriver down and they started asking a lot of questions, good questions, and it became more than my 20 percent could handle. They reached out to my manager and we negotiated a month-long loan deal and I went down to Sydney to help them build out their test infrastructure.

HGTS: I take it you were successful.

Simon: Yes, the team was good about pitching in to help and we made it work. It drove a bunch of new requirements for WebDriver and it also served as an example to other Google teams that WebDriver was a tool that could handle cutting edge web applications. From that point on, WebDriver never lacked for customers and it made sense for me to work on it full time.

HGTS: The first customer is always the hardest. How did you handle both developing WebDriver and making it work for Wave?

Simon: I used a process called DDD, defect-driven development. I would declare WebDriver flawless and when a customer found a bug I would fix it and once again declare it flawless. That way I fixed only the bugs that people actually cared about. It's a process that is good for refining an existing product and making sure you are fixing the most important bugs and not spinning on bugs people don't care about.

HGTS: And are you still the only engineer on WebDriver?

Simon: No, we have a team and are an official project internally at Google and very active in open source. With the ever increasing numbers of browsers, browser versions, and platforms, I tell people that we must be crazy, but we do the impossible every day. It's something I think most sane engineers shy away from!

HGTS: So post-Wave you had a lot of momentum. Is that where WebDriver pulled away from the older Selenium infrastructure in terms of users?

Simon: I think so. A lot of the original Selenium engineers had moved onto other things and I had all this puppy energy for WebDriver coming off the Wave success. People I never met like Michael Tam from Germany had already started doing really significant work on WebDriver as well and I was careful to nurture those relationships. Michael was the first person I'd not met in person who got permission to submit code to the project's source repository.

But I didn't really track the spread of WebDriver all that closely. What was clear was that the closer teams were to me physically, the more likely they were to adopt WebDriver. I think Picasa Web Albums was actually the first team before Wave, and then afterwards Ads picked it up. There is still a silo effect of web automation used at Google. Chrome uses PyAuto, Search uses Puppet (which has an open source versions called Web Puppeteer), and Ads uses WebDriver, etc.

HGTS: What about the future of WebDriver? What's the direction your team is taking?

Simon: Well the landscape is really getting crowded. Even a few years ago we were looking at a market with one dominate browser. Not anymore. Internet Explorer, FireFox, Chrome, Safari, Opera to name only a few and that's only the desktop. The proliferation of random WebKit browsers for mobile devices is insane. And the commercial tools ignore them all but IE, which isn't a sensible strategy post 2008! The next logical step for WebDriver is to standardize it so we can guarantee different web app implementations across browsers. Of course it will help to have the browser makers involved so we can ensure compliance with the WebDriver API.

HGTS: Sounds like a standards committee issue. Any progress there?

Simon: Yes. Unfortunately it means I have to write English instead of code but there is a spec in front of W3C now and that's a place that all browser vendors get involved.

HGTS: So what is your wish for the future? How will browser automation tools work in the future?

Simon: My hope is that they disappear into the background. That automation APIs are an expectation for every browser and that people stop worrying about the infrastructure and they just use it. I want people thinking about new features in their web apps, not how to automate them. WebDriver will be successful when people forget it is even there.

CHAPTER 3
The Test Engineer

Testability and long-term viability of test automation infrastructure is the purview of the Software Engineer in Test (SET). The Test Engineer (TE) plays a related but different role where the focus is on user impact and risk to the overall mission of the software product. Like most technical roles at Google, there is some coding involved, but the TE role is by far the most broad of all the engineers. He contributes to the product, but many of the tasks a TE takes on require no coding.[1]

A User-Facing Test Role

In the prior chapter, we introduced the TE as a "user-developer" and this is not a concept to take lightly. The idea that all engineers on a product team fit the mold of a developer is an important part of keeping all stakeholders on an equal footing. At companies like Google where honoring "the writing of code" is such an important part of our culture, TEs need to be involved as engineers to remain first-class citizens. The Google TE is a mix of technical skills that developers respect and a user facing focus that keeps developers in check. Talk about a split personality!

TEs need to be involved as engineers to remain first-class citizens. The Google TE is a mix of technical skills that developers respect and a user facing focus that keeps developers in check.

---

[1] This is a general view. Many TEs perform work more akin to the SET role and write a lot of code. Some TEs perform a role more closely aligned with a release engineer and write little code.

The TE job description is the hardest to nail down as one size definitely does not fit all. TEs are meant as an overseer of all things quality as the various build targets come together and ultimately comprise the entire product. As such, most TEs get involved in some of this lower-level work where another set of eyes and more engineering expertise is needed. It's a matter of risk: TEs find and contribute to the riskiest areas of the software in whatever manner makes the most sense for that particular product. If SET work is the most valuable, then that's what a TE does; if code reviews are the most valuable, then so be it. If the test infrastructure is lacking, then it gets some TE attention.

These same TEs can then lead exploratory testing sessions at some other point in a project or manage a dogfood or beta testing effort. Sometimes this is time-driven as early phase work means far more SET-oriented tasks are needed, and later in the cycle, TE-oriented work is prevalent. Other cases are the personal choice of the TEs involved and there are a number of cases where engineers convert from one of these roles to another. There are no absolutes. What we describe in the following section is essentially the ideal case.

The Life of a TE

The TE is a newer role at Google than either Software Engineers (SWEs) or SETs. As such, it is a role still in the process of being defined. The current generation of Google TEs is blazing a trail that will guide the next generation of new hires for this role. Here we present the latest emerging TE processes at Google.

Not all products require the attention of a TE. Experimental efforts and early-stage products without a well defined mission or user story are certainly projects that won't get a lot of (or any) TE attention. If the product stands a good chance of being cancelled (in the sense that as a proof of concept, it fails to pass muster) or has yet to engage users or have a well defined set of features, testing is largely something that should be done by the people writing the code.

Even if it is clear that a product is going to get shipped, TEs often have little testing to do early in the development cycle when features are still in flux and the final feature list and scope are undetermined. Overinvesting in test engineering too early, especially if SETs are already deeply engaged, can mean wasted effort. Testing collateral that gets developed too early risks being cast aside or, worse, maintained without adding value. Likewise, early test planning requires fewer TEs than later-cycle exploratory testing when the product is close to final form and the hunt for missed bugs has a greater urgency.

TEs often have little to do early in the development cycle when features are still in flux and the final feature list and scope are undetermined.

The trick in staffing a project with TEs has to do with risk and return on investment. Risk to the customer and to the enterprise means more testing effort and requires more TEs, but that effort needs to be in proportion with the potential return. We need the right number of TEs and we need them to engage at the right time and with the right impact.

After they are engaged, TEs do not have to start from scratch. There is a great deal of test engineering and quality-oriented work performed by SWEs and SETs, which becomes the starting point for additional TE work. The initial engagement of the TE is to decide things such as:

- Where are the weak points in the software?

- What are the security, privacy, performance, reliability, usability, compatibility, globalization, or other concerns?

- Do all the primary user scenarios work as expected? Do they work for all international audiences?

- Does the product interoperate with other products (hardware and software)?

- In the event of a problem, how good are the diagnostics?

Of course these are only a subset. All of this combines to speak to the risk profile of releasing the software in question. TEs don't necessarily do all of this work, but they ensure that it gets done and they leverage the work of others in assessing where additional work is required. Ultimately, TEs are paid to protect users and the business from bad design, confusing UX, functional bugs, security and privacy issues, and so on. At Google, TEs are the only people on a team whose full-time job is to look at the product or service holistically for weak points. As such, the life of a TE is much less prescriptive and formalized than that of an SET. TEs are asked to help on projects in all stages of readiness: everything from the idea stage to version 8 or even watching over a deprecated or "mothballed" project. Often, a single TE even spans multiple projects, particularly those TEs with specialty skill sets such as security, privacy, or internationalization.

Clearly, the work of a TE varies greatly depending on the project. Some TEs spend much of their time programming, but with more of a focus on medium and large tests (such as end-to-end user scenarios) rather than small tests. Other TEs take existing code and designs to determine failure modes and look for errors that can cause those failures. In such a role, a TE might modify code but not create it from scratch. TEs must be more systematic and thorough in their test planning and completeness with a focus on the actual usage and systemwide experience. TEs excel at dealing with ambiguity in requirements and at reasoning and communicating about fuzzy problems.

Successful TEs accomplish all this while navigating the sensitivities and, sometimes, strong personalities of the development and product team members. When weak points are found, TEs happily break the software and drive to get these issues resolved with the SWEs, PMs, and SETs. TEs are generally some of the most well known people on a team because of the breadth of interactions their jobs require.

Such a job description can seem like a frightening prospect given the mix of technical skill, leadership, and deep product understanding required. Indeed, without proper guidance, it is a role in which many would expect to fail. However, at Google, a strong community of TEs has emerged to counter this. Of all job functions, the TE role is perhaps the best peer-supported role in the company. The insight and leadership required to perform the TE job successfully means that many of the top test managers in the company come from the TE ranks.

> The insight and leadership required to perform the TE job successfully means that many of the top test managers in the company come from the TE ranks.

There is fluidity to the work of a Google TE that belies any prescriptive process for engagement. TEs can enter a project at any point and must assess the state of the project, code, design, and users quickly and decide what to focus on first. If the project is just getting started, test planning is often the first order of business. Sometimes TEs are pulled in late in the cycle to evaluate whether a project is ready for ship or if there are any major issues before an early "beta" goes out. If they are brought into a newly acquired application or one in which they have little prior experience, they often start doing some exploratory testing with little or no planning. Sometimes projects haven't been released for quite a while and just need some touchups, security fixes, or UI updates—calling for an even different approach.

One size rarely fits all for TEs at Google. We often describe a TE's work as "starting in the middle" in that a TE has to be flexible and integrate quickly into a product team's culture and current state. If it's too late for a test plan, don't build one. If a project needs tests more than anything else, build just enough of a plan to guide that activity. Starting at "the beginning" according to some testing dogma is simply not practical.

Following is the general set of practices we prescribe for TEs:

- Test planning and risk analysis
- Review specs, designs, code, and existing tests
- Exploratory testing
- User scenarios

- Test case creation

- Executing test cases

- Crowd sourcing

- Usage metrics

- User feedback

Of course, TEs with a strong personality and excellent communication skills are the ones who do all these things to maximum impact.

Test Planning

Developers have a key advantage over testers in that the artifact they work on is one that everyone cares about. Developers deal with code and because that code becomes the application that users covet and that makes profit for the company, it is by definition the most important document created during project execution.

Testers, on the other hand, deal with documents and artifacts of a far more temporal nature. In the early phases of a project, testers write test plans; later, they create and execute test cases and create bug reports. Still, later they write coverage reports and collect data about user satisfaction and software quality. After the software is released and is successful (or not), few people ask about testing artifacts. If the software is well loved, people take the testing for granted. If the software is poor, people might question the testing, but it is doubtful that anyone would want to actually see it.

Testers cannot afford to be too egotistical about test documentation. In the throes of the coding, reviewing, building, testing, rinsing, and repeating cycle that is software development, there is little time to sit around and admire a test plan. Poor test cases rarely achieve enough attention to be improved; they simply get thrown out in favor of those that are better. The attention is focused on the growing codebase and as the only artifact that actually matters, this is as it should be.

As test documentation goes, test plans have the briefest actual lifespan of any test artifact.[2] Early in a project, there is a push to write a test plan (see Appendix A, "Chrome OS Test Plan," for an early Chrome OS test plan). Indeed, there is often an insistence among project managers that a test plan must exist and that writing it is a milestone of some importance. But, once such a plan is written, it is often hard to get any of those same managers to take reviewing and updating it seriously. The test plan becomes a beloved stuffed animal in the hands of a distracted child. We want it to be there at all times. We drag it around from place to place without ever giving it any real attention. We only scream when it gets taken away.

---

[2] Clearly in the event a customer negotiates the development of a test plan or some government regulation requires it, the flexibility we talk about here disappears. There are some test plans that have to be written and kept up to date!

Test plans are the first testing artifact created and the first one to die of neglect. At some early point in a project, the test plan represents the actual software as it is intended to be written but unless that test plan is tended constantly, it soon becomes out of date as new code is added, features veer from their preplanned vision, and designs that looked good on paper are re-evaluated as they are implemented and meet feedback from users. Maintaining a test plan through all these planned and unplanned changes is a lot of work and only worthwhile if the test plan is regularly consulted by a large percentage of the projects' stakeholders.

Test plans are the first testing artifact created and the first one to die of neglect.

This latter point is the real killer of the idea of test planning: How much does a test plan actually drive testing activity throughout the entire lifecycle of a product? Do testers continually consult it as they divvy up the features among them so as to divide and conquer the app? Do developers insist the test plan be updated as they add and modify functionality? Do development managers keep a copy open on their desktop as they manage their to-do list? How often does a test manager refer to the contents of a test plan in status and progress meetings? If the test plan is actually important, all of these things would be happening every day.

Ideally, the test plan should play such a central role during project execution. Ideally, it should be a document that lives as the software lives, getting updates as the codebase gets updates and representing the product as it *currently* exists, not as it existed at the start of a project. Ideally, it should be useful for getting new engineers up to speed as they join a project already in progress.

That's the ideal situation. It's also a situation few testers have actually achieved here at Google or anywhere else for that matter.

Here are some features we want in a test plan:

- It is always up to date.

- It describes the intent of the software and why it will be loved by its users.

- It contains a snapshot of how the software is structured and the names of the various components and features.

- It describes what the software should do and summaries how it will do it.

From a purely testing point of view, we have to worry about the test plan being relevant while not making its care and feeding such a burden that it becomes more work than it is worth:

- It cannot take long to create and must be readily modifiable.

- It should describe what must be tested.

- It should be useful during testing to help determine progress and coverage gaps.

At Google, the history of test planning is much the same as other companies we've experienced. Test planning was a process determined by the people doing it and executed according to local (meaning the individual team) custom. Some teams wrote test plans in Google Docs (text documents and spreadsheets), shared with their engineering team but not in a central repository. Other teams linked their test plans on their product's home page. Still others added them to the internal Google Sites pages for their projects or linked to them from the engineering design documents and internal wikis. A few teams even used Microsoft Word documents, sent around in emails to the team in a proper old-school way. Some teams had no test plans at all, just test cases whose sum total, we must suppose, represented the plan.

The review path for these plans was opaque and it was hard to determine the authors and reviewers. Far too many of the test plans had a time and date stamp that made it all too clear that they had been written and long forgotten like the sell-by date on that old jar of jam in the back of the refrigerator. It must have been important to someone at some time, but that time has passed.

There was a proposal floated around Google to create a central repository and template for *all* product test plans. This was an interesting idea that has been tried elsewhere, but one clearly contrary to Google's inherently distributed and self-governed nature where "states rights" was the norm and big government a concept that brought derision.

Enter ACC (Attribute Component Capability) analysis, a process pulled together from the best practices of a number of Google test teams and pioneered by the authors and several colleagues in various product areas. ACC has passed its early adopter's phase and is being exported to other companies and enjoying the attention to tool developers who automate it under the "Google Test Analytics" label.

ACC has the following guiding principles:

- **Avoid prose and favor bulleted lists**. Not all testers wish to be novelists or possess the skill set to adequately capture in prose a product's purpose in life or its testing needs. Prose can be hard to read and is easily misinterpreted. Just the facts please!

- **Don't bother selling**. A test plan is not a marketing document or a place to talk about how important a market niche the product satisfies or how cool it is. Test plans aren't for customers or analysts; they are for engineers.

- **No fluff**. There is no length expectation for a test plan. Test plans are not high school term projects where length matters. Bigger is not better. The size of the plan is related to the size of the testing problem, not the propensity of the author to write.

- **If it isn't important and actionable, don't put it in the plan**. Not a single word in the plan should garner a "don't care" reaction from a potential stakeholder.

- **Make it flow**. Each section of the test plan should be an expansion of earlier sections so that one can stop reading at anytime and have a picture of the product's functionality in his head. If the reader wants more detail, he can continue reading.

- **Guide a planner's thinking**. A good planning process helps a planner think through functionality and test needs and logically leads from higher-level concepts into lower-level details that can be directly implemented.

- **The outcome should be test cases**. By the time the plan is completed, it should clearly describe not just what testing needs to be done but that it should also make the writing of test cases obvious. A plan that doesn't lead directly to tests is a waste of time.

> A plan that doesn't lead directly to tests is a waste of time.

This last point is crucial: If the test plan does not describe in enough detail what test cases need to be written, then it hasn't served its primary purpose of helping us test the application we are building. The *planning of tests* should put us in a position to know what tests need to be written. You are finished planning when you are at exactly that spot: You know what tests you need to write.

ACC accomplishes this by guiding the planner through three views of a product corresponding to 1) *adjectives* and *adverbs* that describe the product's purpose and goals, 2) *nouns* that identify the various parts and features of the product, and 3) *verbs* that indicate what the product actually does. It follows that testing allows us to test that those capabilities work and the components as written satisfy the application's purpose and goals.

A is for "Attribute"

When starting test planning or ACC, it is important to first identify why the product is important to users and to the business. Why are we building this thing? What core value does it deliver? Why is it interesting to customers? Remember, we're not looking to either justify or explain these things, only to label them. Presumably the PMs and product planners, or developers, have done their job of coming up with a product that matters in the marketplace. From a testing perspective, we just need to capture and label these things so we can ensure they are accounted for when we test it.

We document the core values in a three-step process called Attribute, Component, Capability analysis and we do so in that order, with attributes as the first target.

Attributes are the adjectives of the system. They are the qualities and characteristics that promote the product and distinguish it from the competition. In a way, they are the reasons people would choose to use the product over a competitor. Chrome, for example, is held to be fast, secure, stable, and elegant, and these are the attributes we try to document in the ACC. Looking ahead, we want to get to a point where we can attach test cases to these labels so that we know how much testing we have done to show that Chrome is fast, secure, and so on.

> Attributes are the adjectives of the system. They are the qualities and characteristics that promote the product and distinguish it from the competition. Attributes are the reasons people would choose to use the product over a competitor.

Typically, a product manager has a hand in narrowing down the list of attributes for the system. Testers often get this list by reading the product requirements document, the vision and mission statement of the team, or even by simply listening to a sales guy describe the system to a prospective customer. Indeed, we find at Google that salespeople and product evangelists are an excellent source of attributes. Just imagine back-of-the-box advertising or think about how the product would be pitched on QVC, and you can get the right mindset to list the attributes.

Some tips on coming up with attributes for your own projects:

- **Keep it simple**. If it takes more than an hour or two, you are spending too long on this step.

- **Keep it accurate**. Make sure it comes from a document or marketing information that your team already accepts as truth.

- **Keep it moving**. Don't worry if you missed something—if it's not obvious later, it probably wasn't that important anyway.

- **Keep it short**. No more than a dozen is a good target. We boiled an operating system down to 12 key attributes (see Figure 3.1), and in retrospect, we should have shortened that list to 8 or 9.

FIGURE 3.1 Original Chrome risk analysis.

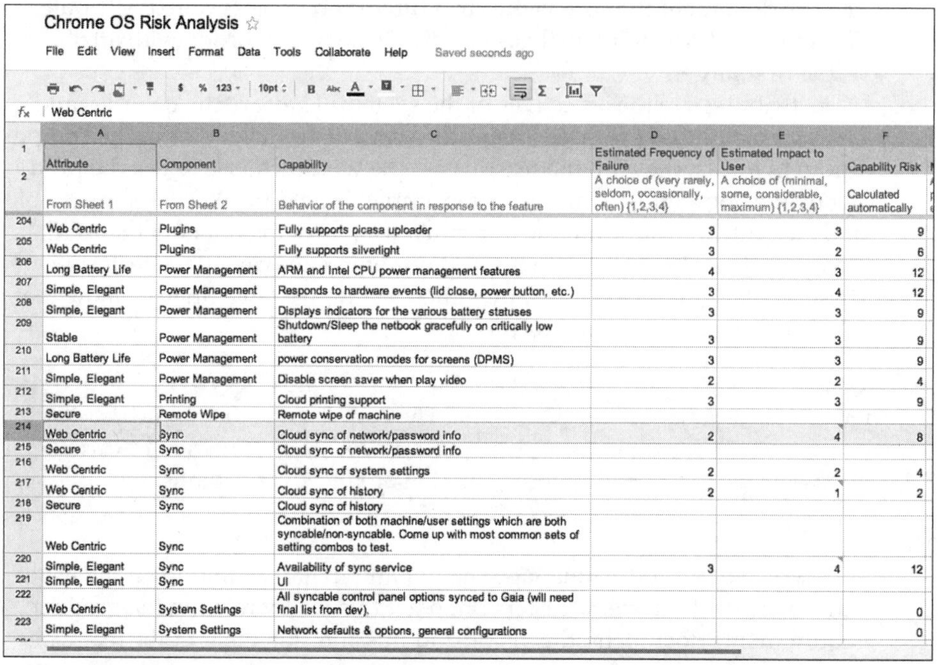
Chrome OS Risk Analysis

File Edit View Insert Format Data Tools Collaborate Help Saved seconds ago

fx Web Centric

	A	B	C	D	E	F
1	Attribute	Component	Capability	Estimated Frequency of Failure	Estimated Impact to User	Capability Risk
2	From Sheet 1	From Sheet 2	Behavior of the component in response to the feature	A choice of (very rarely, seldom, occasionally, often) {1,2,3,4}	A choice of (minimal, some, considerable, maximum) {1,2,3,4}	Calculated automatically
204	Web Centric	Plugins	Fully supports picasa uploader	3	3	9
205	Web Centric	Plugins	Fully supports silverlight	3	2	6
206	Long Battery Life	Power Management	ARM and Intel CPU power management features	4	3	12
207	Simple, Elegant	Power Management	Responds to hardware events (lid close, power button, etc.)	3	4	12
208	Simple, Elegant	Power Management	Displays indicators for the various battery statuses	3	3	9
209	Stable	Power Management	Shutdown/Sleep the netbook gracefully on critically low battery	3	3	9
210	Long Battery Life	Power Management	power conservation modes for screens (DPMS)	3	3	9
211	Simple, Elegant	Power Management	Disable screen saver when play video	2	2	4
212	Simple, Elegant	Printing	Cloud printing support	3	3	9
213	Secure	Remote Wipe	Remote wipe of machine			
214	Web Centric	Sync	Cloud sync of network/password info	2	4	8
215	Secure	Sync	Cloud sync of network/password info			
216	Web Centric	Sync	Cloud sync of system settings	2	2	4
217	Web Centric	Sync	Cloud sync of history	2	1	2
218	Secure	Sync	Cloud sync of history			
219	Web Centric	Sync	Combination of both machine/user settings which are both syncable/non-syncable. Come up with most common sets of setting combos to test.			
220	Simple, Elegant	Sync	Availability of sync service	3	4	12
221	Simple, Elegant	Sync	UI			
222	Web Centric	System Settings	All syncable control panel options synced to Gaia (will need final list from dev).			0
223	Simple, Elegant	System Settings	Network defaults & options, general configurations			0

Note

Some figures in this chapter are representational and are not intended to be read in detail.

Attributes are used to figure out what the product does to support the core reasons for the product's existence and to surface these reasons to testers so they can be aware of how the testing they do impacts the application's ultimate reason for existence.

As an example, consider the attributes for a product called Google Sites, which is a freely available application for building a shared website for some open or closed community. Sites, as you'll find with many end-user applications, is kind enough to provide most of its attributes for you in its own documentation, as shown in Figure 3.2.

Indeed, most applications that have some sort of Getting Started page or sales-oriented literature often do the work of identifying attributes for you. If they do not, then simply talking to a salesperson, or better yet, simply watching a sales call or demo, gets you the information you need.

Attributes are there for the taking. If you have trouble enumerating them in anything more than a few minutes, then you do not understand your product well enough to be an effective tester. Learn your product and listing its attributes becomes a matter of a few minutes of work.

If you have trouble enumerating attributes in anything more than a few minutes, then you do not understand your product well enough to be an effective tester.

At Google, we use any number of tools for documenting risk; from documents to spreadsheets to a custom tool built by some enterprising engineers called *Google Test Analytics* (GTA). It doesn't really matter what you use, just that you get them all written down (see Figure 3.3).

FIGURE 3.3   Attributes for Google Sites as documented in GTA.

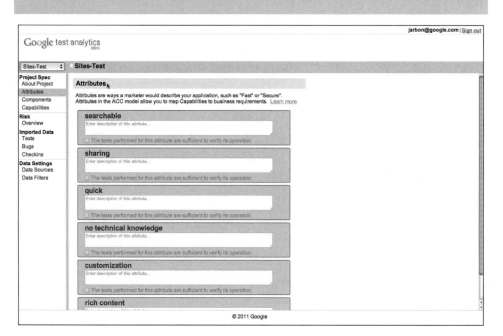

C is for "Component"

Components are the nouns of the system and the next target of enumeration after the attributes are complete. Components are the building blocks that together constitute the system in question. They are the shopping cart and the checkout feature for an online store. They are the formatting and printing features of a word processor. They are the core chunks of code that make the software what it is. Indeed, they are the very things that testers are tasked with testing!

> Components are the building blocks that together constitute the system in question. They are the core components and chunks of code that make the software what it is.

Components are generally easy to identify and often already cast in a design document somewhere. For large systems, they are the big boxes in an architectural diagram and often appear in labels in bug databases or called out explicitly in project pages and documentation. For smaller projects, they are the classes and objects in the code. In every case, just go and ask each developer: "What component are you working on?" and you will get the list without having to do much else.

As with attributes, the level of detail in identifying components of the product is critical. Too much detail and it becomes overwhelming and provides diminishing returns. Too little detail, and there's simply no reason to bother in the first place. Keep the list small; 10 is good and 20 is too many unless the system is very large. It's okay to leave minor things out. If they are minor, then they are part of another component or they don't really matter enough to the end user for us to focus on them.

Indeed, for both the attributes and the components, spending minutes tallying them should suffice. If you are struggling coming up with components, then you seriously lack familiarity with your product and you should spend some time using it to get to the level of a power user quickly. Any actual power user should be able to list attributes immediately and any project insider with access to the source code and its documentation should be able to list the components quickly as well. Clearly we believe it is important for testers to be both power users and, obviously, project insiders.

Finally, don't worry about completeness. The whole ACC process is based on doing something quick and then iterating as you go. If you miss an attribute, you might discover it as you are listing the components. Once you get to the capability portion, which is described next, you should shake out any attributes or components you missed earlier.

The components for Google Sites appear in Figure 3.4.

FIGURE 3.4 Components for Google Sites as documented in GTA.

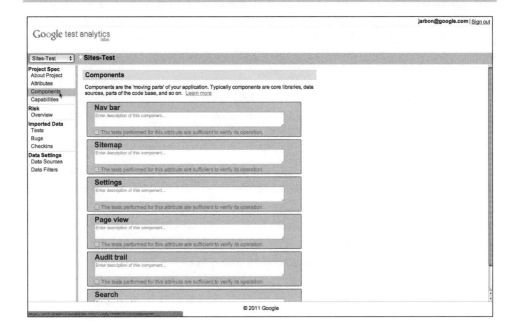

C is for "Capability"

Capabilities are the verbs of the system; they represent the actions the system performs at the command of the user. They are responses to input, answers to queries, and activities accomplished on behalf of the user. Indeed, they are the very reason users choose to use your software in the first place: They want some functionality and your software provides it.

> Capabilities are the actions the system performs at the command of the user. They are responses to input, answers to queries, and activities accomplished on behalf of the user.

Chrome, for example, has the capabilities of rendering a web page and playing a Flash file. Chrome can synchronize between clients and download a document. All these are capabilities and these and many more represent the full set of capabilities of the Chrome web browser. A shopping app, on the other hand, has the capability of performing a product search and completing a sale. If an application can perform a task, then this task is labeled as one of its capabilities.

Capabilities lie at the intersection of attributes and components. Components perform some function to satisfy an attribute of the product and the result of this activity is providing a capability to a user. Chrome renders a web page *fast*. Chrome plays a Flash file *securely*. If your product does something that isn't covered by the intersection of an attribute and a component, it probably doesn't matter and warrants raising the question as to why we are bothering to have it in the product. A capability that doesn't serve a core value to the product sounds very much like fat that can be trimmed and represents potential points of failure with little to be gained. Either that or there is an explanation for the capabilities' existence and you don't understand it. Not understanding your product is unacceptable in the testing profession. If any single engineer on a project understands his product's value proposition to its users, that someone is a tester!

Here are some examples of capabilities for an online shopping site:

- **Add/remove items from the shopping cart.** This is a capability of the Cart component when trying to meet the Intuitive UI attribute.

- **Collect credit card and verification data.** This is a capability of the Cart component when trying to meet the Convenient attribute and the Integrated (for instance, integrated with the payment system) attribute.

- **Processes monetary transactions using HTTPS.** This is a capability of the Cart component when trying to meet the Secure attribute.

- **Provide suggestions to shoppers based on the products they are viewing.** This is a capability of the Search component when trying to meet the Convenient attribute.

- **Calculate shipping cost.** This is a capability of the UPS Integration component when trying to meet the Fast and Secure attribute.

- **Display available inventory.** This is a capability of the Search component when trying to meet the Convenient and Accurate attribute.

- **Defer a purchase for a later date.** This is a capability of the Cart component when trying to meet the Convenient attribute.

- **Search for items by keyword, SKU, and category.** This is a capability of the Search component when trying to satisfy the Convenient and Accurate attributes. In general, we prefer to treat each search category as a separate capability.

Obviously there can be a large number of capabilities and if it feels like you are listing everything you *could* test, then you are getting the hang of ACC! The entire idea is to list, quickly and succinctly, the most important capabilities of the system that need to be verified to be in working order.

Capabilities are generally user-oriented and written to convey a user's view of what the system does. They are also far more numerous than either attributes or components. Whereas brevity rules in the first two stages of ACC, capabilities should in sum total describe everything the system is capable of doing and therefore be greater in number based on the feature richness and complexity of the application in question.

For systems, we have worked on at Google, capabilities tend to be in the hundreds for larger more complicated applications (Chrome OS has more than 300, for example) and in the dozens for smaller applications. Surely there is a case to be made for products with only a few capabilities to not require testing beyond what the developers and a few early users could accomplish. So if you are testing something with fewer than 20 capabilities, you might want to question your presence on the project!

The most important aspect of capabilities is that they are testable. This is the primary reason we write them in an active voice. They are verbs because they require action on our part, specifically that we will write test cases to determine whether each capability is implemented correctly and that the user will find the experience useful. We discuss more about translating capabilities into test cases later.

> The most important aspect of capabilities is that they are testable.

The right level of abstraction for capabilities is a point that gets argued about a great deal among Google TEs. Capabilities, by definition, are not meant to be atomic actions. A single capability can describe any number of actual use cases. In the previous shopping example, the capabilities don't specify which items are in the cart or the outcome of a specific search. They describe general activities a user might be involved in. This is intentional as such details are too voluminous to document unless they are actually going to be tested. We cannot test all possible searches and shopping cart configurations, so we only bother translating these capabilities into test cases for the ones that actually get tested.

Capabilities are not meant to be test cases in the sense that they contain all the information necessary to run them as actual tests. We don't put exact values and specific data into a capability. The capability is that a user can shop. The test case specifies what they shop for. Capabilities are general concepts of actions the software can take or a user can request. They are meant to be general. They imply tests and values but are not tests themselves.

Continuing with the Google Sites example, we show in Figure 3.5 a grid showing attributes across the x axis and components across the y axis. This is the way we link capabilities back to attributes and components. The first thing to note is the large number of empty squares. This is typical as not every component has an impact on every attribute. For Chrome, only some of the components are responsible for making it fast or secure; the others will have blanks representing no impact. These blank entries mean that we don't have to test this particular attribute component pair.

FIGURE 3.5   Capabilities are tied to attributes and components in GTA.

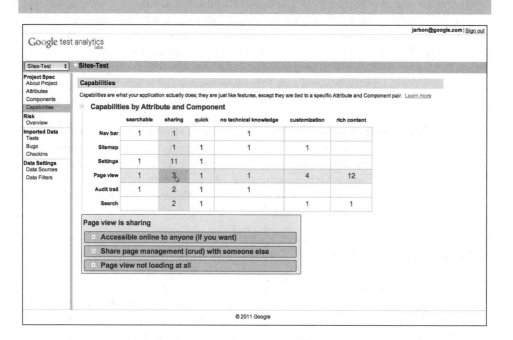

Each row or column of the table of capabilities represents a slice of functionality that is related in some fashion. A single row or column is a good way to break the application's functionality into testable sessions. A test manager might take each row and assign it to separate test teams or have a bug bash to really hit a row or column hard. They also make excellent targets for exploratory testing and when each exploratory tester takes a different row and column, you can manage overlap and get better coverage.

For entries that contain a numeric value, this is the number of capabilities provided by that component to satisfy that attribute. The higher the number, the more test points for that particular intersection. For example, the Page View components impact the Sharing attributes with the following three capabilities:

- Make the document accessible to collaborators.

- Share page management duties with a collaborator.

- View collaborator position within a page.

These capabilities conveniently specify things that need to be tested for the Page View/Sharing pair. We can either write test cases for them directly or test a combination of capabilities by combining them into a larger use case or test scenario.

Writing good capabilities requires some discipline. Here are some properties we've found to be useful guidance for writing capabilities:

1. A capability should be written as an *action* and convey the sense of the user accomplishing some activity using the application under test.

2. A capability should provide enough guidance for a tester to understand what variables are involved in writing test cases for the behavior it describes. For example, *process monetary transactions using https* requires that the tester understands what types of monetary transactions the system is capable of performing and a mechanism to validate whether the transaction occurs over https. Obviously, there is a great deal of work to be done here. If we believe there are monetary transactions that might be missed by, say, a new tester on the team, then by all means, replicate this capability to expose the various transaction types. If not, then the level of abstraction is good enough. Likewise, if https is something well understood by the team, then the capability is fine as it is worded. Don't fall into the trap of trying to document everything as capabilities; they are supposed to be abstract. Leave it to the test cases or exploratory testers themselves to provide that level of detail.[3]

---

[3] Leaving such variation to the tester is a good idea. It creates variety in how capabilities are interpreted and cast into actual test cases. This translates to better coverage.

3. A capability should be composed with other capabilities. In fact, a *user story* or *use case* (or whatever terminology you may prefer) should be describable with a series of capabilities. If a user story cannot be written with only the existing capabilities, then there are missing capabilities or the capabilities are at too high a level of abstraction.

Transforming a set of capabilities into user stories is an optional interim step that can add a great deal of flexibility to testing. In fact, there are several groups in Google that prefer more general user stories over more specific test cases when engaging with external contractors or when organizing a crowd-sourced exploratory testing effort. Test cases can be specific and cause boredom as they are executed over and over by a contractor, whereas a user story provides enough leeway in deciding specific behaviors that it makes testing more fun and less prone to mistakes from boring, rote execution.

Whether it is user stories, test cases, or both that are the ultimate goal, here is the general guidance for translating capabilities to test cases. Keep in mind these are goals, not absolutes.

- Every capability should be linked to at least one test case. If the capability is important enough to document, it is important enough to test.

- Many capabilities require more than one test case. Whenever there is variation in the inputs, input sequences, system variables, data used, and so on, multiple test cases are required. The attacks in *How to Break Software* and the tours in *Exploratory Software Testing* provide good guidance in test case selection and ways to think through data and inputs that are more likely to turn a capability into a test case that finds a bug.

- Not all capabilities are equal and some are more important than others. The next step in the process (described in the next section) addresses how risk is associated with the capabilities to distinguish their importance.

Once the ACC is complete, it specifies everything we *could* test if budget and time were not a problem. Given that both of these are pretty major problems, it helps to prioritize. At Google, we call such prioritization *risk analysis* and that's the subject matter we turn to next.

Example: Determining Attributes, Components, and Capabilities for Google+

ACC can be performed quickly in a document, spreadsheet, or even on a napkin! Here is an abbreviated example of ACC for Google+.

- **Google+ Attributes** (derived exclusively by watching an executive discuss Google+)

  Social: Empowers users to share information and what they're up to.

Expressive: Users can express themselves through the features.

Easy: Intuitive. Easy to figure out how to do what you want to do.

Relevant: Shows only information the user cares about.

Extensible: Capable of integrating with Google properties and third-party sites and applications.

Private: Users' data won't be shared.

- **Google+ Components** (derived from architecture documents)

Profile: Information and preferences for the logged in user.

People: Profiles that the user has connected with.

Stream: A ranked stream of posts, comments, notifications, photos, and so on.

Circles: Groups to put contacts into "friends," "co-workers," and so on.

Notifications: Indicators for when you are mentioned in a post.

Interests or +1: Indication for user likes.

Posts: Buzz posts from the users and their contacts.

Comments: Comments on posts, photos, videos, and so on.

Photos: Photos uploaded by the users and their contacts.

- **Google+ Capabilities:**

Profile:

Social: Share profiles and preferences with friends and contacts.

Expressive: Users can create an online version of themselves.

Expressive: Personalize your experience with Google+.

Easy: Easy to enter and update information and have it propagate.

Extensible: Serves profile information to applications with appropriate access.

Private: Enables a user to keep private data private.

Private: Share data only with approved and appropriate parties.

People:

Social: Users can connect with users' friends, coworkers, and families.

Expressive: Profiles of other users are personalized and easily distinguishable.

Easy: Provides tools to easily manage a user's contacts.

Relevant: Users can filter their contacts based on criteria for relevance.

Extensible: Serves contact data to authorized services and applications.

Private: Keeps data about a user's contacts private to approved parties.

Stream:

Social: Informs the users of updates from their social networks.

Relevant: Filters for updates the user would be interested in.

Extensible: Serves stream updates to services and applications.

Circles:

Social: Groups contacts into circles based on social context.

Expressive: New circles can be created based on the context of the user.

Easy: Facilitates adding, updating, and removing contacts to and from circles.

Easy: Facilitates creating and modifying circles.

Extensible: Serves data about circles for use to services and applications.

Notifications:

Easy: Presents notifications concisely.

Extensible: Posts notifications for use by other services and applications.

Hangouts:

Social: Users can invite their circles to hang out.

Social: Users can open hangouts to the public.

Social: Others are notified of hangouts they access in their streams.

Easy: Hangouts can be created and participated in within a few clicks.

Easy: Video and audio inputs can be disabled with a single click.

Easy: Additional users can be added to an existing hangout.

Expressive: Before joining a hangout, users can preview how they will appear to others.

Extensible: Users can chat through text while in a hangout.

Extensible: Videos from YouTube can be added to a hangout.

Extensible: Devices can be configured and adjusted in Settings.

Extensible: Users without a webcam can participate in hangouts through audio.

Private: Only invited guests can access a hangout.

Private: Only invited guests are notified of a hangout.

Posts:

Expressive: Expresses the thoughts of the user through Buzz.

Private: Posts are restricted to the intended audience.

Comments:

Expressive: Expresses the thoughts of the user through comments.

Extensible: Posts data on comments for use by other services and applications.

Private: Posts are restricted to the intended audience.

Photos:

Social: Users can share their photos with their contacts and friends.

Easy: Users can easily upload new photos.

Easy: Users can easily import photos from other sources.

Extensible: Integration with other photo services.

Private: Photos are restricted so that they're only visible to the intended audience.

An ACC in basic spreadsheet form is shown in Figure 3.6.

FIGURE 3.6 ACC spreadsheet grid for Google+.

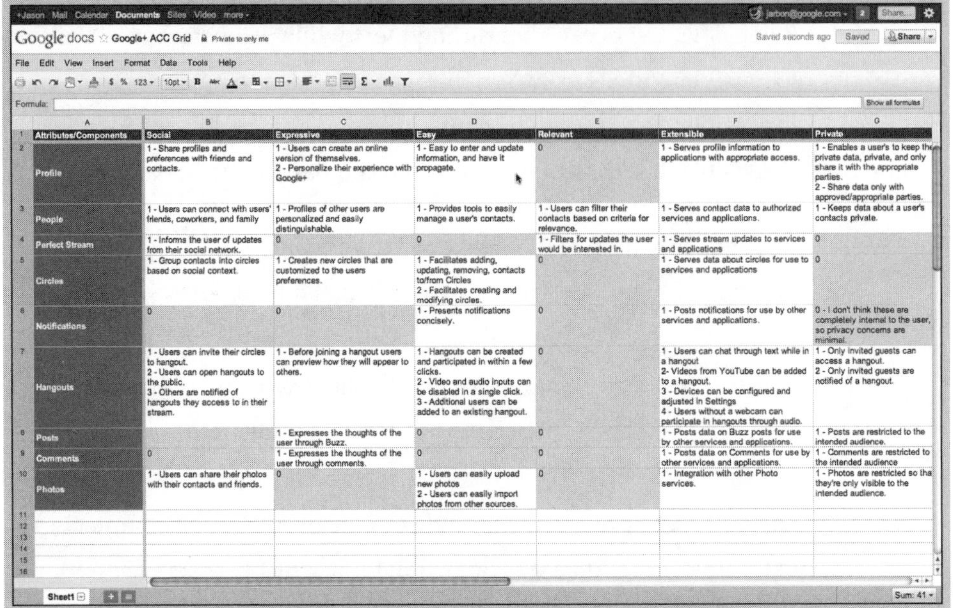

See Figure 3.7 for an alternate grid view of this data.

FIGURE 3.7 Google+ ACC grid.

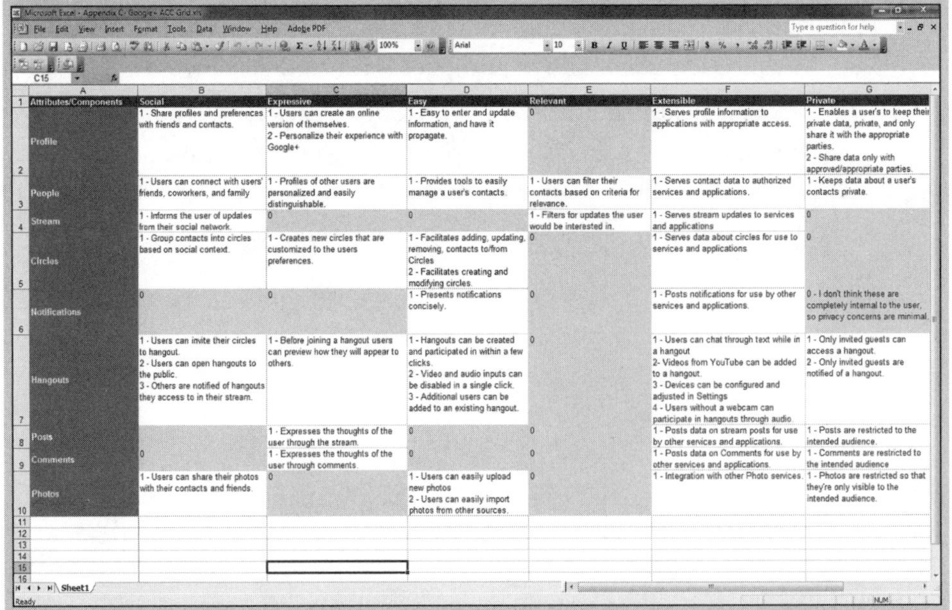

Risk

Risk is everywhere. At home, on the roads, and at our workplace, everything we do has an element of risk, and shipping software is no different. We buy safer cars and practice defensive driving to mitigate the risk of driving. At work, we watch what we say in meetings and try to find projects suitable to our skill set to mitigate the risk of losing our job. How do we mitigate the risk of shipping software? How can we navigate the overwhelming odds that the software will fail (after all, no software is perfect) and cause untold damage to our company's reputation?

Certainly *not shipping* the software isn't an option despite its complete negation of the risk of failure. The enterprise benefits from well calculated risks.

Note that we did not say "well quantified" risks. Risk, at least for our purposes, isn't something that requires mathematical precision. We walk on sidewalks and not the street not because of a formula that shows a 59 percent decrease in risk but a general knowledge that roads are not a safe place for pedestrians. We buy cars with air bags not because we know the math behind increasing our survival chances in case of a wreck but because they represent an obvious mitigation to the risk of breaking our faces on the steering wheel. Risk mitigations can be incredibly powerful without a great deal of precision and the process of determining risk is called *risk analysis*.

Risk Analysis

For software testing, we follow a common sense process for understanding risk. The following factors have been helpful to us when understanding risk:

- What events are we concerned about?
- How likely are these events?
- How bad would they be to the enterprise?
- How bad would they be for customers?
- What mitigations does the product implement?
- How likely is it that these mitigations would fail?
- What would be the cost of dealing with the failure?
- How difficult is the recovery process?
- Is the event likely to recur or be a one-time problem?

There are many variables in determining risk that makes quantifying it more trouble than mitigating it. At Google, we boil risk down to two primary factors: *frequency of failure* and *impact*. Testers assign simple values for each of these factors to each capability. We've found that risk is real as a qualitative number rather than as an absolute number. It isn't about assigning an accurate value; it's about determining whether one capability is more or less risky than another capability. This is enough to determine which capabilities to test and which order to test them in. GTA presents the options, as shown in Figure 3.8.

FIGURE 3.8   Estimating risk in terms of frequency and impact in GTA for Google+.

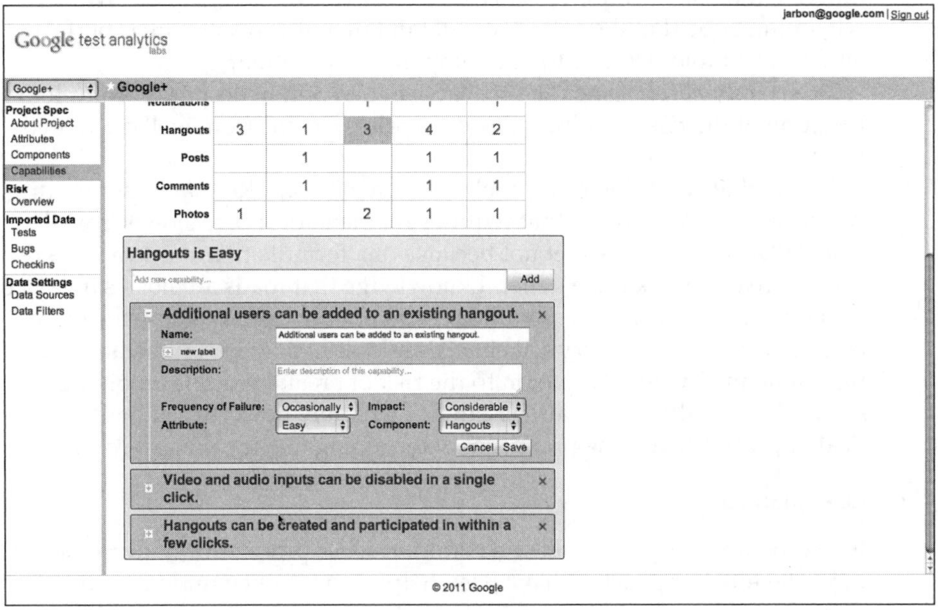

GTA uses four predefined values for frequency of occurrence:

- **Rarely:** It's hard to imagine a case where failure would occur and recovery would not be trivial.

  - Example: Download page for Chrome.[4] The content is largely static with parameterization for only auto-detection of the client OS, even if there was a break in the core HTML or script on the page that would be detected quickly by monitoring code.

- **Seldom:** There are cases where failure can occur, but low complexity or low usage would make such occurrences rare.

  - Example: The Forward button in Chrome. This button is used, but far less frequently than the Back button. Historically, it doesn't fail often, and even if it did regress, we would expect our early adopters on the early release channels to catch this issue quickly as it would be fairly obvious.

---

[4] The web page where people can download Chrome is http://www.google.com/chrome.

- **Occasionally:** Failure circumstances are readily imaginable, somewhat complex, and the capability is one we expect to be popular.

  - Example: Chrome Sync capabilities. Chrome synchronizes the bookmarks, themes, form-fill, history, and other user profile data across clients. There are different data types and multiple OS platforms, and merging changes is a somewhat complex computer science problem in its own right. Users are also likely to notice if this data isn't synchronized. Synchronization happens only when data to be synchronized changes, like when a new bookmark has been added.

- **Often:** The capability is part of a high-use, high-complexity feature that experiences failure on a regular basis.

  - Example: Rendering web pages. This is the primary use case of a browser. Rendering HTML, CSS, and JavaScript code of whatever origin and quality is the principle task a browser performs. If any of this code fails, it's the browser that the user blames. Risk increases when you consider such a failure on a high-traffic site. Rendering issues aren't always caught by users either; they often result in elements misaligned slightly, but still functional, or elements go missing, but the user wouldn't know they aren't there.

Testers choose one of these values for each capability. We used an even number of values on purpose to keep testers from simply picking the middle value. It's important to think about it a bit more carefully.

Estimating impact takes a similarly simplistic approach and is also based on choosing from an even number of possibilities (more examples from the Chrome browser):

- **Minimal:** A failure the user might not even notice.

  - Example: Chrome Labs. This is optional functionality. Failure to load the chrome://labs page would affect few users. This page contains optional Chrome experimental features. Most users don't even know they are there; the features themselves are labeled "use at your own risk" and don't pose a threat to the core browser.

- **Some:** A failure that might annoy the user. If noticed, retry or recovery mechanisms are straightforward.

  - Example: Refresh button. If this fails to refresh the current page, the user can retype the URL in the same tab, simply open a new tab to the URL, or even restart the browser in the extreme case. The cost of the failure is mostly annoyance.

- **Considerable:** A failure would block usage scenarios.

  - Example: Chrome extensions. If users installed Chrome extensions to add functionality to their browser and those extensions failed to load in a new version of Chrome, the functionality of that extension is lost.

- **Maximal:** A failure would permanently damage the reputation of the product and cause users to stop using it.

    - Example: Chrome's autoupdate mechanism. Should this feature break, it would deny critical security updates or perhaps even lead the browser to stop working.

Sometimes the impact to the enterprise and the user are at odds. A banner ad that fails to load is a problem for Google but might not even be noticed by a user. It is good practice to note whether risk to the enterprise or risk to the user is being considered when assigning a score.

We can generate a heat map of risk areas of Google Sites based on the values entered by the tester and the Attribute-Component grid shown earlier. This appears in Figure 3.9.

FIGURE 3.9   Heat map of risk for attribute-component grid for an early version of Google+.

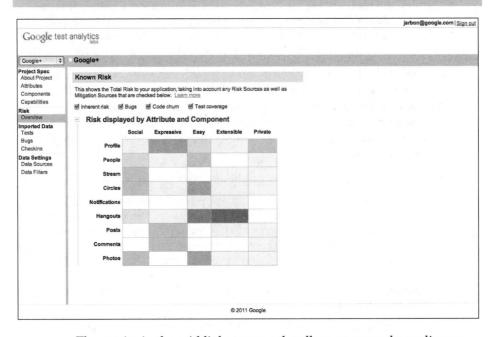

The entries in the grid light up as red, yellow, or green depending on the risk level of the components assigned to those intersections. It is a simple calculation of risk for each of the values you've entered—we simply take the average of each capability's risk. GTA generates this map, but a spreadsheet can also be used.

This diagram represents the testable capabilities of the product and their risk as you assign the values. It's difficult to keep bias from these numbers, and testers do represent a specific point of view. We're careful to solicit feedback from other stakeholders as well. Following is a list of stakeholders and some suggestions about getting them involved in assigning these risk values:

- **Developers:** Most developers, when consulted, will assign the most risk to the features they own. If they wrote the code, they want tests for it! It's been our experience that developers overrate the features they own.

- **Program Managers:** PMs are also humans and introduce their own biases. They favor the capabilities they see as most important. In general, they favor the features that make the software stand out from its competition and make it "pop."

- **Salespeople:** Sales are the ones who get paid for attracting users. They are biased toward features that sell the product and look good in demos.

- **Directors and VPs:** Executives often highlight the features that set the software apart from its major competitors.

Obviously, all stakeholders have significant biases so our approach has been to solicit all their opinions and have them each separately score the capabilities using the previous two scales. It isn't always easy to get their participation, but we've hit upon a strategy that has been successful. Instead of explaining the process and convincing them to help, we simply do it ourselves and present them with our heat map. Once they see our bias, they are quick to supply their own. Developers participate in mass if they know we are using the map to prioritize testing; the same goes for PMs and salespeople. They all have a stake in quality.

There is power in this approach. In determining risk ourselves, we have undoubtedly come to a conclusion they will argue with. Indeed, in presenting our risk analysis as the basis for all forthcoming tests, we have *given them* something to argue about! And that is the point. Instead of asking their opinions about a concept they consider nebulous, we have shown them a specific conclusion they can argue against. People are often ready to tell you what the answer is *not*. We also avoid having everyone wade through all data for which they have little interest or context. With this little ruse in our toolkit, we generally get a lot of focused input that we can factor into the risk calculations.

Once risk is generally agreed upon, it's time to start mitigating it.

Risk Mitigation

Risk can rarely be eliminated. Driving is risky, yet we have places to go. Travel is risky, yet we do it anyway, and more often than not, the risk never manifests as any real injury. Why is this the case? Because we mitigate risks based on our actions. There are certain times of the day we choose not to drive and certain destinations to which we choose not to travel. This is mitigation.

For software, the ultimate mitigation is to simply eliminate the riskiest components: the less software we ship, the less risk we assume. But besides outright elimination of risk, there are many things we can do to mitigate risk:

- We can write user stories around risky capabilities to define paths of less risk and feed this back to development so that more constraints can be added to the app.

- We can write regression test cases to ensure that failures cannot be reintroduced without being detected.

- We can write and run tests to show the need for recovery and fallback features.

- We can add instrumentation and watchdog code to detect failures early.

- We can add instrumentation that notices behavioral changes across versions of the software that indicate a bug has regressed.

The exact mitigation needed depends greatly on the application and what users expect of its safety and security. For testers, we might be involved in the actual mitigation, but we are most certainly involved in exposing the risk. We proceed by prioritizing the capabilities marked in red over those in yellow or green. We want to test in the order of risk. This is important: *If you can't test everything, test the most important stuff first,* and the most important stuff is the riskiest stuff.

Depending on the type of project, it is up to you the tester to advise about readiness to ship. A tester should be able to glance at the risk heat map and make a recommendation to other engineers whether the product is ready for release. If it is a Google Labs Experiment, it is probably fine to ship with some red areas as long as they don't deal with privacy or security. If it is a major new release of Gmail, any yellows will likely be a blocking concern. The colors are also simple enough that even test directors can understand them.

Concerns about risk fade over time and a significant amount of successful testing is a good indication that risk is at acceptable levels. This makes it crucial that we tie test cases back to individual capabilities and back to attributes and components in the risk grid. Indeed, ACC fits this requirement perfectly and it's why we designed it the way we did.

The 10-Minute Test Plan by James Whittaker

Anything in software development that takes 10 minutes or less to perform is either trivial or is not worth doing in the first place. If you take this rule of thumb at face value, where do you place test planning? Certainly it takes more than 10 minutes. In my capacity as test director at Google, I presided over teams that wrote a large number of test plans, and every time I asked how long one would take, I was told "tomorrow" or "the end of the week" and a few times, early in the day, I was promised one "by the end of the day." So I'll establish the task of test planning to be of the hours-to-days duration.

As to whether it is worth doing, well, that is another story entirely. Every time I look at any of the dozens of test plans my teams have written, I see dead test plans—plans written, reviewed, referred to a few times, and then cast aside as the project moves in directions not documented in the plan. This begs the question: If a plan isn't worth bothering to update, is it worth creating in the first place?

Other times, a plan is discarded because it went into too much detail or too little; still, others because it provided value only in starting a test effort and not in the ongoing work. Again, if this is the case, was the plan worth the cost of creating it given its limited and diminishing value?

Some test plans document simple truths that likely didn't need to be documented at all or provide detailed information that isn't relevant to the day-to-day job of a software tester. In all these cases, we are wasting effort. Let's face facts here: There is a problem with the process and content of test plans.

To combat this, I came up with a simple task for my teams: write a test plan in 10 minutes. The idea is simple. If test plans have any value at all, then let's get to that value as quickly as possible.

Given 10 minutes, there is clearly no room for fluff. It is a time period so compressed that every second must be spent doing something useful, or any hope you have of actually finishing the task is gone. This was the entire intent behind the exercise from my point of view: Boil test planning down to only the essentials and cut all fat and fluff. Do only what is *absolutely necessary* and leave the details to the test executors as opposed to the test planners. If I wanted to end the practice of writing test plans that don't stand the test of time, this seemed a worthwhile exercise.

However, I didn't tell the people in the experiment any of this. I told them only: Here is an app, create a test plan in 10 minutes or less. Remember that these people work for me and are paid to do as I tell them. Technically, I am uniquely positioned to begin termination procedures with respect to their Google employment. On top of that, I am presuming they have some measure of respect for me, which means they were likely convinced I actually thought they could do it.

As preparation, they could spend some time with the app in question and familiarize themselves with it. However, because many of the apps we used (Google Docs, App Engine, Talk Video, and so on) were tools they used every week, this time was short.

In each case, the teams came up with methodologies similar to ACC. They chose to jot down lists and create grids over writing long paragraphs of prose.

Sentences ... yes, paragraphs ... no. They wasted little time on formatting and explanations and chose instead to document capabilities. Indeed, capabilities, as described in this text, were the one commonality of all the plans. Capabilities were the one thing that all the teams gravitated toward as the most useful way to spend the little time they were given.

None of the teams finished the experiment in the 10 minutes allotted. However, in 10 minutes they were all able to get through both the attributes and components (or things that served a similar purpose) and begin documenting capabilities. At the end of an additional 20 minutes, most of the experiments had a large enough set of capabilities that it would have been a useful starting point for creating user stories or test cases.

This, at least to me, made the experiment a success. I gave them 10 minutes and hoped for an hour. They had 80 percent of the work complete in 30 minutes. And really, isn't 80 percent enough? We know full well that we are not going to test everything, so why document everything? We know full well that as we start testing, things (schedules, requirements, architecture, and so on) are going to change, so insisting on planning precision when nothing else obeys such a calling for completeness seems out of touch with reality.

80 percent complete in 30 minutes or less. Now that's what I call a 10-minute test plan!

Last Words on Risk

Google Test Analytics supports risk analysis based on values of the categories (very rarely, seldom, occasionally, often) we presented earlier. We specifically do not want to turn risk analysis into a complicated effort or it won't get done. We also aren't concerned about the actual numbers and math because a single number in isolation means little anyway. Simply knowing something is more risky than something else is often enough. Risk is about choice, choosing one test over another because it tests a more risky area of the application. It is enough to know that A is riskier than B without paying too much attention to the exact risk value of either. Simply knowing that one feature is riskier than another allows an individual test manager to distribute testers to features more optimally and on an organizational level, it allows someone like Patrick Copeland to decide how many testers each product team is allocated. Understanding risk provides benefit at every level of the organization.

Risk analysis is a field of its own and taken very seriously in many different industries. We use a lightweight version here, but remain interested in additional research that can improve the way we test. If you want to read more about risk analysis, we suggest searching for Risk Management Methodology on Wikipedia. It will get you to a good starting point for a more in-depth treatment of this important topic.

GTA helps us identify risk, and testing is what helps us mitigate it. The Google TE is a facilitator of this mitigation. A TE might decide to perform tests in house on some of the riskier areas and might request regression tests to be added by SWEs and SETs. Other tools at the TE's disposal include manual and exploratory testing and the use of dogfood users, beta users, and crowd sourcing.

The TE is responsible for understanding all the risk areas and creates mitigations using any and every tool he or she can get his hands on.

Here is a set of guidelines we've found helpful.

1. For every set of high-risk capabilities and attribute-component pairs that appear red in the GTA matrix, write a set of user stories, use cases, or test guidance that address them. Google TEs take personal responsibility for the highest risk areas, and even though they might coordinate with other TEs or use tools, the ultimate responsibility is their own.

2. Take a hard look at all the previous SET- and SWE-oriented testing that has occurred and assess its impact on the risk levels exposed in GTA. Was this testing well placed to manage the risk? Are there additional tests that need to be added? A TE might need to write these tests or negotiate with the attending SET or SWE to get them written. The important thing is not who does the coding, but that it gets done.

3. Analyze the bugs that have been reported against every high-risk attribute-capability pair and ensure that regression tests are written. Bugs have a tendency to recur as code is modified. Every bug in every high-risk component should have a regression test.

4. Think carefully about the high-risk areas and inquire about fallback and recovery mechanisms. Surface any concerns about user impact by coming up with worst-case scenarios and discussing them with other engineers. Try and determine how realistic the scenarios are. TEs who cry wolf too often won't be listened to again. It's important to reduce the shrill warnings unless they cover high-risk scenarios that are also very realistic and unmitigated by existing tests.

5. Involve as many concerned stakeholders as possible. Dogfood users are often internal and if left on their own will just use the system without providing a lot of input. Actively engage dogfood users. Specifically ask them to run certain experiments and scenarios. Ask them questions such as, "How does this work on your machine?" and "How would you use a feature like this one?" Dogfood users are numerous at Google, and TEs should be very active in pushing them for more than just casual use.

6. If none of the previous is working and a high-risk component continues to be under-tested and fails often, lobby hard for its removal. This is a chance to explain the concept of risk analysis to project owners and underscore the value a TE provides.

User Stories by Jason Arbon

User stories describe real-world or targeted user paths through the application under test. They describe user motivation and perspective and ignore product implementation and design details. User stories might refer to capabilities, but only tangentally, as they serve a user action. A user has a need and the story generally describes how he uses the software to satisfy that need. A story is deliberately general. There are no specific steps, no hard-coded inputs, just a need to do some actual work and a general way to go about performing that work with the application under test.

When writing user stories, we focus on a view of the product that reflects its user interface. Nothing technical should ever be described in a user story. This generality allows a tester to create his own variations for every new test pass in how to extract value from the software in a way that the variety of real users might also choose to accomplish that same task. That's the whole idea!

User stories focus on value to the user as opposed to a more specific test case that might specify exact inputs to be applied and results achieved. They should use fresh user accounts when necessary and at Google, we often create any number of test user accounts that represent the users we describe in our stories. Also, use "old" accounts full of state. Projects such as Google Documents see many of their most interesting bugs from older accounts with documents crafted in previous versions of the application loading into the newer version.

When possible, we vary the tester executing these scenarios to add as much variety and different sets of eyes as possible.

For less risky capabilities, we can be somewhat less insistent in our execution. We may decide that writing specific test cases for lower risk areas is too much investment for too little return. Instead, we might choose to perform exploratory testing or use crowd sourcing to handle these areas. The concept of "tours" as high-level guidance for exploratory testing[5] is often used as direction for crowd source testers. "Run the Fed Ex tour on this set of capabilities" will often get far better results from the crowd than simply tossing them an app and hoping for the best. At once, we have identified the features we want testing and instructed them how to go about testing it.

---

[5] Tours are described in detail in James A. Whittaker, *Exploratory Software Testing: Tips, Tricks, Tours, and Techniques to Guide Test Design* (Addison Wesley, 2009).

Crowd Sourcing *by James Whittaker*

Crowd sourcing is a new phenomenon on the testing scene. It is a solution for the fact that testers are few in number and have limited resources and that users are great in number and possess every variation of hardware and environment combinations we could ever wish to test our application on. Surely there is a subset of those users who would be willing to help us?

Enter the crowd: a set of power users who are test savvy and willing to help for reasonable compensation. All they need is access to some staging area where they can execute the application under test and a mechanism for them to provide feedback and bug reports. On projects like our open-source Chromium work, the crowd is ideal. For more sensitive and secretive projects that exist only on the corporate network, it's a bit more problematic and requires some level of trusted tester to be able to pull it off.

The key value the crowd brings in addition to its large array of hardware and configurations is the sheer volume of perspective. Instead of one tester trying to figure out the way 1,000 users will work, you have 1,000 users acting like testers. What better way to find the user scenarios that will cause your application to fail than to sign up the users to apply those scenarios and give you feedback? It's about variation and scale, and the crowd has both.

The crowd willing to do software testing these days is large and available 24/7. Let's say we'd like the top 1,000 websites to be tested in the latest version of Chrome. 1 tester = 1,000 iterations. 20 testers = 50 iterations. The math favors the crowd!

The main weakness of the crowd is the time it takes for them to learn an application and put it through its paces. Much of this time is washed out by the sheer size of the crowd but it can also be managed. For Chrome, we wrote tours and had the crowd follow the tours when doing their exploratory testing and running their user scenarios (see Appendix B, "Test Tours for Chrome," for a sample of Chrome Tours executed by crowd testers). Tours made the work more prescriptive and guided them to specific parts of the application. The trick was to write multiple sets of tour guidance and distribute them to different members of the crowd.

Crowd testing is an extension of the progression of Google's canary/dev/test/dogfood channels. It's a way for us to engage with early adopters and people who just like to find and report bugs. In the past, we've used an internal crowd of testers who like to early adopt our products, captive vendors who cycle through various product teams on demand, and commercial crowd sourcing companies such as uTest.com. We've also put programs in place to pay the best bug finders.[6]

---

[6] Chrome's cash-for-bugs program is discussed at http://blog.chromium.org/2010/01/encouraging-more-chromium-security.html.

The real power of the ACC is that it presents a set of capabilities that can be rank-ordered by risk and also parceled out in sections to various quality collaborators. The set of actual project TEs can be given different sets of capabilities to validate. Dogfood users, 20-percent contributors, contract testers, crowd testers, SWEs, SETs, and so on can all take a subset of capabilities and the TE can feel good about getting coverage of important areas with less overlap than simply throwing out the application to a free for all of usage.

The range of a TE, unlike that of an SET, does not stop when our software is released.

Life of a Test Case

Whether they come from user stories or from direct translation of capabilities, Google TEs create a large number of test cases that prescribe, in terms ranging from general to precise, inputs and data to test an application. Unlike code and automated test artifacts that are managed by common infrastructure, test case management is still a group-by-group thing, but a new tool is beginning to change all that.

Spreadsheets and documents have often been the tool of choice for storing test cases. Teams with rapid feature development and fast ship cycles aren't too concerned with keeping test cases around for long. As new features arrive, they often invalidate the scripts, requiring all the tests to be rewritten. In such cases, documents that can be shared and then trashed are as suitable as any other format. Documents are also a suitable mechanism to describe the context of a test session as opposed to specific test case actions. Such tests are less prescriptive and more general suggestions about which feature areas to explore.

Of course, some teams have rather elaborate spreadsheets for storing test procedures and data and some teams even document ACC tables in spreadsheets because they are more flexible than Google Test Analytics (GTA). But this takes discipline and some continuity in the TE team as one TE's procedure will be another TE's shackles. Large team turnover requires a more structured approach, a structure that can outlast any individual team member.

Spreadsheets are preferred over documents because they provide convenient columns for procedure, data, and pass or fail tags, and they are easy to customize. Google Sites and other types of online wikis are often used to display the test information to other stakeholders. They can be easily shared and edited by anyone on the team.

As Google grew, many teams had a growing set of prescriptive test cases and regression tests that needed better management. Indeed, the test cases documented grew so large, they became burdensome to search and to share. Another solution was needed and some enterprising testers built a system called Test Scribe that was loosely based on any number of commercial tools and other homegrown test case management systems our testers were familiar with from previous employers.

Test Scribe stored test cases in a rigid schema and had the capability to include or exclude test cases from a specific test pass. It was a basic implementation and enthusiasm over using it and maintaining it was waning; however, many teams had taken dependencies on it and after nursing it along for a few quarters, it was trashed and a new tool was written in 2010 by a Senior SET named Jordanna Chord. Google Test Case Manager (GTCM) was born.

The idea behind GTCM was to make it simple to write tests, provide a flexible tagging format that can be tailored to any project, make the tests easily searchable and reusable, and, most importantly, integrate GTCM with the rest of Google's infrastructure so that test results could become a first-class citizen. Figures 3.10 through 3.14 show various screenshots of GTCM. Figure 3.11 shows the page for creating test cases. Test cases can have arbitrary sections or labels. This allows GTCM to support everything from classic test and validation steps, to exploratory tours, cukes,[7] and user-story descriptions, and some test teams even store code or data snippets in the GTCM test case itself. GTCM had to support a wide variety of test teams and their varied test case representations.

FIGURE 3.10 The GTCM home page is focused on the search experience.

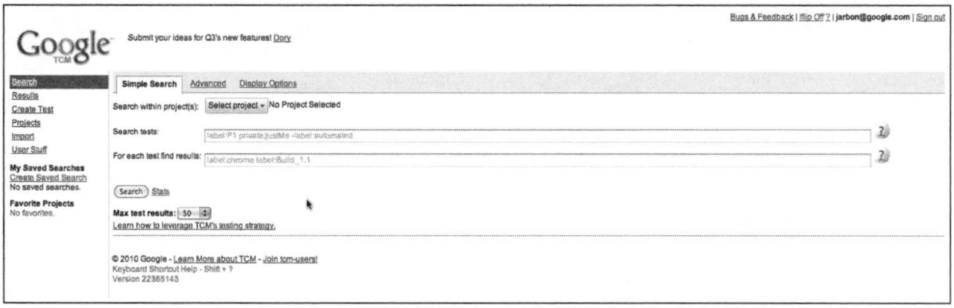

---

[7] Cukes are a behavioral test case definition. See http://cukes.info.

FIGURE 3.11   Creating a project in GTCM.

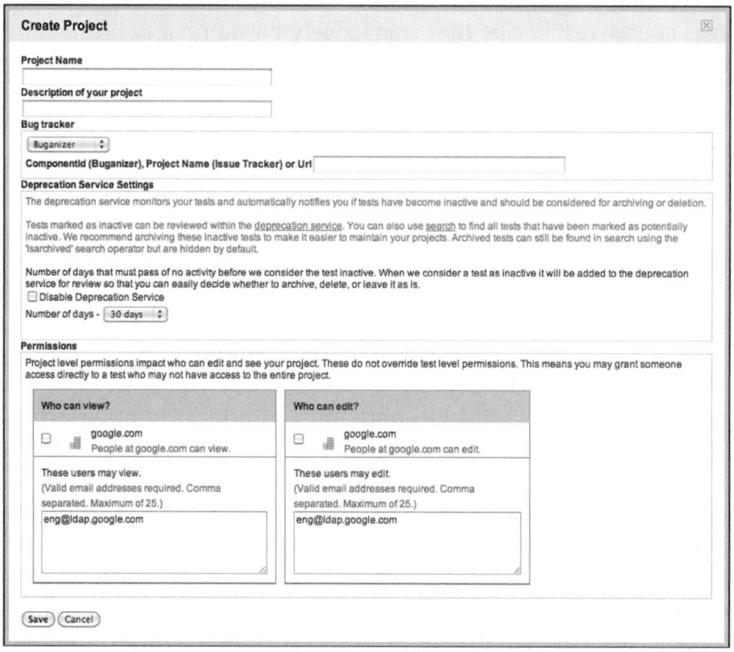

FIGURE 3.12   Creating a test in GTCM.

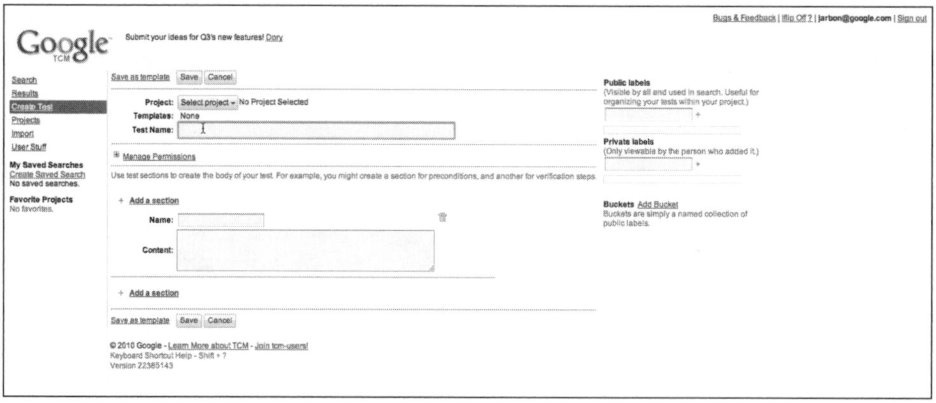

FIGURE 3.13 View of test cases when searching for Chrome in GTCM.

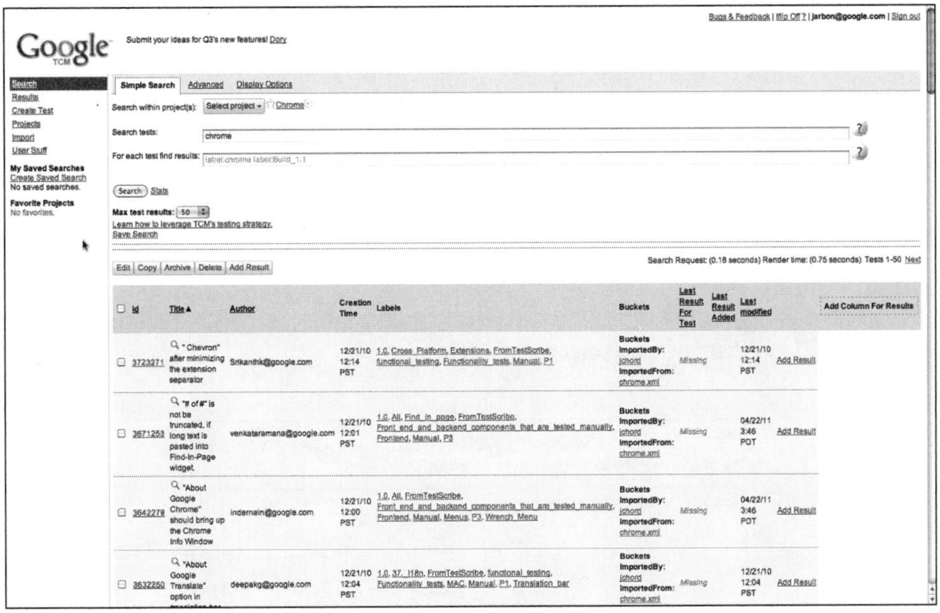

FIGURE 3.14 Simple test case for Chrome's About dialog.

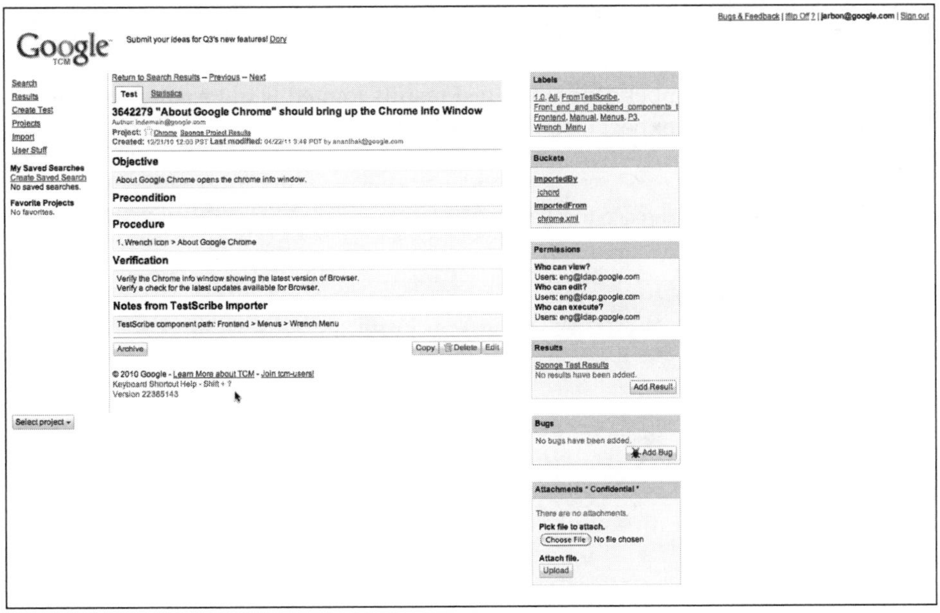

The metrics around GTCM are interesting to get a feel for what testers are doing with test cases in aggregate. The total number of tests and tests result trends are interesting, as shown in Figures 3.15 and 3.16. The total number of tests is reaching an asymptote. Basic analysis of why this is so is that Google is also deprecating older, more manual-regression focused projects, along with their tests. Also, GTCM largely holds manual tests, and many teams are replacing their manual testing with automation or external crowd-sourcing and exploratory testing, which is putting downward pressure on total test case counts in our internal TCM—even while coverage is going up. The numbers of tests logged are increasing as these numbers are dominated by several large and necessarily manually focused teams such as Android.

FIGURE 3.15   Test case counts over time in GTCM.

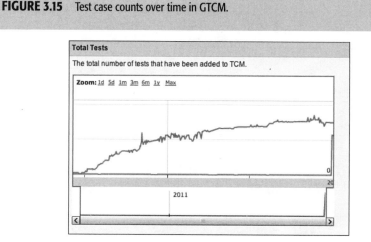

The total number of manual test results logged is increasing, as one would generally expect (see Figure 3.16).

FIGURE 3.16   Test result counts over time in GTCM.

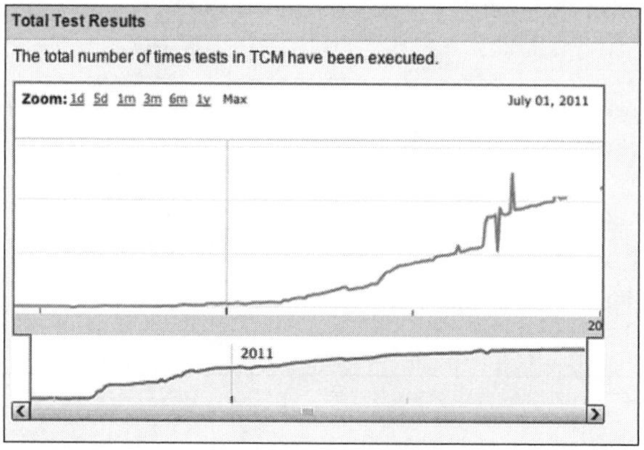

Taking a look of a plot of the number of bugs associated with GTCM, in Figure 3.17, is interesting to look at, but it also doesn't tell the whole story. Google is bottom-up, so some teams are particular about tracking which bugs came from which test cases; others are much looser with their data, as they don't find that information too valuable for the project. Also, some of these logged bugs are filed via automation; not all of these are from manual test execution.

FIGURE 3.17 Total number of bugs logged during GTCM test execution over time.

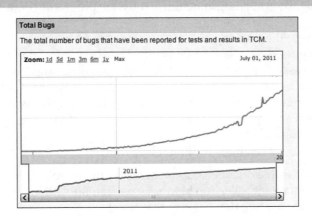

A primary requirement of GTCM from day one was to have a clean and simple API. TestScribe technically had an API, but was SOAP-like and the authentication scheme was so painful that few people used it. And, as security tightened internally, the original authentication mode used made it too awkward to use. To resolve all these issues, GTCM now has a restful JSON API.

The team intends to open GTCM up for general external usage soon. We also hope to open source this test case database for the world to collectively maintain. GTCM was also designed with external re-use in mind. It is built on a Google App Engine for scalability and also to allow other testers outside of Google to host their own instance if they prefer. GTCM's internals are also designed to abstract much of the logic and UI from Google App Engine, so it can be ported to other stacks if people prefer. Watch the Google Testing Blog for any updates on these efforts.

Life of a Bug

Bugs and bug reports are the one artifact every tester understands. Finding bugs, triaging bugs, fixing bugs, and regressing bugs are the heartbeat and workflow for software quality. This is the part of testing that is the most conventional at Google, but there are still a few interesting deviations from the norm. For this section, we ignore the bugs that are filed to track work items and use the term to identify actual broken code. As such, bugs often represent the hour-to-hour and day-to-day workflow for engineering teams.

A bug is born. Bugs are found and filed by everyone at Google. Product Managers file bugs when they catch issues in the early builds that differ form their specifications/thoughts. Developers file bugs when they realize they accidentally checked in an issue, or find an issue somewhere else in the codebase, or while dogfooding Google products. Bugs also come in from the field, from crowd-sourced testers, external vendor testing, and are filed by Community Managers monitoring the product-specific Google Groups. Many internal versions of apps also have quick one-click ways to file bugs, like Google maps. And, sometimes, software programs create bugs via an API.

Because the tracking and workflow around a bug is such a large part of what engineers do, a great deal of effort has been expended to automate this process. Google's first bug database was called BugsDB. It was nothing more than a few database tables to store information and a set of queries to retrieve bugs and compute statistics about them. BugDB was used until 2005 when a couple of enterprising engineers, Ted Mao[8] and Ravi Gampala, created "Buganizer."

The key motivations for Buganizer were:

- More flexible n-level component hierarchy to replace the simple Project > Component > Version hierarchy used in BugDB (and all the other commercial bug databases at that time)

- Better accountability for bug tracking and a new workflow around triage and maintenance

- Easier tracking of a group of bugs with the capability to create and manage hotlists

- Improved security with login authentication

- The capability to create summary charts and reports

- Full text search and change history

- Default settings for bugs

- Improved usability and a more intuitive UI

Some Buganizer Trivia and Metrics

The oldest bug filed and still in existence: May 18, 2001, 15:33. The title is Test Bug. The body of the documentation is "First Bug!." Interestingly, this bug is often used accidentally when developers are asked to provide a bug that their CL fixes.

The oldest active bug was filed in March of 1999. This bug suggests a performance investigation to reduce latency for serving for ads based on

---

[8] We interviewed Ted Mao in Chapter 2.

geographic region. The last activity was in 2009. The last edit said that this could be investigated, but that it would require architectural work, and the latency metrics are just fine.

Here are some bug charts of overall bug activity at Google. Some of these are filed automatically and some manually; these are aggregate information. Some of the automation dominates these bug trends, and we don't highlight any single teams here, but it is interesting nonetheless.

As you can see in Figure 3.18, there are many P2[9] bugs, far fewer P1, and even fewer P0 bugs. Correlation is not causation, but it can be a sign that the engineering methodology described in this book works. It might also be that no one bothers to file P1 issues, but that isn't what we see anecdotally. P3 and P4 bugs are often not filed as they are rarely looked at.

FIGURE 3.18   Number of bugs in Buganizer by priority.

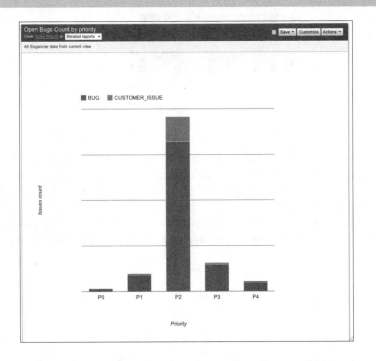

The average age of bugs is also generally what would be expected (see Figure 3.19). The anomaly seems to be with P0 bugs. In practice, though, P0 bugs are often more difficult to fix as they represent severe design or deployment issues, which are often complex to debug and resolve. The rest of the bugs on average take longer to fix, with increasing priority numbers, as they are less important.

---

[9] Like many bug-filing systems, we use PX, where X is an integer, to define how high a priority the bug is. P0 bugs are the worst, P1 less awful, and so on.

FIGURE 3.19   Average age of bugs in Buganizer.

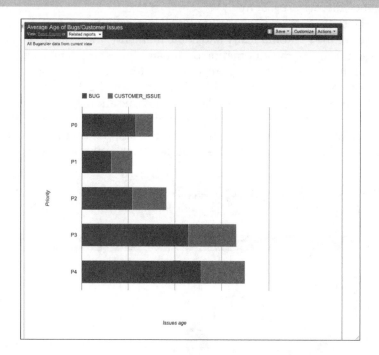

The chart for the number of bugs found over time in Figure 3.20 shows a slight uptick in bugs found each month. We don't systematically understand why this is increasing. The obvious explanation is that we have more code and more coders over time, but the bug rate increases at a rate lower than the increase in number of testers and developers. Perhaps either our code is getting better with quality controls or we aren't finding as many of them.

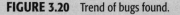

FIGURE 3.20 Trend of bugs found.

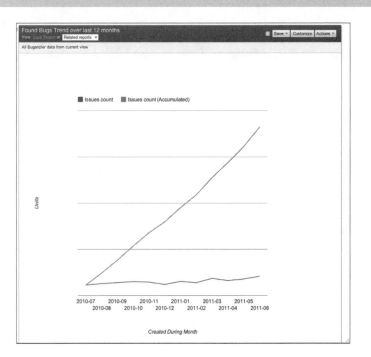

Our fix rate in Figure 3.21 shows that teams generally have a handle on the bug rate. Many teams simply stop adding features when the incoming bug rate exceeds the team's ability to fix them. This practice is highly recommended versus focusing on the feature or code-complete milestones. Focus on small bits of tested code, incrementally testing, and dogfooding help keep bug rates in check.

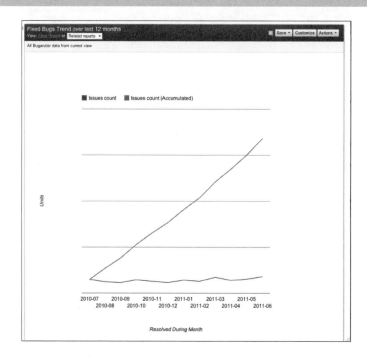

FIGURE 3.21   Bugs fixed over time. It's a good thing this looks similar to the trend of bugs found!

As Google's products have moved more into the open, such as Chrome and Chrome OS, it's no longer possible to maintain a single bug database. These projects also deal with externally visible bug databases such as Mozilla's Bugzilla for WebKit issues and issue tracker for chromium.org issues. Googlers are encouraged to file issues in any product they see, including those from competitive products. The primary goal is making the Web as a whole better.

Issue Tracker is the core repository for all Chrome and Chrome OS bugs. Its bug database is public. This means anyone can look at the bug activity, even the press. Security bugs are sometimes hidden between the time they are found and fixed to avoid tipping off hackers, but other than that, it is a public bug database. External users are free to file bugs, and they are a valuable source of bug information. Figures 3.22 and 3.23 show searching and finding a bug related to the Chrome logo in the About box.

FIGURE 3.22   Issue tracker search.

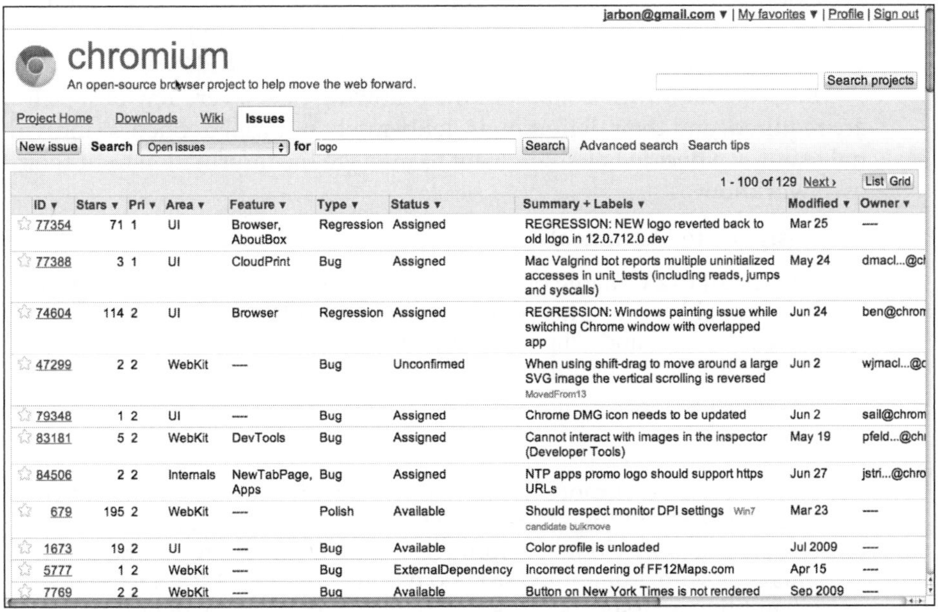

jarbon@gmail.com ▼ | My favorites ▼ | Profile | Sign out

chromium
An open-source browser project to help move the web forward.

[Search projects]

Project Home   Downloads   Wiki   **Issues**

[New issue]   Search   [Open issues ▼] for logo   [Search]   Advanced search   Search tips

1 - 100 of 129 Next ›   List Grid

ID ▼	Stars ▼	Pri ▼	Area ▼	Feature ▼	Type ▼	Status ▼	Summary + Labels ▼	Modified ▼	Owner ▼
☆ 77354	71	1	UI	Browser, AboutBox	Regression	Assigned	REGRESSION: NEW logo reverted back to old logo in 12.0.712.0 dev	Mar 25	---
☆ 77388	3	1	UI	CloudPrint	Bug	Assigned	Mac Valgrind bot reports multiple uninitialized accesses in unit_tests (including reads, jumps and syscalls)	May 24	dmacl...@ch
☆ 74604	114	2	UI	Browser	Regression	Assigned	REGRESSION: Windows painting issue while switching Chrome window with overlapped app	Jun 24	ben@chrom
☆ 47299	2	2	WebKit	---	Bug	Unconfirmed	When using shift-drag to move around a large SVG image the vertical scrolling is reversed MovedFrom13	Jun 2	wjmacl...@c
☆ 79348	1	2	UI	---	Bug	Assigned	Chrome DMG icon needs to be updated	Jun 2	sail@chrom
☆ 83181	5	2	WebKit	DevTools	Bug	Assigned	Cannot interact with images in the inspector (Developer Tools)	May 19	pfeld...@ch
☆ 84506	2	2	Internals	NewTabPage, Apps	Bug	Assigned	NTP apps promo logo should support https URLs	Jun 27	jstri...@chro
☆ 679	195	2	WebKit	---	Polish	Available	Should respect monitor DPI settings Win7 candidate bulkmove	Mar 23	---
☆ 1673	19	2	UI	---	Bug	Available	Color profile is unloaded	Jul 2009	---
☆ 5777	1	2	WebKit	---	Bug	ExternalDependency	Incorrect rendering of FF12Maps.com	Apr 15	---
☆ 7769	2	2	WebKit	---	Bug	Available	Button on New York Times is not rendered	Sep 2009	---

FIGURE 3.23   Open issue in Chromium Issue Tracker.

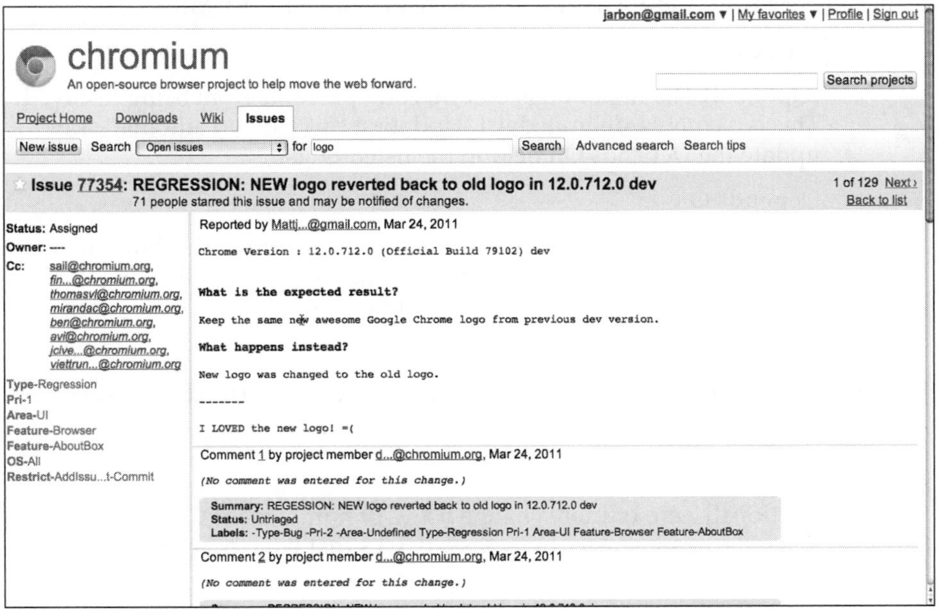

jarbon@gmail.com ▼ | My favorites ▼ | Profile | Sign out

chromium
An open-source browser project to help move the web forward.

[Search projects]

Project Home   Downloads   Wiki   **Issues**

[New issue]   Search   [Open issues ▼] for logo   [Search]   Advanced search   Search tips

☆ **Issue 77354: REGRESSION: NEW logo reverted back to old logo in 12.0.712.0 dev**   1 of 129 Next ›
71 people starred this issue and may be notified of changes.   Back to list

Status: Assigned
Owner: ---
Cc: sail@chromium.org,
fin...@chromium.org,
thomasvl@chromium.org,
mirandac@chromium.org,
ben@chromium.org,
avi@chromium.org,
jclive...@chromium.org,
viettrun...@chromium.org

Type-Regression
Pri-1
Area-UI
Feature-Browser
Feature-AboutBox
OS-All
Restrict-AddIssu...t-Commit

Reported by Mattj...@gmail.com, Mar 24, 2011

```
Chrome Version : 12.0.712.0 (Official Build 79102) dev
```

What is the expected result?

```
Keep the same new awesome Google Chrome logo from previous dev version.
```

What happens instead?

```
New logo was changed to the old logo.

-------

I LOVED the new logo! =(
```

Comment 1 by project member d...@chromium.org, Mar 24, 2011

(No comment was entered for this change.)

> **Summary:** REGESSION: NEW logo reverted back to old logo in 12.0.712.0 dev
> **Status:** Untriaged
> **Labels:** -Type-Bug -Pri-2 -Area-Undefined Type-Regression Pri-1 Area-UI Feature-Browser Feature-AboutBox

Comment 2 by project member d...@chromium.org, Mar 24, 2011

(No comment was entered for this change.)

However, the longest-lived and most widely used piece of testing infrastructure at Google is Buganizer and it deserves further discussion. For the most part, it is a typical bug database, but it also supports the core quality cycle of tracking problems in our software, from discovery to resolution, and in building regression test cases. Buganizer is also built on top of Google's latest core storage technology for scale and speed.

Bugs are filed with a subset of the following fields, very few of which are required, and their definition is deliberately not well defined so individual teams can decide how they want to manage the information to fit their own workflow.

- **Assigned to (Assignee)**

  [Optional] LDAP name of one person who should take the next step in handling this issue. This person is automatically emailed when the issue is created and whenever anyone changes the value of any field in the issue. Buganizer administrators specify a default assignee for every component.

- **CC**

  [Optional] Zero or more LDAP names of people to email when an issue is created or modified. Names are LDAP or mailing list names only, no @google, so only Google mailing lists or employees are valid entries. This is a comma-delimited list. Do not include the "Assign to" name when filing an issue, because this person is emailed by default.

- **Attachments**

  [Optional] Zero or more attachments to the bug. Any file type is accepted. There is no limit to the number of attachments for an issue, but the maximum total size of each attachment is 100MB.

- **Blocking**

  [Optional] The IDs of bugs that this bug prevents from being resolved. This is a comma-delimited list. Updating this list will automatically update the Depends On field in the listed bugs.

- **Depends On**

  [Optional] The IDs of bugs that must be fixed before this bug can be fixed. Updating this list will automatically update the Blocking field of all listed bugs. This is a comma-delimited list.

- **Changed**

  [Read-only] The date and time when any value in the issue was last changed.

- **Changelists**

  [Optional] Zero or more change list (CL) numbers for CLs dealing with this issue in some way. Only specify CLs that have been submitted; do not specify pending CLs.

- **Component**

  [Required] The thing that has the bug or feature request if it is known. When filing an issue, this should be a complete path to the component. An infinitely long path is now supported. When filing an issue, you do not need to assign the issue to a leaf component (that is, one without children).

  Additional components can be created only by project and engineering managers.

- **Created**

  [Read-only] The date when the bug was created.

- **Found In**

  [Optional] Use for versioning by entering the number of the software version where you found the issue, such as 1.1.

- **Last modified**

  [Read-only] The date that any field in the issue was last modified.

- **Notes**

  [Optional] Detailed description of the problem and running comments as the issue is handled over time. When filing the issue, describe the steps required to reproduce a bug or how to get to a screen involving a feature request. The more information you put here, the less likely future issue handlers will need to contact you. You cannot edit previous entries in the Notes field, not even if you added them; you can add only new values to the Notes field.

- **Priority**

  [Required] The importance of a bug, where P0 is the highest priority. This indicates how soon it should be fixed and how many resources should be allocated to fix it. For example, misspelling "Google" in the search page logo would be low severity (the page function would not be affected), but high priority (it would be a Very Bad Thing). Setting both fields lets the bug fix team allocate its time more wisely. See also the Severity description.

- **Reported by (Reporter)**

  [Read-only] The Google login of the person who originally reported the bug. The default value is assigned to the person creating the bug, but this can be modified to give credit where credit is due.

- **Resolution**

  [Optional, entered by Buganizer] The final action chosen by the verifier. Values include Not feasible, Works as intended, Not repeatable, Obsolete, Duplicate, and Fixed.

- **Severity**

  [Required] How much the bug affects the use of the product, where S0 is the most severe. Setting both priority and severity can help prioritize the importance of this bug to bug fixers. For example, misspelling "Google" in the search page logo would be low severity (the page function would not be affected), but high priority (it would be a Very Bad Thing). Setting both fields lets the bug fix team allocate its time more wisely. Severity values have the following text equivalents:
  - s0 = System unusable
  - s1 = High
  - s2 = Medium
  - s3 = Low
  - s4 = No effect on system

- **Status**

  [Required] The current state of the bug. See Life of an issue (see Figure 3.24) for details on how these values are set in the issue. Available statuses include the following:
  - **New:** The issue has just been created and not assigned yet.
  - **Assigned:** An assignee has been specified.
  - **Accepted:** The assignee has accepted the issue.
  - **Fix later:** The assignee has decided that the issue will be fixed in the future.
  - **Will not fix:** The assignee has decided that the issue will not be fixed for some reason.
  - **Fixed:** The issue has been fixed, but the fix has not been verified.
  - **Verifier assigned:** A verifier has been assigned to the issue.
  - **Verified:** The fix has been verified by the verifier.

- **Summary**

  [Required] A descriptive summary of this issue. Be sure to make this as descriptive as possible; when scrolling through a list of issues in a search result, this is what helps the user decide whether or not to examine the issue further.

- **Targeted To**

  [Optional] Use for versioning by entering the number of the software version in which the issue should be fixed, such as 1.2.

- **Type**

  [Required] What type of issue:
  - — **Bug:** Something that causes the program not to work as expected
  - — **Feature request:** Something you would like to see added to the program
  - — **Customer issue:** A training issue or general discussion
  - — **Internal cleanup:** Something requiring maintenance
  - — **Process**: Something tracked automatically via the API

- **Verified In**

  [Optional] Use for versioning by entering the number of the software version where the issue fix was verified, such as 1.2.

- **Verifier**

  [Required before issue can be resolved] Each issue is assigned one person who has the right to mark the issue as resolved. This person need not be assigned until the issue is ready to be resolved, but the verifier is the only one who can change the status to "Verified" (the issue is closed). The verifier can be the same person as the assignee.
  Figure 3.24 summarizes the life of an issue.

FIGURE 3.24 The basic workflow for bugs in a Buganizer world.

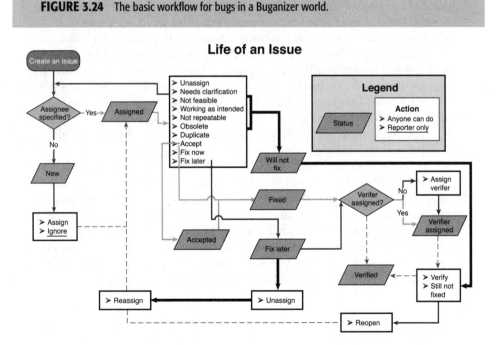

A few key differences between bugs at Google and elsewhere:

- For the most part, the bug database is completely open. Any Googler can see any bug in any project.

- Everyone files bugs, including engineering directors and (Senior Vice Presidents (SVPs). Googlers file bugs against products they use even if they are not part of that product team. Groups of testers often "dog pile" on a product just to be helpful.

- There are no formal top-down bug triage processes. How bugs are triaged[10] varies widely from team to team. Sometimes it's an individual task or a TE and SWE do it together informally at one or the other's desk. Sometimes triage is part of a weekly or daily standup meeting. The team figures out who should be there and what works best. There are no formal methods or dashboards for triaging or big brothers checking in on a team. Google leaves this up to the individual teams to decide.

Google projects are often in one of two states: new and rapid development swamped with a continual stream of issues or established infrastructure released incrementally and with so much upfront unit testing and fault tolerance that bugs aren't very common and kept to a small and manageable number.

The dream of a unified dashboard has haunted Googlers, much like it has at many other companies. Every year or so, a new effort tried to take root to build a centralized bug or project dashboard for all projects at Google. It makes sense, even if confined only to Buganizer data. But, as each group has different ideas of what metrics are important for shipping and for day-to-day health of the projects, these projects have consistently not gotten far off the ground. This idea may be useful at more uniform companies, but at Google, well-intentioned folks often keep ending up frustrated due to the variety of projects and engineering at Google.

A Google-scale approach to filing bugs was started by the Google Feedback team[11] (http://www.google.com/tools/feedback/intl/en/index.html). Google Feedback enables end users to file bugs against select Google services. The general idea is that external users don't have full context on what bugs have already been filed, or even already fixed, and we want to make it quick and easy to get feedback from users. So, Google testers and software engineers have made it point-and-click simple for users to file a bug. The engineers on this team have gone to great lengths to ensure that users can intuitively omit parts of the page that might contain private data when filing bugs back to Google (see Figure 3.25).

---

[10] Triage is the process of reviewing incoming bugs and deciding what order and who should fix them. It is much like triage in a hospital emergency room.

[11] An interview with Brad Green, engineering manager for Google Feedback appears in Chapter 4.

FIGURE 3.25 Google Feedback shown with privacy filtering.

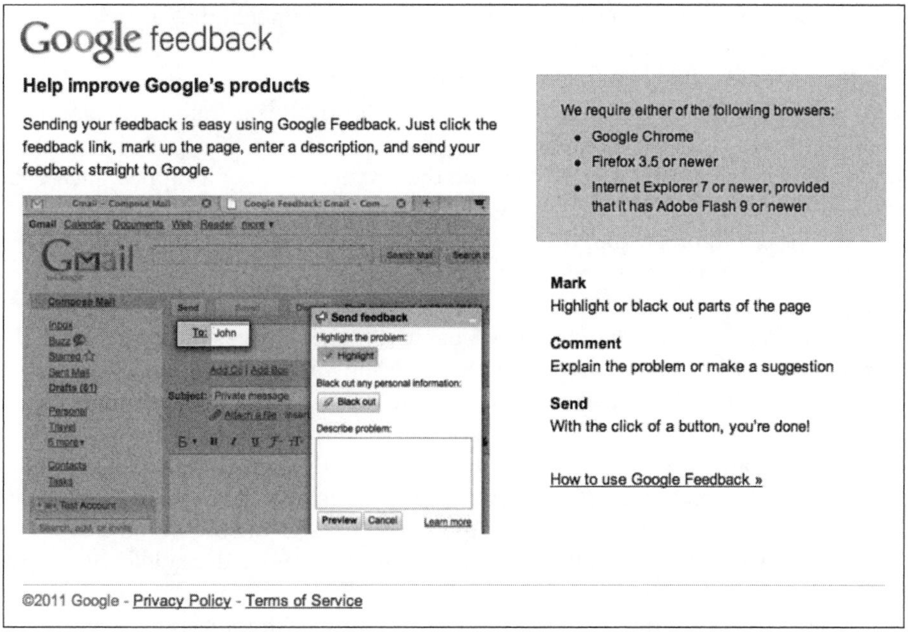

The Google Feedback team has done some very cool work to avoid blindly dropping these bugs from the wild into our bug databases, as duplicate issues can overwhelm the bug triage process. They use clustering algorithms automatically to de-dupe and identify the top issues coming in. Google Feedback has a helpful dashboard showing this processed data of user-reported issues to the product team for analysis. It is not unusual for many tens of thousands of pieces of feedback to pour in the week after a major application launch—and have them boil down to just 10 or so major and common issues. This saves a lot of engineering time and makes it possible for Google to actually listen to end users without having to process each individual piece of feedback that would be prohibitive. The team is beta testing this with a small set of Google properties, but aims to provide this for all Google properties in the future.

It's a Bug's Life *by James Whittaker*

Bugs are like over-parented kids. They get a lot of attention. They might be born in the relative quiet of a developer's IDE, but the moment they are exposed to the rest of the world, they live their lives amidst a great deal of fanfare.

For tester-identified bugs, the lifecycle looks something like this: A tester finds a bug and takes a moment or two to savor it. Seriously, this is important. Not only are we allowed to take a moment to enjoy the fruits of our labor, it's important to understand subtle nuances of the bug and the circumstances of its appearance. Is it on a path that users will tread? How likely are such paths? Are there more paths that will lead to it other than the one on which it appeared? Are there side effects that might affect data or some other application (increasing its severity)? Does it have privacy, security, performance, or accessibility ramifications? A parent who hears a small cough from his child and imagines the worst possible debilitating illness would feel right at home thinking through software bugs!

Like a parent calling a friend or relative to discuss the cough, a tester should seek company for his discovery as well. Invite a colleague to watch you demo it. Get her input and talk through your thinking about the bug, its severity, its priority, and its side effects. Clarity is often found through such a discussion. A parent can often save a trip to the emergency room, and a tester can often find that what he thought was a P0 is actually pretty minor after all and the whole crying wolf thing can be avoided.

Now it's time for the bug report. Like a parent reaching for a thermometer, a tester seeks out his tools. A parent wants to make the child's illness easy to diagnose. A mother wants to convince the doctor just how seriously ill her child has become. A tester also wants to impact severity, but even more importantly, a tester wants to make the bug easy to fix. Screen captures, keystroke recorders, stack traces, and DOM dumps are the ways a bug can be documented. The more information a developer has, the less daunting a fix is and the higher the chances of getting the bug fixed.

The bug report triggers an email to all concerned stakeholders, and a CL is prepared for the fix. The CL is queued for review and once approved, it is queued for a build target. This is the medicine for the bug and as parents monitor their child's reaction to antibiotics, a tester is reminded by email that a new test build is ready. He installs the build and reruns the revealing test case.

This test now becomes part of the regression suite for the application. Every attempt is made to automate it lest the bug regress or, at the least, a manual test case is authored and checked into the Test Case Management system. In this way, the system builds immunity to future infection just as the child builds immunity to the bacteria that made her sick in the first place.

Recruiting TEs

Google takes hiring engineers seriously. In general, our engineers have computer science or related degrees from accredited universities. However, few schools systematically teach software testing. This makes hiring good testers a challenge for any company, because the right mix of coding and testing skills is truly rare.

The TE role is particularly difficult to hire because the best ones aren't raw algorithm, theorem-proving, function-implementing people. Google TEs break the mold of the SWE/SET that we have traditionally built our recruiting and interviewing process around. To be honest, we haven't always gotten it right. Indeed, we owe apologies to all the testers caught up in our early attempts to perfect our TE interview process. TEs are rare individuals. They are technical, care about the user, and understand the product at a system and end-to-end perspective. They are relentless, great negotiators, and most importantly, they are creative and able to deal with ambiguity. It's a small wonder Google, or any company for that matter, struggles to hire them.

It is often forgotten, but testing is also largely about validation. Does the application do what it is supposed to do? Much of the testing work is planning the execution and performing the validation. Crashes happen, but aren't always the goal. Bending the software until it breaks might be interesting, but even more interesting is bending it a little bit over and over repeatedly, simulating actual usage, and making sure it *doesn't* break under those conditions. We look for this positive viewpoint of testing when we interview.

Over the years, we tried a number of interview styles for TEs:

- **Interview them as an SET**. If a candidate is smart and creative but doesn't meet the coding bar, then we'd consider him for a TE role. This caused lots of problems, including a virtual hierarchy within the test team, and worse, it filtered out a lot of folks focused on user-centric things, such as usability and end-to-end testing, that we were wrong to exclude.

- **Deemphasize the coding requirement:** If we focus only on user-centric and functional testing, then we vastly increase the size of the candidate pool. A candidate who can't write code to solve a Sudoku puzzle or optimize a quick sort algorithm doesn't mean he doesn't have the ability to be a tester. This might be a route to get more TEs into the company, but it is not a route that sets them up for success once they are inside. The Google coding culture and computer science-centric skills among its engineering population are at odds with the career development of a strictly high-level tester.

- **Use a hybrid middle ground:** Today we interview for general computer science and technical skills combined with a strong requirement for testing aptitude. Knowledge of coding is necessary but tends toward the coding skills necessary for the TE work described previously: the modification of code over its creation and the ability to script end-to-end user scenarios. This, combined with excelling in TE-specific attributes such as communication, system-level understanding, and user empathy usually get you in the door and set the stage for internal advancement and promotion.

TEs are difficult to hire because they have to be good at many things, any one of which has the chance to derail the interview process. They are the jack-of-all-trades, and the stronger ones are often looked to as the final go or no-go decider in releasing products and new versions into the wild. If we didn't take the quality of these individuals seriously, we would be in some serious trouble.

As a result of these filters, TEs can adapt to almost any product and role needed. From building tools, engaging customers, coordinating with other teams and dependencies, and so on, TEs often take a leadership role with respect to SETs as they have a broader perspective of what needs to get done and they can understand the design issues and risks.

Google has built up its TE ranks as our products have become more complex and with more UI than google.com. As our products have impacted many more users and become a more critical piece of users' lives, the TE role has emerged as crucial to the Google culture.

The Difference Between SETs and TEs by Jason Arbon

SETs' roles and TEs' roles are related but different in fundamental ways. I've been both and managed both. Look at the lists that follow and find which description most fits you—maybe you should switch roles.

You might be an SET if

- You can take a specification, a clean whiteboard, and code up a solid and efficient solution.

- When you code, you guiltily think of all the unit tests you should be writing. Then, you end up thinking of all the ways to generate the test code and validation instead of hand crafting each unit test.

- You think an end user is someone making an API call.

- You get cranky if you look at a poorly written API documentation, but sometimes forget why the API is interesting in the first place.

- You find yourself geeking out with people about optimizations in code or about looking for race conditions.

- You prefer to communicate with other human beings via IRC or comments in check-ins.

- You prefer a command line to a GUI and rarely touch the mouse.

- You dream of machines executing your code across thousands of machines, beating up algorithms, and testing algorithms—showing their correctness through sheer numbers of CPU cycles and network packets.

- You have never noticed or customized your desktop background.

- Seeing compiler warnings makes you anxious.

- When asked to test a product, you open up the source code and start thinking about what needs to be mocked out.

- Your idea of leadership is to build out a great low-level unit test framework that everyone leverages or is highly exercised millions of times a day by a test server.

- When asked if the product is ready to ship, you might just say, "All tests are passing."

You might be a TE if

- You can take existing code, look for errors, and immediately understand the likely failure modes of that software, but don't much care about coding it from scratch or making the change.

- You prefer reading Slashdot or News.com to reading other people's code all day.

- You read a spec for a product that is half-baked, you take it upon yourself to fill in all the gaps, and just merge this into the document.

- You dream of working on a product that makes a huge impact on people's lives, and people recognize the product you work on.

- You find yourself appalled by some websites' UI and wonder how they could ever have users.

- You get excited about visualizing data.

- You find yourself wanting to talk to humans in meat space.

- You don't understand why you have to type "i" to start typing in a certain text editor.

- Your idea of leadership is nurturing other engineers' ideas and challenging their ideas with an order of magnitude more scale.

- When asked if the product is ready to ship, you might say, "I think it's ready."

It is important for testers to figure out who they are. Often, TEs are simply seen as SETs who don't code as much or as well. The reality is that they see things that people with their head in the code all day will never see. SETs should also realize they aren't TEs and let go of any guilt or pressure to find UI issues or think about the system overall or competitive products; focus instead on high quality, testable, and reusable modules and amazing automation.

It takes a diverse family of testers to raise an amazing product.

Interviewing TEs

When we find the right mix of skills, we bring a candidate in for an interview. We are often asked how we interview TEs; indeed, it ranks as the most common question we receive on our blog and when we speak at public events. We're not willing to give up the entire set of questions we ask, but here is a sampling (which will be deprecated now that they are public!) to give you insight into our thinking.

To begin, we probe for test aptitude. Our intent is to find out whether the candidate is more than just bright and creative, and whether he has a natural knack for testing. We are looking for innate curiosity about how things are built and what combinations of variables and configurations are possible and interesting to test. We are looking for a strong sense of how things *should* work and the ability to articulate it. We are also looking for a strong personality.

The idea here is to give a testing problem that requires a variety of input and environmental conditions and then to ask the candidate to enumerate the most interesting ones. On a simple level, we might ask a candidate to test a web page (see Figure 3.26) with single text input box and a button labeled count which, when pressed, computes the number of As in the text string. The question: Come up with a list of input strings you would want to test.

FIGURE 3.26   Sample UI for test question.

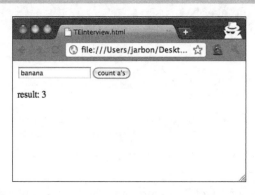

Some candidates just dive right in and start listing test cases. This is often a dangerous signal because they haven't thought about the problem enough. The tendency to focus on quantity over quality is something we have learned to interpret as a negative (mostly through experience) because it is an inefficient way to work. You can learn a lot about a candidate by just looking at how they approach a problem before they even get to their solution.

Better is the candidate who asks clarifying questions: Capital or lowercase? Only English? Is the text cleared after the answer is computed? What about repeated button presses? And so on.

When the problem is clarified, candidates then start listing test cases. It is important to see whether they have some method to their madness. Are they just looking to break the software or also looking to validate that it works? Do they know when they are doing the former or the latter? Do they start with the obvious simple stuff first so they can find big bugs as quickly as possible? Can they figure out how to clearly represent their test plan/data? Random ordering of strings on a white board doesn't indicate clarity of thought, and their test plans are likely to be ragged if they bother to plan at all. A typical list might look something like this:

- "banana": 3 (An actual word.)

- "A" and "a": 1 (A simple legal case with a positive result.)

- "": 0 (A simple legal case with a zero result.)

- null: 0 (Simple error case.)

- "AA" and "aa": 2 (A case where the count is > 1 and all As.)

- "b": 0 (A simple, nonblank legal case with a negative result.)

- "aba": 2 (Target character at the beginning and end to look for an off-by-one loops bug.)

- "bab": 1 (Target character in the middle of the string.)

- space/tabs/etc.: N (Whitespace characters mixed with N As.)

- long string without As: N, where N > 0

- long string with As: N, where N is equal to the number of As

- X\nX in the string: N, where N is equal to the number of As (Format characters.)

- {java/C/HTML/JavaScript}: N, where N is equal to the number of As (Executable characters, or errors or accidental interpretation of code.)

Missing several of the previous tests is a bad indicator.

Better candidates discuss more advanced testing issues and rise above the specifics of input selection. They might

- Question the look and feel, color palette, and contrast. Is it consistent with related applications? Is it accessible for the visually impaired, and so on?

- Worry that the text box is too small/suggest that it be long enough to accommodate the longer strings that can be entered.

- Wonder about multiple instances of this application on the same server. Is there a chance for crosstalk between users?

- Ask the question, "Is the data recorded?" It might contain addresses or other personally identifiable information.

- Suggest automation with some real-world data, such as drawing from a dictionary of words or text selections from books.

- Ask the questions, "Is it fast enough? Will it be fast enough under load?"

- Ask the questions, "Is it discoverable? How do users find this page?"

- Enter HTML and JavaScript. Does it break the page rendering?

- Ask whether it should count capital or lowercase As, or both.

- Try copying and pasting strings.

Some concepts are even more advanced and indicate an experienced and valuable testing mind willing to look past only the problem presented. They might

- Realize that if the count is passed to the server via a URL-encoded HTTP GET request, the string can be clipped as it bounces across the Net. Therefore, there is no guarantee how long the supported URL can be.

- Suggest the application be parameterized. Why count only As?

- Consider counting other As in other languages (such as angstrom or umlaut).

- Consider whether this application can be internationalized.

- Think about writing scripts or manually sampling string lengths, say by powers of 2, to find the limits and ensure that string lengths in between would work.

- Consider the implementation and code behind this. There might be a counter to walk the string and another to keep track of how many As have been encountered (accumulator). So, it's interesting to vary both the total number of As and the length of a string of As around interesting boundary values.

- Ask the questions, "Can the HTTP POST method and parameters be hacked? Perhaps there is security vulnerability?"

- Generate test input and validation with script to create interesting permutations and combinations of string properties such as length, number of As, and so on.

Digging into the issue of what length strings the candidate uses as test cases often reveals a lot about how well they will do on the job. If candidates cannot be more technically specific than "long strings," which is an all too frequent answer, then that is a bad sign. More technical candidates will ask what the specification for the string is and then provide boundary tests around these limits. For example, if the limit is 1,000 characters, they will try 999, 1,000, and 1,001. The best candidates will also try 2^{32}, and many interesting values in between, such as powers of two and ten. It is important that candidates show an understanding of which values are important versus just random numbers—they need to have some understanding of the underlying algorithms, language, runtime, and hardware because this is where the faults most often live. They will also try lengths based on possible implementation details, and think of counters and pointers and off-by-one possibilities. The very best ones will realize the system might be stateful and that tests must take into account previous values entered. Thus, trying the same string multiple times or a zero length after a 1,000-length string become important cases.

Another key characteristic often looked for in interviewing is the ability for the TE to deal with ambiguity and push back on goofy ideas. We often change specifications or specify a behavior that doesn't make sense when candidates ask clarifying questions. How they deal with this ambiguity can reveal a lot about how well they will do on the job. At Google, specifications are often moving targets and open to interpretation and modification given the pace of our release cycles. Suggesting that the maximum length of five characters is odd and would likely frustrate users is a great indicator that they are thinking of the user. Candidates who accept this blindly and move on might do the same on the job and end up validating goofy behavior. Candidates who push back or question specifications will often do wonders on the job, as long as they can do it diplomatically.

The final part of our TE interviews is probing for what we call "Googliness." We want curious, passionate engineers who don't just do what they are told but investigate options and do things outside the direction job description. Job responsibilities must get done, but life and work should be about maximum impact on the world around you. We want people who are connected to the world around them and the larger computer science community. People who file bugs on open-source projects are one example or those who generalize their work for reuse are another. We want to hire people who are enjoyable to work with, get along well with others, and who add to our culture here. We want engineers who want to continue to learn and grow. We also want people who we can learn from as well—people with new ideas and experiences that will add to our collective talent pool. With a corporate motto of "do no evil," we want people who will call out evil if they see it!

Interviewing at big technology companies is intimidating. We know because it was intimidating to us! Many don't make it through the first time around and require a practice round to get it right. We're not trying to be harsh; we are trying to ensure that we find people who can contribute and when they become Google TEs, can grow in their role. It has to be good for the company and the candidate. Google, like most companies intent on keeping a small-company feel despite the big company numbers, tends to err on the side of caution. We want Google to be a place we want to continue to work for many years to come. Hiring the right people is the best way to ensure that!

Test Leadership at Google

We sometimes joke that we are only good at managing highly skilled, highly motivated, and autonomous engineers. The truth about managing TEs at Google is that it is difficult. The problems are focused on inspiring versus commanding and ensuring there is a coherence and focus to the team while encouraging experimentation and trusting folks to make the right decisions as much as possible on their own. This is actually tough work.

Leading and managing testers at Google is likely the thing most different from other testing shops. There are several forces at work at Google driving these differences, namely: far fewer testers, hiring competent folks, and a healthy respect for diversity and autonomy. Test management at Google is much more about inspiring than actively managing. It is more about strategy than day-to-day or week-to-week execution. That said, this leaves engineering management in an open-ended and often more complex position than that typical of the places we've worked before. The key aspects of test management and leadership at Google are leadership and vision, negotiation, external communication, technical competence, strategic initiatives, recruiting and interviewing, and driving the review performance of the team.

Generally, there is tension in Google when there is too much management and structure. Google test directors, managers, and leaders all try to walk this tightrope of trusting the engineers, but ensuring they don't walk off a cliff or waste their time. Google invests in large-scale and strategic solutions and approaches to problems. Managers help avoid developing duplicate of test frameworks, over invest in small tests, and often encourage the pooling of engineers for larger test execution and infrastructure efforts. Without this oversight, test engineering projects often die on the vine if left to individual engineers, or only organic 20 percent time.

Pirate Leadership by Jason Arbon

A pirate's ship is a useful analogy for managing test engineering teams at Google. Specifically, the test organization is a world where engineers are by nature questioning, wanting conclusive data, and constantly measuring their lead's and manager's directives. One of the key aspects we interview for is being a self-starter and self-directed—so how do you manage these folks?

The answer is much like how I imagine the captain of a pirate ship maintains order. The truth is the captain cannot "manage" the ship through brute force or fear as he is outnumbered, and everyone is armed to the teeth with technical talent and other offers for work. He also cannot manage through gold alone, as these pirates often have more than they need for sustenance. What truly drives these pirates is the pirate way of life and the excitement of seeing what they can capture next. Mutiny is always a real possibility, too, as Google's organizations are dynamic. Engineers are even encouraged to move between teams frequently. If the ship isn't finding lots of treasure, or if it's not that fun of a place to work, engineering "pirates" get to step off the ship at the next port and not return when it's time to sail.

Being an engineering leader means being a pirate engineer yourself and knowing just a bit more about what is on the horizon, which ships are sailing nearby, and what treasure they might hold. Leading through technical vision, promises of exciting technical adventures, and interesting ports of call. You always sleep with one eye open as an engineering manager at Google!

There are several types of leaders and managers at Google. The roles are the tech lead, the tech lead manager, the engineering manager, and the director.

- **Tech lead:** Tech leads in test emerge on the larger teams where there is a cluster of SETs or TEs on a larger project where they share common technical problems, infrastructure, and so on. They usually do not manage people. This also happens on teams building product-independent infrastructure. If you think of who this person is, he is the go-to person for technical and or testing problems on the team. This role is often informal and organically decided on based on team dynamics. These folks are focused on a single project at a time.

- **Tech lead manager (TLM):** This interesting creature appears when the go-to person is officially the manager for a set of commonly focused engineers and is also the go-to person for technical issues. These people are often highly respected and effective. They are often focused on only one primary project at a time.

- **Test engineering manager:** Engineering managers oversee the engineering work across multiple teams and almost always "come up through the ranks." These positions are roughly equivalent to the industry standard test manager role, but with the breadth of context typical of a director at many other companies due to lower density of test resources on projects. These folks typically manage from as few as 12 to up to 35 folks depending on the complexity of the work. They focus on cross-team sharing of tools and processes, load balancing people across teams based on risk assessments, and steering the recruiting and interview and hiring pipelines.

- **Test director:** There are only a few test directors. Test directors more or less drive several test-engineering managers across sever products. They work on overall scoping the testing work and driving strategic and sometimes transformative technical infrastructure or testing methodologies. Their focus is on how quality and testing affect the business (rough cost analysis, benefit analysis, and so on), and often has an external bent—sharing externally with the industry. These folks often have between 40 and 70 reports. They are closely aligned with high-level groups or "focus areas," such as Client, Apps, Ads, and so on.

- **Senior test director:** There is only one (Pat Copeland) whose accountability is to the senior leadership at the company for a unified approach to job descriptions, hiring, external communication, and overall testing strategy for Google. His job is often one of sharing best practices and creating and driving new initiatives such as global build or test infrastructure, static analysis, and testing activities that span the breadth of Google's products, user issues, and codebase.

External recruiting and interviewing is something most Google testers are involved with, especially the directors and senior director. There are a few strange quirks about recruiting for Google. Most engineers already know of the company, the basic technology, and that it's a great place to work. Often, candidates are a little leery of the interview process and concerned about getting excited about the possibility and then not making it through the loops. Great candidates are often well taken care of in their current position, but they worry about increased competition at Google. Often the best way to dispel these concerns is to point out who they are talking to. Google engineers are competent and motivated, but a large part of what makes their work seem interesting and sometimes herculean, is simply leveraging the community of like-minded engineers and the raw compute infrastructure at Google to do amazing things.

There is also a lot of internal recruiting going on. Engineers are encouraged to change projects so there is always movement from team to team. Internal recruiting is focused on getting the word out about the projects in your domain and your team's harmony. Most internal recruiting is done engineer-to-engineer, as they talk about their interesting projects, technical issues, and overall happiness about their family of testers, developers, and PMs. There are occasional, semi-formal gatherings where teams looking for engineers present what they are working on, but for the most part, internal recruiting is organic by design—let people flow to where they are interested and think they can add the most value.

- **Technical:** Test managers and especially test leads are expected to be technical. They may write a prototype, perform code reviews, and always strive to know the product and customers better than anyone else on the team.

- **Negotiation:** We can't test everything all the time. Requests for resources and attention from engineering directors are constant. They need to know how to politely say no with great reasoning.

- **External communication.** Test management and leadership often also strike deals for onsite vendor work or external validation where it makes senses. Test management also reaches out to peers and organizes events, such as GTAC, to create forums for discussing and sharing test engineering issues with the larger community.

- **Strategic initiatives:** Test leads and managers also often ask what can we do at Google that can't be done anywhere else? How can we broaden and share our test infrastructure to help make the Web better, not just our product or Google? What things could happen if we pooled our resources and took longer-term bets? Supporting these initiatives with vision, funding, and protection from the onslaught of everyone wanting a tester is truly a full-time job.

- **Reviews/performance:** At Google, reviews are a mix of peer input and cross-team leveling driven by the leads and managers. Googlers are reviewed quarterly. The emphasis is on what have you done lately? What impact have you made on quality and efficiency and for users? The review system doesn't let people coast based on their previous work. The mechanics of this aren't fully disclosed, and they often undergo experimentation and change, so documenting details wouldn't be all that useful anyway. Basically, Googlers submit a short description of what they worked on and how well they think they did. Their peers and manager then get to comment, and neutral committees meet to arbitrate and level the results across teams. It is important to note that Googlers are expected to set goals higher than they think possible. If Googlers meet all their objectives, they aren't aiming high enough.

Part of review and performance management at Google is also identifying or encouraging folks to cross disciplines if they'd be better served. Moves in all directions happen all the time. TE to SET and SET to SWE moves are the most common as engineers often pursue their technical interests and specialize. Moves from SET to TE and TE to PM are the second most occurring, as folks move to generalize, have a wider context, and become disinterested in coding all day.

Managers also help set the quarterly and yearly OKRs[12] for people. They ensure there are some "stretch" OKRs, which are OKRs that are very optimistic or ambitious goals, but not always necessary or likely to be reached to force the function of aiming high even when planning for the near term. The manager also helps ensure the goals represent a blend of the individual TE and SET's abilities and interests with the needs of the project and business.

Test leadership often requires compromise and deferring to the wisdom of the individual SET and TEs. A hallmark of Google leadership and management is mentoring and guiding their report work, not dictating it.

Maintenance Mode Testing

Google is known for shipping early and often, and failing fast. Resources can also rush to the highest-risk projects. What that means to the TE is that features, and sometimes entire projects, are either deprioritized at times or entirely scrapped. This often happens just as you get things under control

---

[12] OKR stands for Objectives and Key Results. OKR is just a fancy way of saying list your goals and how you will measure your success on those goals. At Google, emphasis is placed on quantifiable metrics for success. Hitting 70 percent means you likely aimed high and worked hard. 100 percent means you likely weren't ambitious enough.

and have figured out the hard problems of testing that particular piece of software. TEs at Google have to be prepared and know how to deal with these situations both technically and emotionally. It's not glamorous, but these situations can be some of the most risk-intensive and expensive if not done carefully.

Maintenance Mode Example: Google Desktop by Jason Arbon

I was asked to take on the gargantuan task of testing Google Desktop with tens of millions of users, client and server components, and integration with Google search midway through the projects. I was the latest in a long line of test leads for this project with the usual quality and project debt. The project was large, but as with most large projects, it had begun to slow down feature wise and risk had been reduced through several years of testing and usage.

When two test buddies and I dropped into the project, Google Desktop had some 2,500 test cases in the old TestScribe Test Case Manager (TCM) database and several smart and hardworking vendors in the Hyderabad office running through these tests cases for each release. These test passes were often week-long or longer test cycles. Some previous attempts were made at automating the product via the UI and accessibility hooks, but that effort had failed under the weight of complexity and cost. It wasn't easy to drive both web pages and the desktop window's UI via C++, and then there were the issues of timeouts everywhere.

The two test buddies were Tejas Shah and Mike Meade. There weren't a lot of resources for client testing at Google. As the bulk of Google products were on the Web or moving to the Web quickly, we decided to leverage a Python test framework (previously developed for Google Talk Labs Edition) which drove the product via the web DOM. This quick framework had the basics, such as a test case class, derived from PyUnit. Many TEs and developers knew Python, so we had a quick exit strategy if needed, and a lot of other engineers could help if something broke. Also, Python is amazingly quick to iteratively develop smaller bite-sized chunks of code without a compilation step, and it is installed on everyone's workstations by default at Google so the whole test suite can be deployed with a single command line.

Together, we decided to build out the full breadth of a Python API to drive the product, using ctypes to drive the client-side COM APIs for searching, mocking the server responses for testing injection of local results into google.com results (non-trivial!), using quite a few library functions for users, and manipulating the crawl. We also constructed some virtual machine automation for tests that required a Google Desktop index; otherwise, we would have to wait several hours for the indexing to complete on a fresh install. We built a small, automated smoke suite to cover the high-priority functions of the product.

We then moved to investigate the older 2,500 test cases. Many of these were difficult to understand and referred to code words from prototypes or dropped features from the early days of the project, or they assumed a lot about the context and state of the machines. Much of this documentation was unfortunately locked away in the minds of the vendors in Hyderabad. This wasn't a good idea if we needed to quickly validate a build with a security patch with zero notice. It was also downright expensive. So, we took the brave leap to review all 2,500 tests, identify the most important and relevant ones based on our independent view of the product, and deprecated (deleted) all but around 150 tests. This left us with an order of magnitude fewer test cases. We worked with the vendors to clean up the text of the remaining manual test cases to make the test steps so clear and detailed that anyone who had used Google Desktop for a few minutes could run them. We didn't want to be the only people who could perform a regression run in the future.

At this point, we had automated coverage for every build that started catching some regressions for us and a very small set of manual tests that could be executed by anyone in an afternoon against a release candidate build. This also freed up the vendors to work on higher value targets, it reduced cost, and it reduced ship latency with close to the same amount of functional coverage.

About this time, the Chrome project began and we started looking in that direction as the future of Google services on client machines. We were just about to reap all the benefits of our rush to automate with a rich test API and we were going to build generated and long-running tests, but we were asked to move resources quickly to the Chrome browser.

With our automated regression suites checking every internal build and the public builds, and with a super light manual test pass, we were in good shape to leave Desktop in maintenance mode and focus our energy on the more volatile and risky Chrome project.

But, for us, there was one nagging bug we kept hearing from the forums: For several versions of Google Desktop and for a few people, Google Desktop was gobbling up drive space. The issue kept getting deferred because there wasn't a consistent repro. We reached out through our Community Manager to get more machine information from customers, but no one could isolate the issue. We worried that this would impact more users over time, and without a full crew on board, it would never be resolved or it would be painful if it ended up needing to be dealt with later. So, we invested in deep investigations before moving on. The test team kept pushing on PM and Dev to investigate, even pulling a developer from the original indexing code back onto the project from a remote site thinking he'd know what to look for. He did. He noticed that Desktop kept re-indexing tasks if the user had Outlook installed. The index code kept thinking each old item was a new item each time it scanned, slowly but steadily chewing up hard drives and only for users of Outlook who used the Outlook tasks feature. Because the index was capped at 2GB, it took a long time to fill up, and users would only notice because recent documents weren't indexed. But, diligence in engineering led to its discovery and fix. The last version of Desktop launched with this fix so we wouldn't have a latent issue pop up in 6 to 12 months after shipping with a skeleton crew.

We also time-bombed a feature, giving users the warning it was going away. We also made it simple and reliable. The test team suggested moving this from a code path of pinging the server for a global flag when the feature should be disabled to a more reliable and robust client-only one. This eliminated the need for a subsequent release without this feature and made the feature more robust through simplicity of design.

We set up a quick doc and how-to for executing the automation and kicking the manual tests (a small release requiring only one vendor a few hours), placed a vendor on call for this work, and moved our testing focus to Chrome and the cloud. Incremental releases went off without a hitch. Those automated runs continue today. Desktop customers are still actively using the product.

When putting a project in a quality maintenance mode, we need to reduce the amount of human interaction required to keep quality in check. A funny thing about code is that when left alone, it gets moldy and breaks of its own accord. This is true of product code and test code. A large part of maintenance engineering is about monitoring quality, not looking for new issues. As with all things, when a project is well funded, you don't always build the leanest set of tests so the tester will need to deprecate (remove) tests.

When deprecating manual tests, we use these guidelines:

- We look for tests that always pass or tests that are a low priority when you can't keep up with your higher priority testing. Deprecate them!

- We understand what we are deprecating. We take the time to pick a few representative sample tests from the areas you deprecate. Talk to the original authors if possible to understand their intent so it's not lost.

- We use the newly freed time for automation or to look at a higher priority test or at exploratory testing.

- We also prune automated tests that might have given false positives in the past or are flaky—they just create false alarms and waste engineering work later.

Following are tips to consider before entering maintenance mode:

- Don't just drop the hard problems; fix them before leaving.

- Even a small, automated suite focused on E2E can give a lot of assurance over the long haul for almost zero cost. Build this automated suite if you don't have one already.

- Leave a how-to document, so anyone in the company can run your test suite; it takes you off the firing line for a random interrupt and is the right thing to do.

- Ensure you have an escalation path if something were to go wrong. Be willing to be somewhere on that escalation path.

- Always be ready to dive in and help on projects you used to work on. It's good for the product, the team, and users.

Entering test maintenance mode is a fact of life for many projects, especially at Google. As a TE, we owe it to our users to take prudent steps to make sure it is as painless for them as possible and as efficient as possible engineering wise. We also have to be able to move on and not be married to our code or ideas.

Quality Bots Experiment

What would testing look like if we forgot the state-of-the-art approaches and tools for testing and took on the mindset of a search engine's infrastructure with virtually free CPU, virtually free storage, and expensive brains to work on algorithms— bots, quality bots to be exact.

After working on many projects at Google and chatting with many other engineers and teams, we realized we spent a lot of engineering brains and treasure hand-crafting and running regression suites. Maintaining automated test scenarios and manual regression execution is an expensive business. Not only is it expensive, but it is often slow. To make it worse, we end up looking for behavior we expect—what about the unexpected? Perhaps due to the quality-focused engineering practices at Google, regression runs often show less than a 5 percent failure rate. Importantly, this work is also mind-numbing to our TEs, who we interview for being highly curious, intelligent, and creative—we want to free them up to do the smarter testing that we hired them for: exploratory testing.

Google Search constantly crawls the Web; it keeps track of what it sees, figures out a way to order that data in vast indexes, ranks that data according to static and dynamic relevance (quality) scores, and serves the data up on demand in search result pages. If you think about it long enough, you can start to view the basic search engine design as an automated quality-scoring machine—sounds a lot like the ideal test engine! We've built a test-focused version of this same basic system:

1. **Crawl:** The bots are crawling the Web now.[13] Thousands of virtual machines, loaded with WebDriver automation scripts, drive the major browsers through many of the top URLs on the Web. As they crawl URL to URL like monkeys swinging vine to vine, they analyze the structure of the web pages they visit. They build a map of which HTML elements appear, where they appear, and how they appear.

---

[13] The highest priority crawls execute on virtual machines from Skytap.com. Skytap provides a powerful virtual machine environment that lets developers connect directly to the virtual machine where the failure occurred and manage those debugging instances—all without leaving the browser. Developer focus and time is much more valuable than CPU cycles. Moving forward, Skytap enables bots to execute entirely on other users' virtual machines and accounts, allowing access to their nonpublic staging servers.

2. **Index:** The crawlers post the raw data to the index servers. The index orders the information based on which browser was used and what time the crawl happened; it pre-computes basic statistics about the differences between each run such as how many pages were crawled.

3. **Ranking:** When an engineer wants to view results for either a particular page across several runs or all pages for a single browser, the ranker does the heavy compute to figure out a quality score. The quality score is computed as a simple percent similarity score between the two pages, and also averages it for entire runs. A 100 percent means the pages are identical. Less than 100 percent means things are different and is a measure of how different.

4. **Results:** Results are summarized on a bots dashboard (see Figure 3.27). Detailed results are rendered as a simple grid of scores for each page, showing the percent similarity (see Figures 3.28 and 3.29). For each result, the engineer can dig into visual differences, showing the detailed score on overlays of what was different between the runs with the XPaths[14] of the different elements and their positions (see Figure 3.30). Engineers can also view the average minimum and maximum historical scores for this URL, and so on.

FIGURE 3.27   Bot summary dashboard showing trends across Chrome builds.

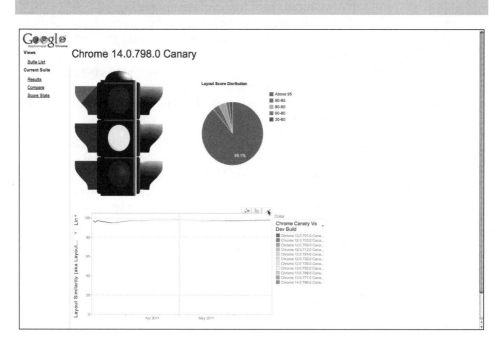

---

[14] XPaths are much like file paths, but work within web pages instead of file systems. They identify the parent-child relationships and other information that uniquely identifies an element within the DOM on a web page. See http://en.wikipedia.org/wiki/XPath.

FIGURE 3.28   Bot typical grid details view.

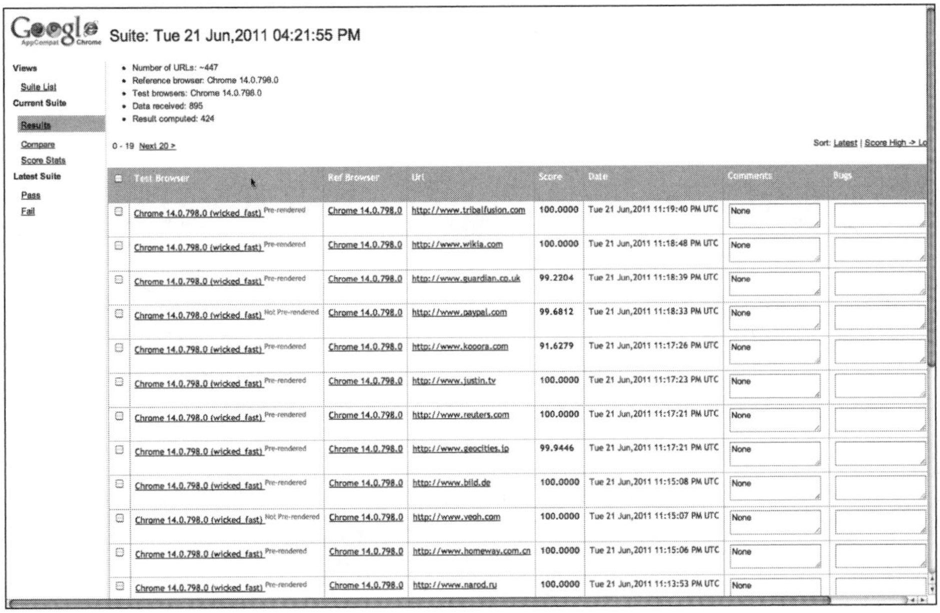

FIGURE 3.29   Bot grid sorted to highlight the largest differences.

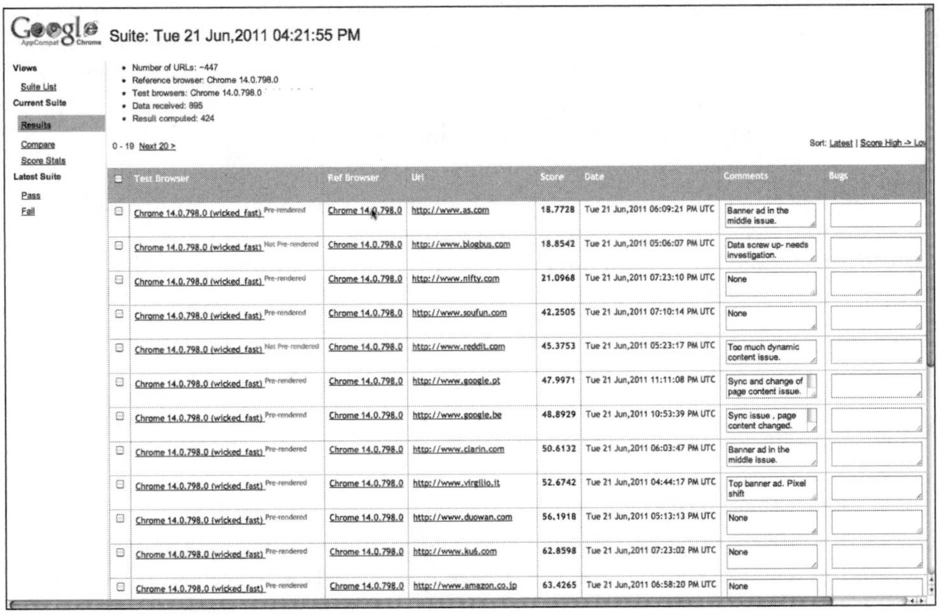

FIGURE 3.30   Bot visual diff inspection for page with no differences.

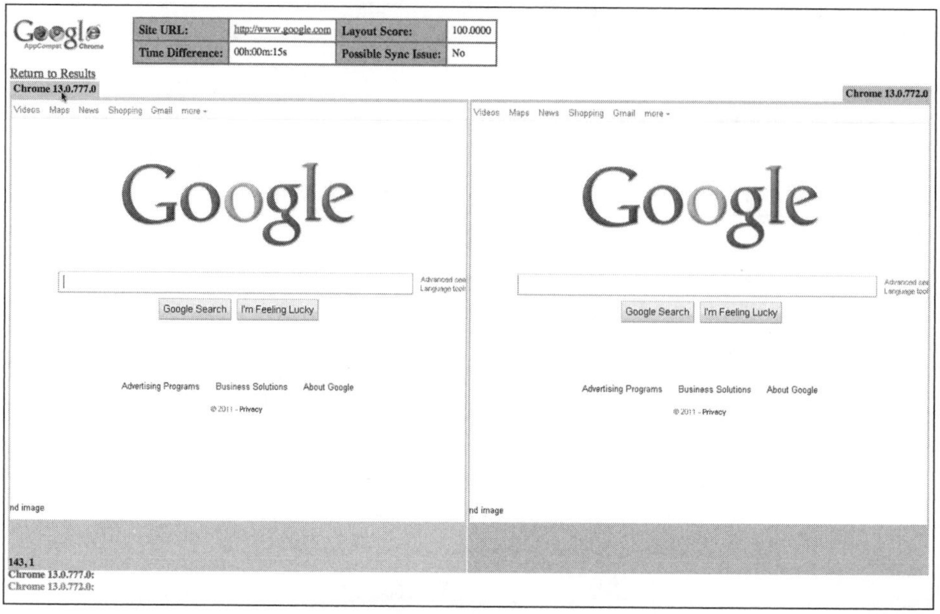

The first official run of Bots caught an issue introduced between two Canary builds of Chrome. The bots executed automatically, and the TE looked at the results grid, which showed this URL to have dropped in percent similarity. Based on this detail view that highlighted the differences, the engineer was able to quickly file the issue based on the detail view in Figure 3.31, which highlighted the exact portion of the page that was different. Because these bots can test every build of Chrome,[15] the engineer quickly isolated any new regressions found as the build contained only a few CLs, quickly isolating the offending code check-in.

Check-in[16] into the WebKit codebase (bug 56859: reduce float iteration in logicalLeft/RightOffsetForLine) caused a regression[17] that forced the middle div on this page to be rendered below the fold of the page. Issue 77261: ezinearticles.com layout looks broken on Chrome 12.0.712.0.

---

[15] Chrome builds many times per day.

[16] URL to check in that caused regression is at http://trac.webkit.org/changeset/81691.

[17] URL to WebKit BugZilla issue https://bugs.webkit.org/show_bug.cgi?id=56859. Tracking the issue in Chromium is http://code.google.com/p/chromium/issues/detail?id=77261.

FIGURE 3.31   View of first bug caught with first run of bots.

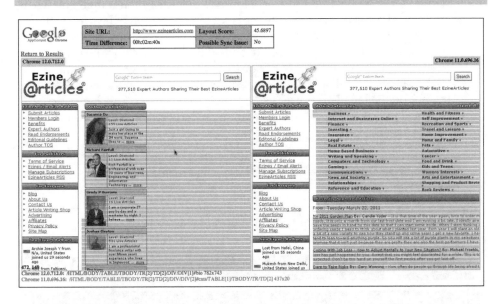

As we predicted (and hoped), the data from the bots looks very much like the data we get from the manual equivalents—and in many ways, it's better. Most of the web pages were identical, and even when they were different, quick inspection using the results viewer enables engineers to quickly note that there was nothing interesting (refer to Figure 3.29). Machines are now able to compute that no regressions happened. The significance of this should not be lost—that means we don't need humans to slog through all these uninteresting web pages—some 90 percent of them. Test passes that used to take days can now be executed on the order of minutes, and they can be executed every day versus every week or so. Those testers are freed to look for more interesting bugs.

If we look at the view where the browser remains the same, but we vary a single website's data over time, we now have something that tests a website, instead of just testing a browser. There are similar views for seeing a single URL across all browsers and across all test runs. This gives a web developer the opportunity to see all changes that have happened for her site. This means a web developer can push a new build, let the bots crawl it, and be pushed a grid of results showing what changed. At a glance, almost immediately, and with no manual testing intervention, the web developer can confirm that any changes the bots found are okay and can be ignored, and those that look like regressions can be turned into bugs with the data on which browsers and what application version and the exact HTML element information where the bug occurred.

What about websites that are data-driven? YouTube and CNN are heavily data-driven sites—their content changes all the time. Wouldn't this confuse the bots? Not if the bots are aware of what the normal "jitter" in data for that site is based on historical data. If run over run, only the article text and images change, the bots measure differences within a range that is normal for that site. If the sites score moves outside of that range, say when an IFRAME is broken, or the site moves to an entirely new layout, the bots can generate an alert, notify the web developer of who can determine this is the new normal, or file appropriate bugs if it was a new layout issue. An example of this small amount of noise can be seen in Figure 3.32 where CNET shows a small ad that appeared during the run on the right side, but not on the left. This noise is small and can be ignored via heuristics or quickly marked ignore by a human in seconds who notices this difference is an ad.

FIGURE 3.32   Bot visual diff inspection for page with noisy differences.

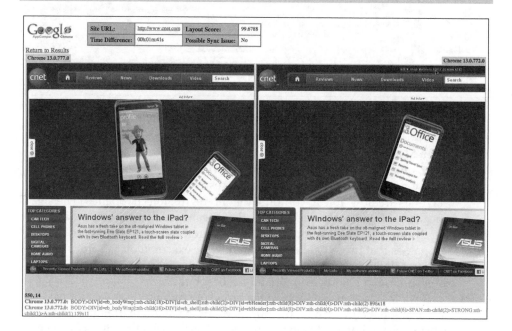

Now, what about all these alerts when they do occur? Does the tester or developer have to see them all? Nope, experiments are underway to route these differences directly to crowd-sourced[18] testers for quick evaluation to shield the core test and development teams from any noise. The crowd-sourced testers are asked to view the two versions of the web page and the differences found, and asked to label it as a bug, or ignore it as it looks like a new feature. This extra layer of filtering can further shield the core engineering team from noise.

---

[18] Our friends at http://www.utest.com have been helpful in setting up these experiments. Their crowd of testers has been amazingly sharp and responsive. At times, the test results from their crowd have found more issues of higher quality than internal repetitive regression test runs.

How do we get the crowd-sourced voting data? We built some infra-structure to take the raw bot data where there are differences and deliver a simple voting page for crowd testers. We've run several experiments with crowd testers versus the standard manual review methods. The standard manual review methods take up to three days latency across two days with onsite vendor testers to evaluate all 150 URLs for regressions. The bots flagged only six of the 150 URLs for investigation. Those didn't need any further evaluation. These flagged URLs were then sent to crowd testers. With bot data and the difference visualization tools, the average time for a crowd-sourced tester to evaluate a site as having a bug or "okay" was only 18 seconds on average. Crowd testers successfully identified all six as nonissues, matching the results of the manual and expensive form of this validation.

Great, but this measures only the static versions of web pages. What about all the interactive parts of a page such as flying menus, text boxes, and buttons? Work is underway to tackle this problem much like movies. The bots automatically interact with interesting elements on the web page, and at each step, take another scrape, or picture, of the DOM. Then, these "movies" from each run can be compared with the same difference tech-nologies frame by frame.

There are several teams at Google already replacing much of their man-ual regression testing efforts with Bots and freeing them up to do more interesting work such as exploratory testing that just wasn't possible before. Like all things at Google, we are taking it slowly to make sure the data is solid. The team aims to release this service and source code publically, including options for self-hosting for testing on other folks' VPNs if they prefer that to opening their staging URLs to the Internet.

The basic Bots code runs on both Skytap and Amazon EC2 infrastruc-ture. The code has been open sourced (see the Google testing blog or Appendix C). Tejas Shah has been the tech lead on Bots from very early on and was joined by Eriel Thomas, Joe Mikhail, and Richard Bustamante. Please join them in pushing this experiment forward.

Measuring the Quality of the Entire Internet

In information retrieval, it is common practice to take a random, representative sample of search queries. If you measure how well a search engine performs on that set of queries, much like presidential polls, you can have statistical confidence in the quality of all search queries. For Bots, the promise is that if we run Bots against a representative sample of URLs on the Internet, we might actually be able to quantify and track the quality of the Internet as a whole.

FIGURE 3.33   Early WebKit layout testing used single hashes of the entire page layout. We can now test full pages and fail at the element versus page level.

The Singularity[19]: Origin of the Bots *by Jason Arbon*

A long time ago, in a Google office far, far away… Chrome was at version 1. We could see the early data coming in and realized that there were quite a few issues where Chrome was rendering web pages differently than Firefox. The early method of measuring these differences was limited to tracking the incoming rate of bugs reported by users and seeing how many users complained of application compatibility problems when they uninstalled the browser after trying it out.

I wondered if there could be a more repeatable, automated, and quantifiable way of measuring how well we were doing in this area. Many folks before had tried to automatically diff screenshots of web pages across browsers, and some even tried to use fancy image and edge detection to identify exactly what was different between the renderings, but this often failed because you still end up with a lot of differences due to different images from ads, content changing, and so on. Basic WebKit layout tests used only a single hash of the entire layout of the page, as shown in Figure 3.33. Even when a real issue was found, engineers still had little clue about what was technically broken in the application, as they had only a

---

[19] The singularity is a term often used to describe the moment computers surpass human intelligence. It should be an interesting time and we are seeing glimpses of that today (http://en.wikipedia.org/wiki/Technological_singularity).

picture of the failure. The many false positives[20] often created more work for engineers than they saved.

My mind kept coming back to the early simple ChromeBot that crawled millions of URLs via Chrome browser instances across thousands of virtual machines using spare compute cycles in the data centers, looking for crashes of any sort. The tool was valuable as it caught crashes early on, and some functional testing of browser interaction was bolted on later. However, it had lost its shine and become primarily just a tool for catching the rare crash. What if we built a more ambitious version of this tool and interacted with the page itself instead of just the "chrome" around it, and, just called this Bots.

So, I considered a different approach: going inside the DOM.[21] I spent about a week putting together a quick experiment that would load many web pages one after the other, injecting JavaScript into the page to scrape out a map of the inner structure of the web page.

There were many smart people who were highly skeptical of this approach when I ran it past them. A small sampling of reasons people gave to suggest not trying this:

- Ads keep changing.

- Content on sites such as CNN.com keep changing.

- Browser-specific code means pages will render differently on different browsers.

- Bugs in the browsers themselves cause differences.

- Such an effort requires overwhelming amounts of data.

All this just sounded like a fun challenge and if I failed, well, I could fail quietly. I'd also worked on another search engine in the past, so I probably had more confidence than I should have that the signals could be pulled from the noise. I realized I would have little internal competition on such a project. I pressed on quietly. At Google, data speaks. I wanted to see the data.

To run an experiment, I needed control data to compare the data with. The best resource was the actual testers driving this work. I chatted with the two test engineering leads who routinely drove vendor-testers manually though the top 500 or so websites in Chrome, looking for differences with Firefox.[22] They said that at the time of launch, a little less than half of the top websites had some issues, but it had been steadily getting better to the point that they were few and far between—less than 5 percent of sites.

---

[20] False positives are test failures that aren't really failures of the product, but rather the testing software and can become expensive, aggravating to engineers, and quickly slow engineering productivity with fruitless investigations.

[21] The DOM is the Document Object Model, the internal representation of all that HTML under the hood of a web page. It contains all the little objects that represent buttons, text fields, images, and so on.

[22] Firefox was used as the benchmark, as it more closely adhered to the HTML standard, and many sites had IE-specific code, which wasn't expected to render well in Chrome.

I then constructed the experiment using WebDriver (the next generation Selenium). WebDriver had better Chrome support and a cleaner API. I performed the first run to collect data using the early versions of Chrome through the current version to see if the machines would find a similar trend line. It simply loaded up the same top websites, and at every pixel checked to see which HTML element (not the RGB value) was visible at that point[23] and pushed this data to the server. This run was on my local machine and took about 12 hours to run so I let it run over-night.

The next day, the data looked good, and so I swapped out Firefox for Chrome and reran the same tests. Yes, there would be jitter from site content changing, but this was a first pass to see what the data might look like and would later run both in parallel. I came into the office in the morning to find my Windows desktop physically disconnected from every cable and pulled out away from the wall! I usually came in later than my desk neighbors who gave me a strange look and said all they knew what that I was supposed to chat with the security folks. I can only imagine what they thought. The crawl had infected my machine with a virus with an unknown signature and it had started behaving very badly overnight. They asked if I wanted to try to remove any data from the machine in a controlled environment before they physically destroyed the drive. Thanks to my data in the cloud, I said they could just take the entire machine. I moved all runs to external VMs after that.

The data looked similar to the anecdotal data from the TEs (see Figure 3.34). The machines independently produced data in 48 hours that was eerily similar to perhaps a year worth of manual testing efforts. Eerily similar data.

FIGURE 3.34   Early data showing similarity between bot and human measures of quality.

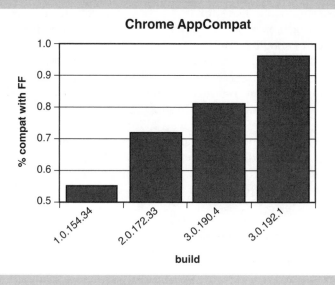

---

[23] Just a hash of elements returned from getElementFromPoint(x,y) for a 800 x 1,000 section of the web pages. There are more efficient ways to do this, but it is simple and works for illustration.

The data looked promising. A few days of coding and two nights of execution on a single machine seemed to quantify the work of many testers for more than a year. I shared this early data with my director who will go unnamed. He thought it was cool, but he asked that we keep focus on our other experiments that were much further along. I did the Googley thing, and told him I'd put it on hold, but didn't. We had two fantastic interns that summer and we roped them into productizing these runs and richer views to visualize the differences. They also experimented with measuring the runtime event differences. Eric Wu and Elena Yang demo'd their work at the end of the summer and made everyone a believer that this approach had a lot of promise.

Tejas Shah was inspired by the data and as the interns rolled off, Tejas built an engineering team to take this experiment and make it real.

Bots: Personal Bet and Scaling to the Web by Tejas Shah

I'm currently the technical lead on the Bots project and my focus is to scale bots to the web and share them with the world. The Bots project has developed from early experiments into a full-fledged project used by multiple teams at Google.

It was late 2010, and I was busy working on automation framework (also known as SiteCompat) for Chrome that used directed JavaScript tests to automatically catch functional bugs in Chrome on popular websites. It did things such as automatically validate search functionality on google.com or view an article on CNN for nearly every Chrome build. It was working great and caught some regressions and added automated functional checks for runtime behavior of websites.

About that same time, Jason's interns were working on an early demo of this super cool Bots project. I kept an eye on the intern's progress and when they finally demonstrated their results, it totally changed my approach and view at how to validate websites. When I saw Elena's demo with the first renderings of the bot data, I was totally sold on it. I realized this had a chance to fundamentally change the approach to web testing. My directly scripted tests were important, but only scaled linearly, and I had to maintain them. Bots hinted at something more generally useful. I immediately fell in love and became obsessed with this new idea. The interns were leaving, and everyone knew the code was demonstration code. It would need a lot of work to be part of core infrastructure and to make it a web-scalable solution.

Initially, I was the only engineer working on the Bots project. At that time, Bots was still considered experimental, and many still felt it was "mission impossible." But I believed someone had to make this real.

There was a brief time that I worked alone, avoiding questioning and skeptical eyes. This lasted about a quarter. There was a lot of work to do on the scaling issues, performance, scoring methods, and usability of the difference pages. The system would not be useful to others until all these pieces were working as a whole. It's hard to do this kind of work when you are on your own and you know that you are taking a risk with your career by working on such a risky project. If it doesn't work out, you don't have much to show for your work. Google encourages a lot of experimentation, but it wants results. My management chain shielded me from skeptical questioning during reviews as I worked on this longer-term project.

Then we had our first demo with the Chrome team's engineering director. He liked the idea enough that it seemed like an obvious thing to be doing now that it was built, and he decided to incorporate Bots' results into Chrome's day-to-day testing work. That validation was important and gave me a big confidence boost to keep plowing ahead. I also realized that if the Chrome team could use this for difficult quality problems that span all of the Web, then so could any website.

Immediately after that, we had several demos with many internal teams at Google. Everyone who saw the demo wanted to use Bots for their team, which validated our original dream of making it useful for all web apps. After working on it for another quarter, I was able to create some trend lines and scores for the Chrome Canary build. Now, Bots is not only functioning as an early alert system, but it catches real bugs at an early stage in the cycle with much more precise data around failures, so developers can make a decision based on real-world facts. My favorite bug was the first production Bots ran that compared two daily builds against each other. The Bots caught an issue just hours after a developer from Apple had made a change in a WebKit attribute. There were unit tests for this feature, but only the bots caught the issue because it tests real-world web pages.

My team often gets the question after a demo, "Can I soon eliminate my manual testing?" Our answer is a definite no. They can now do the work you hired them for: intelligent exploratory testing, risk analysis, and thinking about the user.

Chrome's success story got us more funding and resources. Now, we have a couple of engineers working on Bots and helping us take it to the next level. In the meantime, we were asked to help out the search team that was in the middle of releasing a new cool feature called Instant Pages. After spending a few weeks on Instant Pages, as it required running Chrome in different modes, we were able to put together a special Bots run for them that helped them ship with confidence because they knew that this same automation could run automatically for any changes they might make in the future.

My message to TEs out there: If you believe in something, build it! My advice to management out there: Give these engineers some room to breathe and experiment and they will do amazing things for the business and the customer.

BITE Experiment

BITE stands for Browser Integrated Test Environment. BITE is an experiment in bringing as much of the testing activity, testing tools, and testing data into the browser and cloud as possible, and showing this information in context. The goal is to reduce distraction and make the testing work more efficient. A fair amount of tester time and mental energy is spent doing all this manually.

Much like a fighter pilot, so much of a tester's time is spent context switching and dealing with a lot of data. Testers often have multiple tabs open: one for the bug database, one for email for product mailing lists or discussion groups, one for their test case management system, and one for a spreadsheet or test plan. The tester is constantly flipping between these tabs. This might seem like we are overly obsessing on efficiency and speed, but there is a greater problem in all this. The testers end up missing valuable context while they are testing:

- Testers waste time filing duplicate bugs because they don't know the right keywords to find the existing bug.

- Testers do not actually file a bug for seemingly obvious issues because they don't want to sift through the bug database looking for the right keyword to confirm it's already filed.

- Not every tester is aware of all the hidden and relevant debug information that is useful for later bug triaging and debugging by developers.

- It takes a lot of time to manually enter the reproduction steps, debug info, and where the bug was found in the application. A lot of time and mental energy is wasted, and often this mundane work takes the creativity and focus out of the TE in the process at the exact time he should be most alert for bugs.

BITE tries to address many of these issues and lets the engineer focus on actual exploratory and regression testing—not the process and mechanics.

Modern jet fighters have dealt with this information overload problem by building Heads Up Displays (HUDs). HUDs streamline information and put it in context, right over the pilot's field of view. Much like moving from propeller-driven aircraft to jets, the frequency with which we ship new versions of software at Google also adds to the amount of data and the premium on the speed at which we can make decisions. We've taken a similar approach with BITE for regression and manual testing.

We implemented BITE as a browser extension because it allows us to watch what the tester is doing (see Figure 3.35) and examine the inside of the web application (DOM). It also enables us to project a unified user experience in the toolbar for quick access to data while overlaying that data on the web application at the same time, much like a HUD.

FIGURE 3.35   BITE extension popup window.

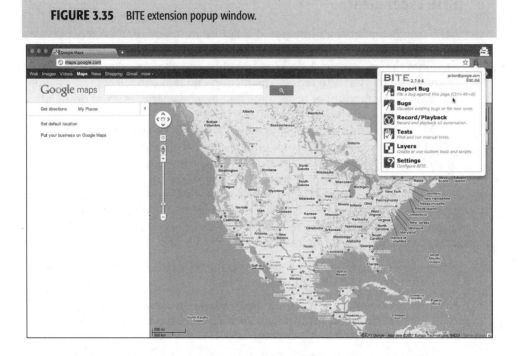

Lets walk through these experimental features using some real world Google web applications.

Reporting Bugs with BITE

When the tester finds a bug on a web application she is testing, or dogfooding, she can make one click on the Chrome extension icon, and then select which part of the page is buggy. Much like Google Feedback, the tester can highlight the part of the page where the bug lives, and with one more click, automatically file that as a bug. The tester can add more text to describe the problem, but the bug already automatically has most of the interesting and tedious information added to it automatically: the URL, the offending element/text on the page, and a screenshot. For a few deeply supported web applications, the tool automatically goes deeper and extracts application-specific debug URLs and information useful for debugging in the page itself.

Let's say the tester tried searching on maps.google.com for "Google offices" and saw a possibly irrelevant maps search result: the White House. The tester simply clicks the BITE menu button to Report Bugs. He then gets a cursor to select the part of the page that he thinks has a bug in it: the fourth search result in this case (see Figure 3.36). He can also pick any of the controls, images, or map tiles on the page, and individual words, links, or icons.

FIGURE 3.36   BITE highlighting the irrelevant search result in yellow, the White House.

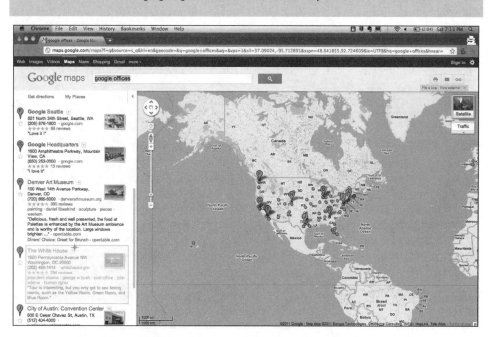

Clicking the highlighted part of the page brings up the bug-filing form (see Figure 3.37) directly on top of the page they file the bug against. There is no tab switching here. They can enter a quick bug title and click Bug It to file it immediately or add additional information. There are a few cool things that are automatically added here by BITE—things that make triage and debugging a lot easier, and most testers don't take the time to do, or it takes quite a bit of manual labor, distracting the tester from actually testing:

1. A screenshot is automatically taken and attached to the bug.

2. The HTML of the element that was highlighted is attached to the bug.

3. The actions taken since landing on maps.google.com are recorded in the background and recorded as a JavaScript that can be executed to replay what the tester was doing on that page before the bug was found. A link to this is automatically attached to the bug, so the developer can watch a replay live in his own browser. See Figure 3.38.

4. Map-specific debug URLs are automatically attached to the bug (often the URL doesn't contain enough information for a full repro).

5. All browser and OS information is attached to the bug.

FIGURE 3.37   BITE: the in-page bug-filing form.

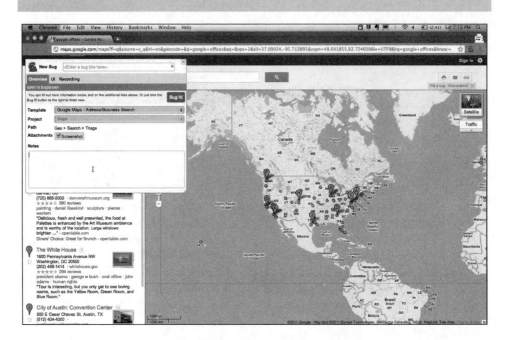

FIGURE 3.38   BITE: the JavaScript recorded during testing.

The bug is added to the bug database with all this information for triaging. All this leads to quick bug filing.

BITE Impact on Maps

BITE is currently used for Googlers filing bugs against maps.google.com. Google maps is interestingly difficult to file bugs against because much of its application state isn't captured in the URL, and the backend data constantly changes. As users browser around maps, zoom in and out, none of that state is captured. With bugs coming in from BITE, the Product Manger driving the triage process was more than happy to roll this out to the larger GEO team, as he said the bugs coming in from even random Googlers were now on par with the debug information coming in from their best dedicated maps testers. This speeds up the bug triage process, and many more bugs can be reproduced and debugged by engineers, where in the past they might have gone into the "no repro" bucket.

Viewing Bugs with BITE

As the testers explore the application or runs regression tests, they can automatically see relevant bugs for the page they are on, floating over the application under test. This helps testers know whether a bug has already been filed before or what other bugs have been found, indicating the classes of bus in this part of the application.

BITE displays bugs from both our internal bug database and from the chromium.org issue tracker—where external developers, testers, and users can file bugs about Chrome in general.

The number next to the BITE icon in the browser indicates how many bugs might be related to the current web page. This a simple matter for bugs originally filed through BITE for which we have a lot of data including the actual part of the page where the bug manifested itself. For bugs filed the old fashioned way, directly into issue tracker or our internal Buganizer, we have a crawler that looks at every bug to look for URLs and match bugs to pages, ranking them by how closely they match the URL to the current page (for example, exact matches are shown first, then the ones that match the path, and then only the domain of the current URL). It's simple, but it works pretty well.

Figure 3.39 shows how a map's page looks with the BITE bug overlay. One click on the bug IDs takes the engineer to the full bug report page in Buganizer or issue tracker. Figure 3.40 shows a bug overlay on top of YouTube.

FIGURE 3.39   BITE: overlay showing bugs related to maps.google.com.

FIGURE 3.40   BITE: bug overlay on the YouTube home page.

Record and Playback with BITE

A significant amount of SET and TE time is spent developing large, end-to-end regression test case automation. These tests are important because they make sure the product works for the end user with all parts working together. The vast majority of these are written in Java using Selenium to drive the browsers and hold the test case logic. There are a few pain points with this approach:

The test logic is written in a language different from the running application (Java versus JavaScript). This is a common complaint of developers and testers across Google. It slows down debugging and not every engineer wants to learn every language.

The test code lives outside of the browser, so they require a build step and deploying these test binaries to machines. The Matrix test automation infrastructure centralizes this problem, but doesn't completely solve it.

You need to have a full IDE separate from the browser and the application installed locally and configured for the project you want to test.

TEs spend a lot of time bouncing between the application's DOM and the Eclipse IDE. They look at the XPaths of interesting elements, then hand-code this into their Java code. Build, run, and see if it works. This takes time and can be tiresome.

Google web apps change their DOM frequently. That means that test cases break all the time as elements move around the page and their attributes change. After a while, teams spend much of their time just maintaining the existing tests. All these false positives also lead developers and testers to start ignoring test results and just marking them as flaky so they don't block check-in.

In response, we worked to build a pure web solution called the Record and Playback framework (RPF), which is based on pure JavaScript, and we worked on storing the test case scripts in the cloud. This also works on Chrome OS, which doesn't support execution of Selenium or WebDriver test cases.

To record a test, you simply click the Record and Playback menu item in the BITE browser menu. A new recording dialog is then launched. When the record button is pressed, this dialog records all the click activity in the main browser window. A right-click on any element enters validation mode, where the tester can validate either a particular string, image, or an element's value. The validation can also be the presence of the element and its relative position on the page. This relative positioning is useful when working with the YouTube team as they don't always know exactly which video should be on the home page, but they do know the general layout of the page to expect.

One of the core aspects of the RPF approach is that it aims to avoid the pain of viewing the application's DOM and then recalculating the XPaths of the elements as they change. We invested quite a bit of engineering into code that would stop the test; if it couldn't find an element during playback, it would pause, allowing the TE to simply pick the new element and automatically update the script and keep executing. The team has also invested in what we call "relaxed execution." Basically, rather than be incredibly strict about whether the element matches the expected XPath, RPF instead looks at all the attributes of the HTML element and its parent and child elements in the DOM. During replay, RPF first looks for an exact match. If no exact match is found, it looks for elements that closely match. Maybe the ID attribute changed, but everything else is the same. The playback can be set to an arbitrary degree of precision in matching, and if the match is within tolerances, the test keeps marching to the next step and simply logs a warning message. We hoped investment in this approach would save a lot of engineering cycles.

We first tried RPF with the Chrome Web Store test team. RPF worked for about 90 percent of their test scenarios, the key exceptions were file upload dialogs that are native OS file dialogs outside of the browser and some aspects of Google Checkout, as it's not possible to automate some of those money scenarios through web APIs for security reasons. The most interesting thing we found, though, was that the TEs didn't care all that much about the fancy relaxed matching or pause-and-fix features. It was simply quicker for them to just re-record the test from scratch. In this early trial, we did parallel development of the same tests in both WebDriver and RPF. RPF with this approach was seven times more efficient to generate and maintain tests over Selenium and WebDriver. Mileage might vary, but it was a good early sign.

RPF also lives in BITE for the bug-filing scenarios. For certain sites, BITE automatically starts recording the engineer's activity. When the engineer finds a bug and uses BITE to file it, BITE appends a link to the generated repro script. For example, on Maps, it records all the searching and zooming activity. A developer viewing the bug, if he has BITE installed, can make a single click and the playback will start. He can watch what the users do when they encounter the bug. If no bug is filed during that session on the website, during exploratory testing or normal usage, the recorded script is simply discarded.

Origin of BITE with RPF by Jason Arbon

During early Chrome OS testing, we realized that the very core attribute of the platform, security, would make testing difficult. Testability and security are often at odds, and Chrome OS has an extreme focus on security.

There was a partially supported Java virtual machine in the early builds but with poor networking and other core library support. As the core user experience was based on web browsing, we went about building some core Selenium tests to validate basic browser functionality in Chrome OS, hoping we could just port all known Selenium tests to run as regressions.

We were able to get basic tests up and running, but soon hit a lack of deep Chrome support in Selenium and WebDriver. Upon returning from the holidays, we discovered that Java was actually removed from the underlying Linux OS to further reduce the security surface area for Chrome OS. This was not good for running Java-based tests. We had a workaround to build custom builds of Chrome OS with Java installed, but this was only a workaround.

At Google, it is often said that "scarcity brings clarity" and this is nowhere more apparent than in the testing world, and especially in this case. We took stock of where we were and realized that this wasn't a great solution. We were building custom images of Chrome OS that contained Java, the test artifacts (jar files), and some disabled security features, and then we ran our tests. But, we weren't testing the actual product in the same configuration that would ship out to our customers. (See Figure 3.41 for a picture of the early Chrome OS test automation lab.)

FIGURE 3.41 The early Chrome OS test lab.

We soon thought that another effort that Po Hu was working on to generally automate web pages using JavaScript via chrome extensions might be the answer. There was an internal, JavaScript-only WebDriver-like API, called puppet, but it had to be deployed with the web application under test (due to cross-site restrictions). We had the idea to place this puppet script into a Chrome extension to make it magically work on any site. If we installed this single extension and stored our tests in the cloud instead of the local file system, we could run browser tests on Chrome OS, even on a Chromebook purchased from a store. This effort would take longer than we had time for Chrome OS version 1, so it was moved into the engineering tools effort to be ready for post-V1 testing.

Interestingly, we got away with calling the original version of BITE Web Test Framework, or WTF for short. Officially, the acronym was derived from the name, not the other way around. RPF was originally called Flux Capacitor, as it allowed you to go back to the future.

Executing Manual and Exploratory Tests with BITE

Google has tried many ways to distribute tests acoss several testers for a given test pass: painful UI in TestScribe and often via spreadsheets shared with the team (manually mapping peoples' names to sets of tests they should execute).

BITE supports the tester subscribing to the test sets in the Google Test Case Manager (GTCM) for multiple Google products. When the test lead wants to start a test pass, she can click a button on the BITE server, and tests are pushed out to testers via the BITE UX. Each test can have a URL associated with it. If the user accepts the ask to execute the test, BITE drives the browser to the URL and shows the test steps and validation to be performed on that test page. It is just one click to mark it as PASS, which automatically takes the tester to the next URL to be tested. If the test fails, it marks the test as FAIL in the database and launches the BITE bug reporting UX.

This method has been tried with success with crowd-sourced testers. They executed tests with BITE installed, and the tests were distributed via BITE test distribution. This let us avoid the pain of managing the full set of testers and hard coding who will execute which tests. Testers with quickly executed tests were automatically pushed more to execute. If testers took a break or stopped all together, their tests simply timed out and were pushed to another tester. This has also been used to drive exploratory testing with each high-level Tour description defined as a single test case, and then distributed to testers who can file bugs via BITE as they tour the product.

Layers with BITE

As with all software projects, there is a compulsion to make things extensible. BITE has the capability to host arbitrary scripts and inject them into the page under test. There are a few current layers. For example, one of them lets developers systematically remove elements form the page, looking to isolate the cause of a bug. Work is underway to include scripts from the security team. These layers can be turned on or off with a little console. We are just now exploring what layers engineers might find interesting.

BITE strives to be all things to all testers. We originally started with each of these features as a separate extension, but the team realized that the whole is greater than the sum of the parts, and we spend quite a bit of engineering to bring everything together under the BITE umbrella.

As with the other experiments, the team hopes to open this up to the larger testing community soon.

The BITE project has been open sourced (see Appendix C). Alexis O. Torres was the original technical lead; Jason Stredwick is now the technical lead working with Joe Muharsky, Po Hu, Danielle Drew, Julie Ralph, and Richard Bustamante when they can find time away from their current projects. At the time of this writing, several external companies have ported BITE to their own infrastructure, and there is active work on Firefox and Internet Explorer ports.

Google Test Analytics

Risk analysis, as discussed earlier, is critically important, yet it is often implemented in on-off, custom-crafted spreadsheets, or worse, only in people's heads. There are a few shortcomings with this spreadsheet approach:

- Custom spreadsheets don't share a common schema. There is no way to roll up the data and it is confusing for folks looking across multiple projects.

- Some simple but important things such as a four-point rating system, and naming learned in ACC, are sometimes lost in these spreadsheets in the interest of brevity.

- There is limited visibility across multiple teams because there is no central repository and they are only ad-hoc shared on a need-to-know basis.

- The engineering and scripting to connect Risk Analysis to product metrics is expensive and rarely added as a feature in the spreadsheets.

Google Test Analytics (GTA) is an attempt to address these issues. GTA is a simple web application that makes the data entry and visualization of risk a little easier. The UI of GTA works to induce ACC best practices in its design. Keeping the data in a common schema also enables managers and directors to get a single view of risk across their products to help them allocate resources to the highest risk areas.

GTA supports the ACC model of Risk Analysis. Attributes and components are entered into quick-fill forms to produce a grid (see Figure 3.42 and Figure 3.43). The UI enables test planners to add capabilities at the intersections of this grid (see Figure 3.44). Adding risk is simply picking a frequency and impact value from the drop-down lists for each capability. This is all rolled up into the risk view. The summary risk for each area (see Figure 3.45) is simply the average of the risks in that square.[24]

---

[24] Yes, one high-risk capability can be obscured by many other related, but very low-risk capabilities. This doesn't happen very often, but the tool is designed to be simple, and is not a replacement for common sense and due diligence.

FIGURE 3.42   Test Analytics: entering attributes for Google+.

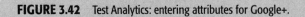

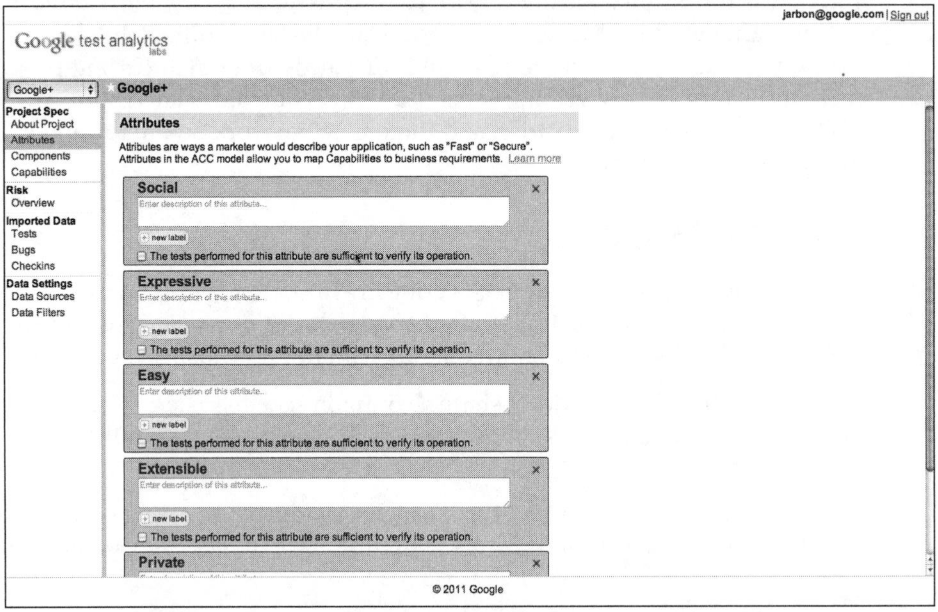

FIGURE 3.43 Test Analytics: entering components for Google+.

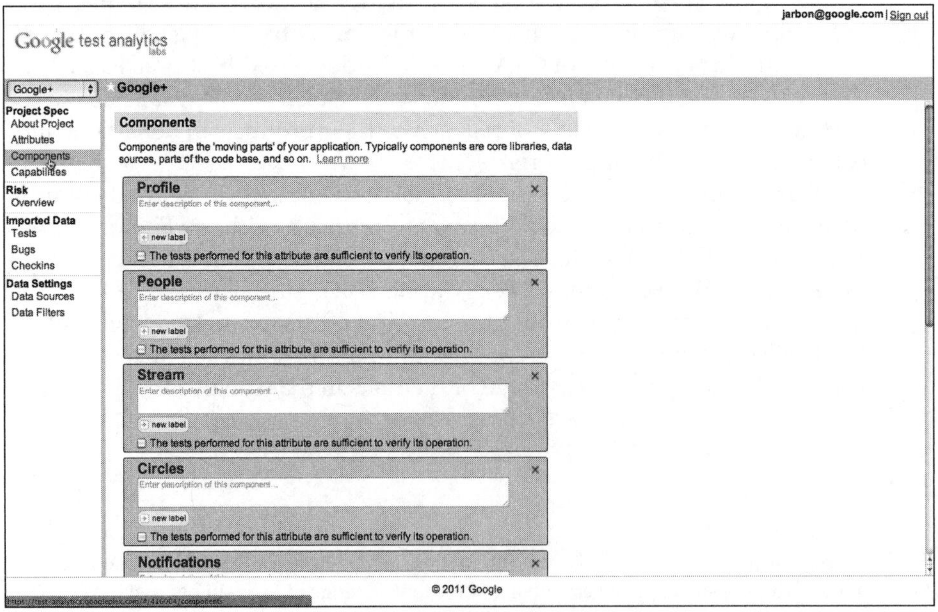

FIGURE 3.44   Test Analytics: entering capabilities on a grid intersection. Note that counts are simply the number of capabilities at the intersection, not risk.

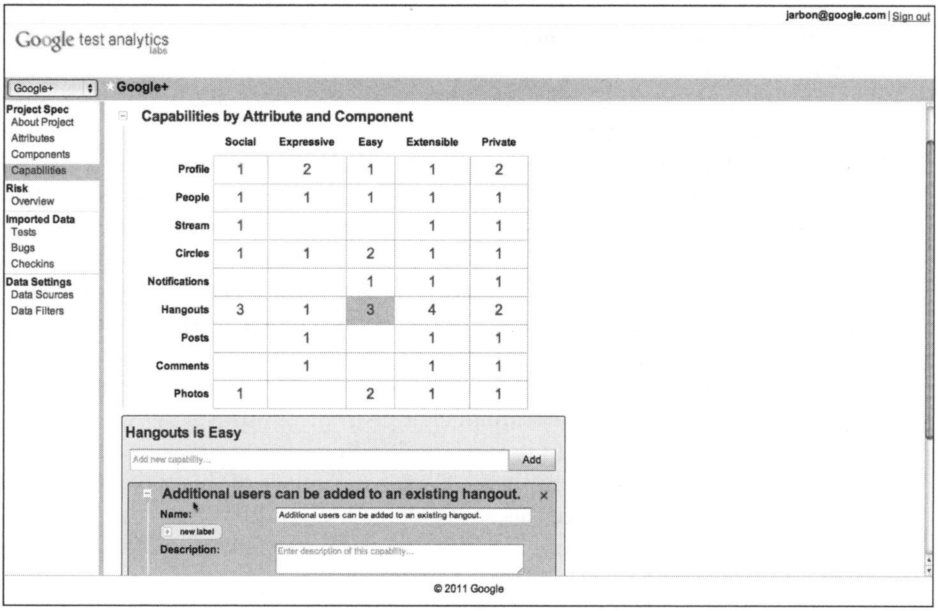

FIGURE 3.45   Test Analytics: risk heat for Google+.

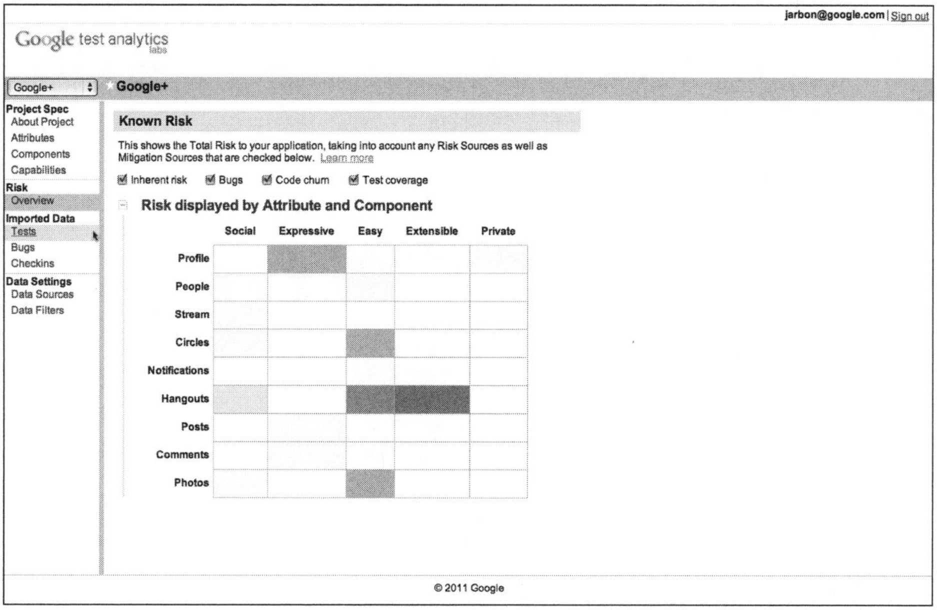

An *optional* and experimental aspect of GTA is the capability to bind the risk calculations to your actual project data. As you add more tests, add more code, and find more bugs, the assessment of risk changes. As TEs, we've always tracked this change in risk in our heads; this is just more systematic and data-driven. Test plans, even ACC/risk-based ones, often drive the initial test planning, which is great, but soon become dead documents themselves. You can always change anything in GTA as you get more data about risk, capabilities, and so on, but we should try to automate even this aspect of test planning where possible.

GTA currently supports only binding to our internal databases, but the work to generalize this is underway. In GTA, testers can enter the locations or queries in the bug database, source tree, and test case manager for the different capabilities. At Google, everyone uses the same databases, so it makes this easy. Then as these metrics change, we do some simple linear algebra to update the risk levels. This aspect is currently under a pilot trial with a few application teams at Google.

The formula we use is constantly evolving, so we won't document it here, but it is basically a measure of change in bug counts, lines of code changed, and the number of passing and failing test cases relative to when the risk assessment was completed. Each component of this risk is scaled to allow for variance in projects as some teams file granular bugs or have high measures of code complexity. Figures 3.46, 3.47, and 3.48 show this for Google Sites.

FIGURE 3.46   Test Analytics: linking data sources to risk.

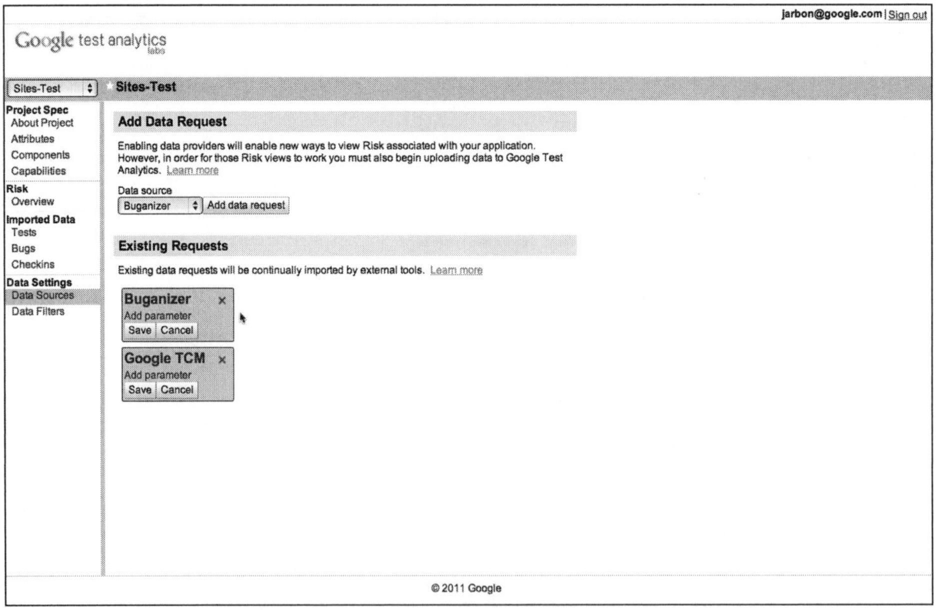

FIGURE 3.47   Test Analytics: linked tests.

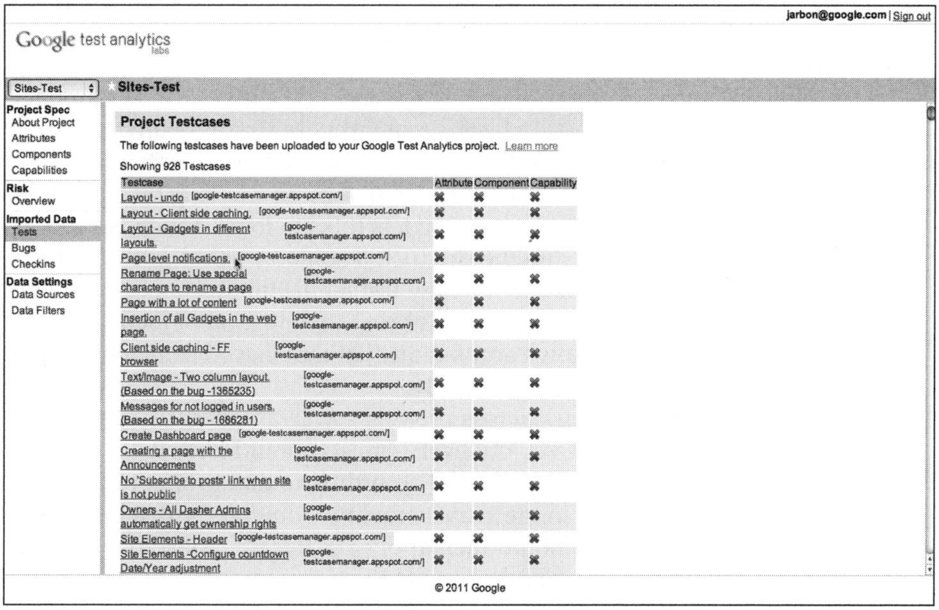

FIGURE 3.48   Test Analytics: linked bugs.

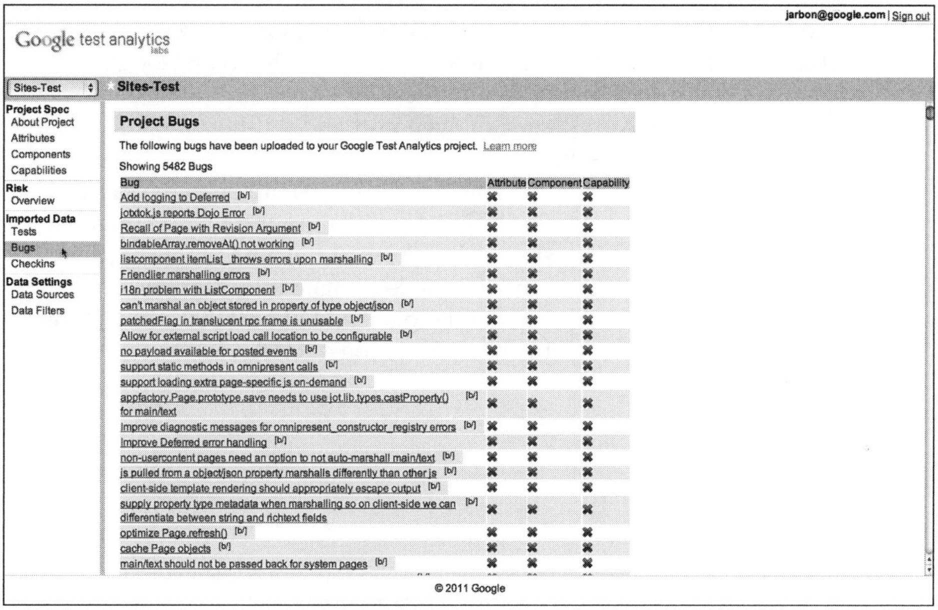

GTA has an easily missed, but very significant feature. Testers can quickly turn the list of capabilities into a test pass. This was the most asked-for feature from teams. The capabilities consist of a simple list of high-level tests that should be tested before releasing the software. For teams that are small or exploratory-driven, such as Google Docs, this list suffices for a test case database.

The ACC matrix behind these test passes in GTA gives the TEs an interesting pivot in which to assign testers to a test pass. Traditionally testers are simply assigned test passes or test development by component area. ACC makes for an interesting pivot that is useful, though—testing by attribute. We've found some success in assigning test folks to focus not on components, but on attributes across the product. If someone is assigned the Fast attribute for a test pass, she can see how fast all the interesting components of the product are in a single pass. This brings a new kind of focus with the ability to find relatively slow components that may have been viewed as fast enough when tested independently.

A note on rolling up risk across projects is warranted. GTA doesn't have this capability built in just yet, but every project should have its own ACC analysis, and risk should be evaluated according to that project only, not relative to other products in the same company. Someone with a broader view across the products should then apply a scalar for risk across all projects when rolling them up and looking at them in aggregate. Just because you work on a small internal tool for only a few other engineers doesn't mean you can't have maximum risk in your ACC assessment. Leave the business of relative risk to others who have visibility across projects. When assessing risk for your product, assess risk as if it was a company's sole product, so it can always have the potential for maximum impact or high frequency.

We hope to have GTA openly available and open sourced shortly. GTA is currently in field testing with large companies other than Google. We hope to open source this, too, so other test teams can host their own instances in Google App Engine or even port and self-host it on different technology stacks if they like.

GTA aims to make risk analysis simple and useful enough that folks actually use it. Jim Reardon built GTA from the ground up and maintains the open sourced code (see Appendix C). As of the time of this writing, other large cloud-testing companies are looking to integrate this approach to risk into their core workflows and tools,[25] and almost 200 external folks have signed up to leverage the hosted version of GTA.

---

[25] An example of other cloud companies looking at this approach is Salesforce. Phil Waligora of Salesforce.com is looking to integrate this into its internal tooling.

Free Testing Workflow

Google strives to shave every last millisecond out of response times and make its systems as efficient as possible in the interest of scaling. Google also likes to make its products free. TEs are doing the same for tools and processes. Google asks us to think big, so why not try to tackle the notion of reducing the cost of testing to near-zero?

If we could make testing free, it would enable small companies to have more testing and it would enable startups to have some level of testing. If testing were free, it would mean a better Web, and a better Web is better for users and for Google.

Following are some thoughts on what free testing would look like:

- Cost next to nothing

- Instantaneous test results

- Require little or no human intervention

- Very flexible because one size does not fit all

We scoped our aspirations to the web to make the problem tractable, relevant, and inline with most projects at Google. We thought that if we tackled the web testing problems first, by the time we finished, the world would have moved to the cloud anyway, so we could ignore inherently painful things such as drivers and COM. We knew if we aimed for free, even if we ended up short, we would have something interesting.

The current model we have for free significantly reduces friction and cost for testing. We are starting to see it in our own labs and engineering efforts (see Figure 3.49). The basic outline of this testing workflow is as follows:

1. **Test planning via GTA**: Risk-based, quick, and automatically updated.

2. **Test coverage**: When new versions of a product are deployed, bots continually crawl the site, index the content, and scan for relevant differences. The bots might not know if it is a regression or a new feature, but they can spot any changes and route these to a human for evaluation.

3. **Bug evaluation**: When differences in the product are found, they are routed automatically to humans for quick evaluation. Are these differences a regression or a new feature? BITE provides rich context on existing bugs and tests during evaluation of these differences.

4. **Exploratory testing**: Continual exploratory testing is performed by crowd testers and early adopters. This catches bugs related to configuration, context, and the really difficult bugs that require human intelligence to induce and report.

5. **Bug filing**: Bugs are filed with just a few clicks of the mouse with rich data about what exactly on the page is broken, screenshots, and debug information.

6. **Triage and debugging**: Developers, or test managers, get near-realtime dashboards of bug trends, rich bugs with the data they need to investigate the failures, and even one-click repros before their eyes in their own browser of how the tester entered that state.

7. **Deploying the new version and returning to step 1**. Rinse and repeat.

Web testing moves to a more automated and search-like stack and workflow. The key value of the previous approach to testing is that testers don't need to grind through hundreds or thousands of regression tests just to find the few features that did change and might have regressed. As these bots can run 24/7 and complete a test cycle in minutes versus hours or days, they can be run more often; thus, they provide earlier detection of regressions.

The best part of this bot workflow is the faster cycle time between a product version being deployed and bugs coming in. The bots can run 24/7, the crowd is available 24/7, so developers can deploy and very quickly have rich feedback on the affects of their code changes. With continual builds and deployments, it is trivial to identify which of a handful of changes could have induced the bugs, and the changes are fresh in the mind of the developer who checked in the regression.

This basic flow works well for web pages, but should also be applicable to pure data applications, client UX projects, or infrastructure. Think about deploying parallel versions of your product or system and think about what the crawl and indexing would look like for that application. It's likely a similar pattern will work for these testing problems, too, but are beyond the scope of this book.

FIGURE 3.49   End-to-end workflow of free testing.

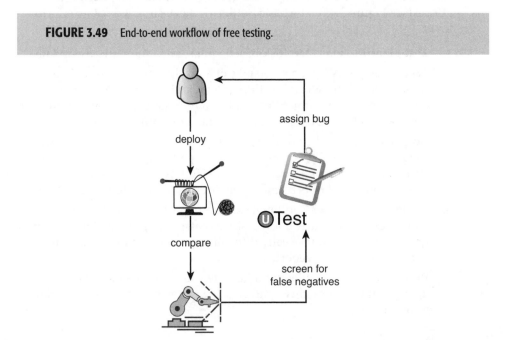

Test Innovation and Experimentation

by Jason Arbon

Google's culture of supporting experimental projects has led to many innovations and a large junk pile of failed experiments. Even when people think there are good solutions already, engineers aren't discouraged from trying to rethink entire approaches to testing, planning, and analyzing—it is actually their job.

When James Whittaker came to Google, one of the first things he did was hold internal tech talks, presenting his latest vision of software testing of the future to anyone who would listen. He said software testing should be much like video games—like first-person shooters where you have full contextual awareness of your surroundings overlaid on the application you were testing. Little did we know that his GTAC talk[26] would inspire work for several years. That sounded like a good idea in theory, but his slides showed pictures of this happening on typical client applications, which would be a pretty difficult and expensive challenge to generalize for all client applications.

During James' talk, I was technically skeptical of his brash ideas until I suddenly realized that I might be able to get James' idea running in the browser and working on web apps in no time at all using the new Chrome extensions API. I was excited enough about this idea to spend the next week focused on a prototype. I immediately halted my day job and spent that Saturday and Sunday at a Starbucks hacking away. The Starbucks folks made conversation and asked if I was job hunting online—I worried it might be an omen of some sort.

I soon had a working demo with a Chrome extension talking to a Python App Engine backend,[27] mocking out calls to a bug database. I was able to demo quite a few interesting things:

- Overlay bug information onto a page and even specific elements on that page.

- Overlay test cases onto the page to be tested with a single Pass/Fail button for logging (see Figure 3.50).

---

[26] James Whittaker's GTAC presentation on the future of testing can be found on You Tube at http://www.youtube.com/watch?v=Pug_5Tl2UxQ.

[27] App Engine is a Google cloud service for hosing a website or service. Testers often leverage App Engine for tools and infrastructure today given its capability to get an application up and running very quickly and still having Google Scale for free. See http://appengine.google.com. It currently supports Java, Python, and the Go languages.

FIGURE 3.50   Test pass UX.

- Heat map showing where other testers had been before and what values they had used (see Figure 3.51).

FIGURE 3.51   Tester coverage heat map.

After getting this to work on google.com, I started trying it on other sites, and sure enough it kept working. I scheduled a quick informal sync with James to show him what I'd built and to see what he thought. James and I became animated and covered a whiteboard with what soon became a roadmap for the experiments detailed in this book. I quickly sent an email to Pat Copeland and James, informing them both that I was pursuing this work and switching to report into James. No questions were asked—this change just happened over an email thread.

Each of the sub-experiments was run similarly—with each engineer owning his mission and design and collaborating at will with their peers. The primary management pull is simply to ensure that their work is reusable, shareable, and avoids limitations. Continually ask them to think bigger even as they code individual features.

Google's culture of sharing ideas—supporting bottom-up experimentation—and organizational flexibility creates a fertile world for test innovation. Whether it ends up valuable or not, you will never know unless you build it and try it out on real-world engineering problems. Google gives engineers the ability to try if they want to take the initiative, as long as they know how to measure success.

External Vendors

For all the great testing talent we have at Google, we do realize our limitations. New and ambitious projects at Google can rise from seemingly nowhere and often require specialized testing expertise. We don't always have the time to ramp up testing specialization or the time to hire someone, because the project can ship before we are ready to add value. Projects at Google are now spanning everything from devices, firmware, and operating systems to payment systems. They include everything from modifying the kernel of an operating system to modifying a rich UI driven by a remote control and to worrying about whether the device works on every television in the market.

We realize our limitations, so we get help from the experts, and sometimes those experts are external vendor agencies. A good example of this is Chrome OS. We realized early that one of the riskiest areas was our Wi-Fi and 3G connection. This part of the operating system and physical devices would vary between manufacturers, and a cloud device without an Internet connection isn't quite as compelling a product. Also, security updates and software fixes are delivered over the network; network connectivity can block these other important features. At the same time, another company was having 3G "conductive connectivity issues." This was not something to be left to well intentioned but nonspecialized testing efforts.

Because Google was just getting into the consumer devices space, we didn't have anyone in house at Google who had the physical test equipment or even knew how to use it if we had it lying around. Our testing at this point was happening by folks trying to manually switch between routers while sitting at a desk next to a rack of about 20 current commercial Wi-Fi routers. In just a few weeks, we had reports from our vendor indicating issues with switching routers and decreased throughput if the user was living in an apartment building with many different routers all within range.[28] Other issues related to using the prototype hardware and boards also occurred. Almost immediately we got graphs like those in Figure 3.52 and Figure 3.53 that showed severe drops in throughput. There shouldn't have been sudden dips in the curve, but there they were. The developers used this data to fix the issues about the time of our internal dogfood.

FIGURE 3.52   Expected curves for rate versus range.

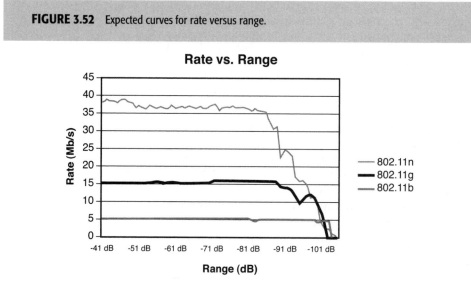

_____

[28] Ryan Hoppes and Thomas Flynn from Allion Test Labs were instrumental in helping us with hardware and network testing and certification.

FIGURE 3.53   Graph of early Chrome OS prototype rate versus range.

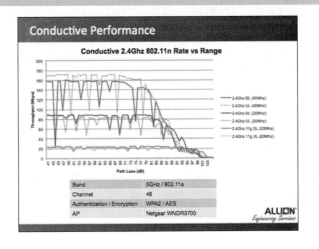

Interestingly, even lower-level engineers at Google can initiate external vendor relationships like this. Our ability to move quickly is a major part of our ability to ship quickly. We now have on-site facilities to measure much of this and continue to leverage vendor expertise, but the ability for us to leverage external vendors and spin these efforts up quickly was critical to successful network connectivity in the field when Chrome OS shipped to the world.

We had another unexpected benefit of partnering with external vendors with experience in this space. We asked them to review our list of Hardware Qualification Tests. These are tests that we ask our hardware vendors to run on their side before sending them to Google for further testing, eliminating much of the back and forth when it comes to sending hardware around. While reviewing our tests, they realized some areas were missing and were kind enough to format all the test cases in a form consistent with other hardware qualification tests that they had seen in the past. This help ensured our first drops of the tests to the large PC manufacturers were easily readable and complete. It pays to be humble and ask for testing help from external experts whenever possible.

An Interview with Google Docs TE Lindsay Webster

Lindsay Webster is a TE for Google Docs in Google's New York City office. Lindsay is a no-nonsense engineer who is known around the company as the go-to tester who can whip a development team into shape with regard to their testing practices. The way she works and the way she impacts both a team and product quality makes her the poster child for the Google TE.

The authors recently sat down with Lindsay to get her take on testing.

HGTS: How do you approach a new project? What are the first questions you ask? What are the first tasks you perform?

Lindsay: For a new project, I first get to know the product from a user perspective. If possible, I become a user myself with my personal account and personal data. I really try to sink myself into the full user experience. The way you look at a product totally changes once you see your own actual data in it. Once I have this user mindset, I do the following:

- Understand the product from end-to-end. If there is a design doc, I'll review that, and if there are design docs for major features, I'll review those. Give me a doc and I will read it!

- Once the docs are absorbed I look to the state of the project, specifically the "quality state" of the project. I review the bug count. I see how issues are grouped. I look at the types of bugs that are open, which have been open the longest, what types of bugs were created recently, and also try to get an idea for a find-to-fix ratio.

HGTS: Per developer or for the whole team?

Lindsay: Both! Seriously, you have to get a complete insight into your team to be truly effective.

I also check the code repository for the actual app code. I look for matching unit tests for each sizeable class. Do they pass if I run them? Are they meaningful and complete unit tests? Are there integration or end-to-end tests? Do these still pass? What is their historical pass rate? Are they very basic scenarios or do they cover corner cases as well? Which packages of the code repository see change most often? Which ones haven't been changed in a long time? The work developers do to document their testing practices is very informative.

I also review any automated tests. Are there any? Are they still running and passing? I'd check the code for these tests either way, though, to understand how they are stepping through the application, if they are complete, and if the assumptions, pass, and fail points are good enough or if they need work. Sometimes automation just covers simple tests. Sometimes there are complicated user scenarios included in the automation suite (this is a very good sign).

Once I hit all the docs, the team is next. I ask them about how they communicate and what their expectations are for testers. If they use mailing aliases, I join all of them, and if there is a team IRC channel or other means of real-time, distributed communication I get involved there.

Asking for testing expectations is where I find out a lot about how and what the dev team doesn't test.

HGTS: I am at once tired just thinking about all this work and incredibly grateful for testers like you! But once you plow through the docs and the people, there's only one thing left, the app right?

Lindsay: Yes! Once the recon is done, it is time to get down to business. I always start by breaking the application down into meaningful components of functionality. If there is a little overlap, that's okay, but I want it high level enough that I am not in the weeds, but low level enough that I am able to get to a point where I am listing subcomponents and features.

Once I have an initial set of functionality buckets, I can prioritize the buckets according to what needs to be tested first. What are the riskiest parts of the application according to the features and capabilities I've discovered?

Once organized here, I review the bug repository again, this time with the goal of creating the same kind of buckets in the repository for these components. This will make it really easy to find already existing bugs, which will lead to less duplicate bug reports and more visibility into what the reoccurring issues are.

Next, I start walking through all of these components in the application in a more detailed way, creating user stories for the components as I step through the prioritized list. For more detailed features that require step-by-step instructions in order to conclude pass/fail, I write test cases and link to those from the larger user story for that component. I try to always include screenshots or video and a quick reference to quirky bugs to look for or a quick link to the current bugs for that section.

Once I have a test set, I look for gaps in coverage by checking the bugs again and reviewing the application (again). So much of what testers do is cyclical! This is also where I go down the list of different types of testing and see how we are covered: security, compatibility, integration, exploratory, regression, performance, load, and so on.

After I have this foundation, I usually just maintain it by keeping it up to date: updating any changes to the tests, adding new documentation for new features, and updating screenshots/video for components that change over time. It's good to watch which bugs make it to production after this because that can also inform where there may be gaps in test coverage.

HGTS: How does the user fit into what you do as a TE?

Lindsay: I try to make myself a user, so users fit in at a very basic level for me. I don't think it's possible to really test an application effectively unless you can somehow place yourself in the perspective of the user. That's why testing can be so much more than checking if a build works; it can be feedback on intuitiveness of the application, industry standards, and just what the right thing to do is, in general.

HGTS: How do developers generally view your work? How do you deal with them if they don't see testing as valuable?

Lindsay: Developers typically underestimate my work until they have worked with me for a couple of months. Once I have completed all the work I just explained, I schedule a meeting with the team and I present the testing process that I have set up. This face-to-face is really important and a chance for me to describe to the developers just how seriously I am taking their application. It results in a lot of questions and give-and-take. I get good feedback, and they know they are in good hands.

After I present the entire process and the changes, updates, and improvements I have made, any question on the value I bring usually flies out the window.

Another thing that might seem a little counterintuitive but also contributes to the developers valuing my work more is when I openly and transparently state the components or areas I will *not* own for testing and communicate justifications for why they should own those. A lot of testers avoid advertising or calling attention to the things they won't be testing for fear of appearing less valuable, but in my experience, it has the opposite effect. Developers respect you for it.

HGTS: Tell us a little about your testing of Google Sites. How did you approach the project? What documents did you produce and what format were they in? How did you communicate your findings and results to developers?

Lindsay: Testing on Sites has been a great challenge because the product is used by such a large number of people, it was an acquired company, and it has been around Google much longer than a lot of other projects.

I ramped up with Sites by using the product, creating sites myself, and just trying to get to know the product in general. I reached out to people who I knew used it a lot. For example, my condo association moved our community website to Google Sites a few months earlier, so I spoke to the board members about that process to find out how it worked for them. Design documents or specification documents aren't really kept up to date on this team, so I had to just start breaking down the product into digestible pieces and documenting components and subcomponents one by one.

The fact that it is an acquisition does play into how it is coded. Google does things differently and the fact that it was outside what I was used to slowed me down a little. The code wasn't where I expected it to be. It was structured differently than I was used to. Also, start-ups aren't known for writing a lot of tests—unit, end-to-end, or automation—so the JotSpot-turned-Google-Sites project has had to bolt that on as they go along and in some places, different styles and approaches were used than others. But this is stuff you learn to deal with as a tester.

With the project having existed so long, this made navigating the bug repository that much more difficult because there were years of bugs. This wouldn't have been so bad if the repository had a good bug structure, but they hadn't really built out detailed subcomponents to help categorize issues, so it took a long time to migrate bugs into a detailed component structure.

I put together a centralized site (using Google Sites of course!) to bring all of the documentation for testing Sites to one place: user stories, testing environment info, test team info, testing per release tracking, and so on. I used a spreadsheet (nothing too fancy) to list all of the components and subcomponents to test in prioritized order as a quick way to organize the testing per release.

As I wrapped up all of my testing overhaul work, I did a presentation for the dev team in order to give them a complete view of the testing process. That presentation really helped a lot for the dev team to understand the scope of testing and the challenges. I certainly felt more appreciated for my effort afterwards!

HGTS: Can you describe a great bug you found and how you found it?

Lindsay: "Dates" testing has always proved entertaining for me in applications with date fields. I like to test for future dates and dates that are far in the past, and I usually catch some pretty strange error behavior or even some pretty fun calculation errors that come out of that. One bug that comes to mind was one where future dates in a date of birth field would result in age calculations that were pretty out of whack. Sue me, I think bugs are funny!

HGTS: How do you determine your impact?

Lindsay: Bugs that make it out to customers are an important measure for me to monitor the impact I am bringing to a team. I like that number to be around 0, roughly! Also, I really take to heart what the buzz is about my project. If my project has a reputation for bugs or a crappy UI, say, in user forums (watch user forums closely!), I take that as signal for me to improve the level of impact I have on a project. A project can also suffer from bug debt, old bugs that never get fixed, so I also measure my impact by how many old bugs exist that still affect users today. I make an effort to escalate these and use the time a bug has existed as part of the justification for upping its priority.

HGTS: How do you know when you are done testing?

Lindsay: It's hard to say. For testing per release, I am usually gated more by the release date than when I would consider testing complete. Also, with the introduction of new browser versions and new devices to access your web app with—even for a web application with no active development—there is still very much a reason to test. I think the gating point for determining when you can stop testing is when you can feel confident that if any bugs do remain, they are in components (or features or browsers or devices) that have a relatively low usage and thus a low impact on users if they are broken in some way. This is where prioritizing the functionality and supported environments for the application really comes into play.

HGTS: How do you get bugs fixed?

Lindsay: Being an advocate for bug resolution is an important facet of my work. I am constantly battling against feature development versus developer time for bug fixes. So I am sure to make user feedback my ally when I am justifying a bug fix. The more user complaints I can find about a bug that might not otherwise be fixed, the more I can prove that the developer's time is not wasted by fixing the issue instead of starting on that new feature. At Google, we have customer service reps for enterprise products like Sites, so I also make sure to be closely aligned and in contact with these groups so that I can stay in touch with what the reoccurring issues are that they hear about from our customers.

HGTS: If you could waive a magic wand and fix one aspect of your job, what would it be?

Lindsay: Wow, the "one aspect" can't be "everything" can it? Okay. If I could fix anything, I would have basic, dummy test cases or user scenarios that did not need to be documented: Every tester would automatically know them somehow. CRUD operations apply to everything, so detailing them for every feature becomes cumbersome. I think moving to higher-level user stories instead of using a prescribed test case model has really helped me to be less impacted by this, but I would still appreciate this problem being gone all together.

HGTS: How does your work impact the decision to release a product?

Lindsay: I justify that a feature or release can't go further by putting it in terms of impact on the user. Thankfully, my teams usually agree. I don't block a release unless there is something pretty serious. So it's important for me to maintain that trust with my team that if I feel strongly enough about blocking it, then they probably don't want it out there either.

HGTS: What do you like best and worst about your role?

Lindsay: I really like the flexibility that having a skill set like this affords me. I am technical but user-facing. What project wouldn't want someone like me? I can bring value to so many different types of projects. I think launching a product or new feature can also be a little scary for teams, so the fact that I can bring calm and confidence to that with my feedback really makes me feel like a positive, helpful force.

HGTS: What is different about testing at Google versus other companies?

Lindsay: The independence. I have a lot of freedom in choosing the projects that I work on fulltime, and also on a 20 percent basis. The 20 percent time is a concept at Google where we can spend one day a week, or 20 percent of my time in general, working on a project of my choice. This has allowed me to broaden my skill set by working on different types of projects, as well as inspired me and kept me enthusiastic about work when I might otherwise feel like it's *Groundhog Day*.

HGTS: How do SETs feel about your work?

Lindsay: SETs can miss the importance of someone tracking the bug repository and testing per release until they get that help and see the difference that it makes in their product. Even if they think automation is covering all testing scenarios (yeah right!), there is no one there doing exploratory testing to develop new test cases that break functionality. Also, there is no one tracking all the bugs uncovered by automation over time and lining those up with or against older smaller bugs and user feedback to advocate getting issues resolved. Because I bring these things to the table, the SETs I have worked with usually really appreciate the changes I bring to a project. But there are some that don't respect my work as much, but they, just like developers who might feel like that, are the ones who haven't worked with me or another TE before. Once they do, those attitudes usually change pretty quickly!

HGTS: How do you interact with SETs?

Lindsay: I organize the testing strategy for the whole team, including SETs. Where SETs normally run into an issue of not knowing where to start coding tests or tools, I can show them prioritized documentation of what needs to be tested most and can back that up with bug data as well. I can also give them feedback on how effective their solutions are for preventing bugs with real data. So my interactions tend to be around the organization and feedback that I can bring to an SET's work.

An Interview with YouTube TE Apple Chow

Apple Chow is a TE for Google Offers and before that a test lead for YouTube in Google's San Francisco office. Apple likes new challenges and is constantly looking to leverage the latest tools and techniques for testing.

The authors recently chatted with Apple about her thoughts on testing in YouTube.

HGTS: Apple, what brought you to Google? And with a name like yours, surely you thought about employment elsewhere?

Apple: Ha! apple@apple.com is very tempting! But I came to Google because of the breadth of our product offerings and the opportunity to work with really smart and knowledgeable people. I like to change projects and I love a wide variety of challenges, so Google seemed like the right place for someone like me. I get a chance to make a difference to millions of users across a lot of different product areas. Every day is a new challenge and I never get bored. Of course the free massages are definitely a plus.

HGTS: What did you think of the interview process for TEs and SETs?

Apple: Google focuses on finding generalists who can learn, grow, and tackle a wide variety of problems. This goes for TEs, SETs, and SWEs in my opinion. A lot of places interview for specific roles on a specific team and the people you meet are all going to be people you will work with closely. A Google interview doesn't work that way. The people interviewing you are from a variety of different teams, so you get a lot of different perspectives. All in all, I think it's a process designed to get good people who can work on almost any team at Google. This is important, too, because it's easy to move around within Google so you can always choose a new product area to work in, a new team to work with. Being a generalist is important in this kind of a structure.

HGTS: You have worked at many other tech companies. What would you say was the most surprising thing about software testing at Google?

Apple: A lot of things are different. Perhaps I am biased because I like Google so much, but I would say that our TEs and SETs are more technical than at most other companies. At other large companies I worked for, we had specialized automation teams and then a bunch of manual testers. SETs at Google have to write code; it's their job. It's also rare to find a TE who can't code here. These coding skills allow us to be more impactful early on when unit testing is far more prevalent and there's nothing really to test end-to-end. I think our technical skills are what make us so impactful here at Google.

Another thing that makes Google unique with respect to test is the sheer volume of automation. Most of this automation executes before manual testers even get hold of the product. When they do, the code they get to test is generally of very high initial quality.

Tooling is another difference. In general, we don't use commercial tools. We have a culture where tooling is greatly appreciated and 20 percent time makes it so that anyone can make time to contribute to the internal Google toolset. Tools help us get past the hard and repetitive parts of testing and focus our manual efforts to really impact things where a human is actually required.

Then, of course, there is the developer-owns-quality and test-centric SWE culture we have here that makes it easy to relate to SWEs. We're all in the quality game together and because any engineer can test any code from any machine, it makes us nimble.

HGTS: What things would you say are pretty much the same about testing at Google?

Apple: Software functionality that is hard to automate is just as hard to test or get right as at any other company. When there is a huge rush to get features out, we end up with code that isn't as well tested as we'd like it to be. No company is perfect and no company creates perfect products.

HGTS: When you were a TE for YouTube, what feature areas were you responsible for?

Apple: I've worked with many teams and helped launch many features at YouTube. Some notable mentions would be the launch of the new Watch page that is a complete redesign of the YouTube video page, one of the most viewed pages on the Internet I am happy to say! Another memorable project is our partnership with Vevo. It is a new destination site for premium music content with YouTube powering the video hosting and streaming. It's a joint venture with Sony Music Entertainment and Universal Music Group. On day one of the launch, more than 14,000 videos went live, and they averaged 14 M views on VEVO premium videos on YouTube.com for the next three months, following the December 8, 2009 launch. I also coordinated test efforts for the major rewrite of the YouTube Flash-based video player during our move from ActionScript 2 to ActionScript 3, and the launch of the new Channel and Branded Partner pages.

HGTS: So what does it mean to be a lead in testing at Google?

Apple: The lead role is a coordination role across the product, across the team, and across any product that our work might impact. For example, for the Vevo project, we had to worry about the YouTube player, the branded watch component, channel hierarchy, traffic assignment, ingestion, reporting, and so on. It's definitely a "forest and not trees" mindset.

HGTS: How have you adapted the concepts of exploratory testing to YouTube?

Apple: With a product that is so human-oriented and visual as YouTube, exploratory testing is crucial. We do as much exploratory testing as we can.

HGTS: How did the YouTube testers take to the idea of exploratory testing?

Apple: Oh, it was a huge morale booster. Testers like to test and they like to find bugs. Exploratory testing increased the level of engagement and interest among the testers. They got to put themselves in the mindset of the person in the tour and, with those specific angles, got creative with the types of tests they conducted to break the software. This made it more fun and rewarding as adding more tests revealed interesting and esoteric bugs that would have otherwise been missed or discovered through more mundane and repetitive processes.

HGTS: You mentioned tours. Did James make you use his book?

Apple: When James first came to Google, that book was new and he did a couple of seminars and met with us a few times. But he's up in Seattle and we're in California, so we didn't get much hand holding. We took the tours in the book and ran with them. Some of them worked, some didn't, and we soon figured out which ones were the best for our product.

HGTS: Which ones worked? Care to name them?

Apple: The "money tour" (focus on money-related features; for YouTube, this means Ads or partner-related features) obviously got a lot of attention and was important for every release. The "landmark tour" (focus on important functionalities and features of the system) and the "bad neighborhood tour" (focus on previously buggy areas and areas that we find to be buggy based on recent bugs reported) have been most effective in uncovering our most severe bugs. It was a great learning experience for each one to look at the bugs others in the team had filed and discussing the strategy in finding them. The concept of tours was really helpful for us to explain and share our exploratory testing strategy. We also had a lot of fun joking about some of the tours such as "antisocial tour" (entering least likely input every chance you get), "obsessive compulsive tour" (repeating the same action), and the "couch potato tour" (provide the minimum inputs possible and accepting default values when you can). It was not only helpful to guide our testing; it built some team unity.

HGTS: We understand you are driving a lot of Selenium testing of YouTube. What are your favorite and least favorite things about writing automation in Selenium?

Apple: Favorite: Easy API, you can write test code in your favorite programming languages such as Python, Java, and Ruby, and you can invoke JavaScript code from your application directly—awesome feature and very useful.

Least favorite: It's still browser testing. It's slow, you need hooks in the API, and tests are pretty remote from the thing being tested. It helps product quality where you're automating scenarios that are extremely difficult for a human to validate (calls to our advertising system backend, for example). We have tests that launch different videos and intercept the Ad calls using Banana Proxy (an inhouse web application security audit tool to log HTTP requests and responses). At a conceptual level, we're routing browser requests from browser to Banana Proxy (logging) to Selenium to Web. Thus, we can check if the outgoing requests include the correct URL parameters and if the incoming response contains what is expected. Overall, UI tests are slow, much more brittle, and have a fairly high maintenance overhead. A lesson learned is that you should keep only a few such high-level smoke tests for validating end-to-end integration scenarios and write as small a test as possible.

HGTS: A large portion of YouTube content and its UI is in Flash; how do you test that? Do you have some magic way of testing this via Selenium?

Apple: No magic, unfortunately. Lots of hard work here. There are some things Selenium does to help and because our JavaScript APIs are exposed, Selenium can be used to test them. And there is the image "diffing" tool pdiff that is helpful to test the rendering of the thumbnails, end of screen, and so on. We also do a lot of proxy work on the HTTP stream to listen to traffic so we know more about changes to the page. We also use As3Unit and FlexUnit to load the player, play different videos, and trigger player events. For verification, we can use these frameworks to validate various states of the software and to do image comparison. I'd like to say it's magic, but there is a lot of code we've written to get to this point.

HGTS: What was the biggest bug you or your team has found and saved users from seeing?

Apple: The biggest bugs are usually not that interesting. However, I recall we had a CSS bug that causes the IE browser to crash. Before that we had never seen CSS crash a browser.

One memorable bug that was more subtle came up during the new Watch Page launch in 2010. We found that when the user moves the mouse pointer outside of the player region, in IE7, the player would freeze after some time. This was interesting because users would encounter this bug if they were watching the same video for an extended period of time and moving the mouse around. Everything got slower until the player finally froze. This turned out to be due to unreleased event handlers and resources sticking around and computing the same things over and over again. If you were watching shorter videos or being a passive viewer, you wouldn't observe the bug.

HGTS: What would you call the most successful aspect of YouTube testing? The least successful?

Apple: The most successful was a tool to fetch and check some problematic URLs. Although it was a simple test, it was really effective in catching critical bugs quickly. We added a feature to make the problems easier to debug by having it provide stack traces that the engineers could then use to track down problems and develop fixes. It quickly became our first line of testing defense during deployment and brought along considerable savings in testing time. With only a little extra effort, we extended it to hit the most popular URLs from our logs plus a list of hand-picked ones. It's been very successful.

The least successful is probably our continued reliance on manual testing during our weekly pushes. Given that we have a very small time window for testing (code goes out live the same day it's frozen) and we have a lot of UI changes that are hard to automate, manual testing is critical in our weekly release process. This is a hard problem and I wish we had a better answer.

HGTS: YouTube is a very data-driven site as much of the content is algorithmically determined; how do you verify that the right videos are displayed the right time and place? Does your team verify the video quality? If so, how do you do this?

Apple: We measure how much and which videos are being watched, their relationship to each other and a whole lot of other variables. We analyze the number of buffer under-runs and cache misses, and we optimize our global-serving infrastructure based on that.

We have unit tests for video quality levels to make sure the right quality is used. After I changed groups, our new team wrote a tool to test this in more depth. The tool is open-sourced[29] and it works by having FlexUnit tests that use the embedded YouTube player to play a variety of test videos and make some assertions about the player state and properties. These test videos have large bar codes on them to mark frames and the timeline that are easily recognizable despite compression artifacts and loss of quality. Measuring state also includes taking snapshots of the video frames and analyzing them. We check for the correct aspect ratio and/or cropping, distortion, color shifts, blank frames, white screens, synchronization, and soon—issues found from our bug reports.

HGTS: What advice do you have for other testers of Web, Flash, and data-driven web services out there?

Apple: Whether it's a test framework or test cases, keep it simple and iterate on the design as your project evolves. Don't try to solve everything upfront. Be aggressive about throwing things away. If tests or automation are too hard to maintain, toss them and build some better ones that are more resilient. Watch out for maintenance and troubleshooting costs of your tests down the road Observe the 70-20-10 rule: 70 percent small unit tests that verify the behavior of a single class or function, 20 percent medium tests that validate the integration of one or more application modules, and 10 percent large tests (commonly referred to as "system tests" and "end-to-end" tests) that operate on a high level and verify the application as a whole is working.

Other than that, prioritize and look for simple automation efforts with big pay-offs, always remembering that automation doesn't solve all your problems, especially when it comes to frontend projects and device testing. You always want smart, exploratory testing and to track test data.

HGTS: So tell us the truth. YouTube testing must be a blast. Watching cat videos all day …

Apple: Well, there was that one April Fool's day where we made all the video captions upside down. But I won't lie. Testing YouTube is fun. I get to discover a lot of interesting content *and* it's my job to do so! And even after all this time, I still laugh at cat videos!

---

[29] You can find the AS3 player helper source code at http://code.google.com/p/youtube-as3-player-helper/source/checkout.

CHAPTER 4
The Test Engineering Manager

As test engineers (TEs) and software engineers in test (SETs) labor to support the user and developer, respectively, there is one role that ties them together, the test engineering manager (TEM). The TEM is an engineering colleague taking on important work as an individual contributor and a single point of contact through which all the support teams (development, product management, release engineers, document writers, and so on) liaise. The TEM is probably the most challenging position in all of Google, requiring the skills of both the TE and SET. He also needs management skills to support direct reports in career development.

The Life of a TEM

The cadence of a Google testing project doesn't just happen with every TE and SET doing his job as we've described in this book. The TEM has a leadership and coordination role of the TEs and SETs who report to him. In general, TEMs report to the director of test who may have many such reports.[1] Test directors all report to Patrick Copeland.

The technical, leadership, and coordination roles of the TEM are generally something that Googlers grow into, and most of the TEMs at Google come from its own ranks as opposed to outside hires. External people are generally (but not always) hired into individual contributor roles. Even James Whittaker, who was hired as a director, didn't get any direct reports for almost three months.

Among current TEMs, well over half came from the TE ranks, which isn't surprising given the broad focus of that role. TEs manage projects and keep a projectwide focus, so it is a smaller step into managing the people

---

[1] At the time of this writing, Google employs six directors of test, each of whom has only a handful of TEMs reporting to them. Individual contributors generally report to a TEM, but senior engineers and technical leads often report to their director. It's a flat structure meant to focus on working together and not heavy on the management side of the equations. Most, if not all, directors at Google also slice off time to perform as an individual contributor.

who work on a project. TEs understand a broad swath of the functional space of their application and come into contact with far more of the engineers working on it than the average SET. However, there is no correlation between success as a TEM and success in either the TE or SET role. At Google, success is a collective issue and we work hard to choose the right managers and we work hard to ensure they are successful.

The first advice toward this end is *know your product*. Given any question about how to use the product, the TEM should be an expert. If you are the TEM for Chrome, I should be able to ask you how to install an extension, change the browser's skin, set up a sync relationship, modify proxy settings, view the DOM, find where cookies are stored, find out how and when it gets updated to a new version, and so on. These answers should come so quickly to a TEM's lips that whatever thought it took to retrieve them from memory is instantaneous. From the UI to the guts of the backend data center implementation, a TEM should know his product cold.

I recall asking the Gmail TEM once why my mail was loading slowly and got an explanation about how the Gmail server parts work and about how a problem in a remote data center happened that weekend. It was way more detailed than I wanted. But it was clear the guy knew how Gmail worked and he was up to date with the latest field information that affected its performance. This is what we expect from all our TEMs at Google: product expertise beyond everyone else associated with the project.

A related second piece of advice is to *know your people*. As a manager, a Google TEM is a product expert and understands the work that needs to get done but plays only a small role in actually performing that work. It's the SETs and TEs who make up the TEM's report structure that gets the work done. Knowing these people and their skills as individuals is crucial in making sure this work gets done quickly and efficiently.

Googlers might be smart, but they are not plentiful. Every TEM we've ever hired from outside of Google makes the comment that their project is understaffed. Our response is a collective smile. We know and we're not going to fix it. It's through knowing your people and their skills well that a TEM can take a small team and make them perform like a larger team.

Scarcity of resources brings clarity to execution and it creates a strong sense of ownership by those on a project. Imagine raising a child with a large staff of help: one person for feeding, one for diapering, one for entertainment, and so on. None of these people is as vested in the child's life as a single, overworked parent. It is the scarcity of the parenting resource that brings clarity and efficiency to the process of raising children. When resources are scarce, you are forced to optimize. You are quick to see process inefficiencies and not repeat them. You create a feeding schedule and stick to it. You place the various diapering implements in close proximity to streamline steps in the process.

It's the same concept for software-testing projects at Google. Because you can't simply throw people at a problem, the tool chain gets streamlined. Automation that serves no real purpose gets deprecated. Tests that find no regressions aren't written. Developers who demand certain types of activity from testers have to participate in it. There are no make-work tasks. There is no busy work in an attempt to add value where you are not needed.

It is the job of the TEM to optimize this equation. If a TEM knows his product well enough, then he can identify the work that is the highest priority and the parts that get appropriate coverage. If a TEM knows her people well enough, then she is able to apply the right skill sets to the parts of the testing problem that need it the most. Obviously, there will be parts that don't get done. If a TEM is doing her job right, those will be the parts that are the lowest priority or are straightforward enough that they can be contracted out or left to crowd source and dogfood testers.

Obviously, a TEM can be wrong about any of these things and because the role is so crucial, such mistakes can be costly. Fortunately, the community of TEMs is a fairly close-knit set of people who know each other well (another benefit of scarcity is small enough numbers of people so that knowing each other on a first name basis and meeting regularly are actually possible) and share experiences that improve the collective.

Getting Projects and People

Project mobility is a hallmark of being a Google engineer. A general rule of thumb is that a Googler is free to change projects every 18 months, give or take a quarter. Of course there is no mandate to do so. If an engineer loves mobile operating systems, putting her on You Tube is unwise. Mobility enables engineers to sample various projects. Many choose to stay on a project for years or for their entire careers, whereas others revel in getting to know a little about everything Google does.

There are a number of benefits in this culture that a TEM can take advantage of. Namely, that there is a good supply of broadly experienced Googlers available for recruiting at any given time. Imagine being a TEM for Google Maps and being able to draw from the Chrome and Google Docs talent pool! There is a wealth of engineers with relevant experience and a fresh perspective to add to your team at any given time.

Of course the downside of this is losing an experienced Googler to another team. It puts the requirement on the TEM to avoid creating dependencies on people. A TEM cannot afford to simply take advantage of a rock star tester. Whatever it is that makes that tester a rock star needs to be embodied in a tool or packaged in a way to be used to turn other testers onto a path of similar superstardom.

TEMs manage a process at Google that we call *allocation*. Allocation is supported by a web app that any TEM can post job openings to and any TE or SET can browse for new opportunities. There are no formal permissions from either a current or future manager that must be obtained before doing so and any engineer with an 18-month longevity on a project is free to leave. Obviously, there are agreements about how fast such a transition occurs so as to not adversely affect a ship date or crucial project milestone, but we've never seen any controversy associated with a re-allocation in our experience.[2]

Nooglers are also allocated with the same web app and process. TEMs can view the resume and interview scores of a Noogler and place a "bid" on the allocation. In heavy hiring seasons, there are generally multiple candidates to be allocated to multiple projects. Competing bids are the norm, and TEMs get to argue their case during an allocation meeting attended by a quorum of test directors who vote with Patrick Copeland or someone he designates breaking a tie. The priorities for allocation are, in general:

- A good skill set match between the Noogler and the project. We want to set the employee up for success.

- The Noogler's wishes. If we can give someone her dream job, she is liable to be a far happier and more productive engineer.

- Project needs. Projects of strategic or economic importance are sometimes given priority.

- Past allocations. If a project hasn't had any new allocations recently, then they might be due.

Allocation is not something to fret over too much. If a TEM doesn't get a Noogler one week, he's liable to the next. On the other hand, there isn't a lot of downside to the Noogler if he is misallocated because transfers are easy.

Getting new projects is also something a TEM must consider. As a TEM's experience and reputation grows, that person can be groomed for a directorship by being given multiple large efforts to manage and have not only individual engineers as reports but also more junior TEMs.

Such recruitment is often done by the development organization that schedules a meeting with a reputable TEM and pitches their project in the hopes the TEM will sign on to build up a test team for them. Of course, as the uber Director, Patrick Copeland has the charter to simply assign such work on projects that are deemed strategically important by executives.

The general rule in the case where a TEM can choose to take a project is simply to avoid toxic projects. Teams that are unwilling to be equal partners in quality should be left on their own to do their own testing. Teams unwilling to commit to writing small tests and getting good unit-level coverage should be left to dig their graves in peace.

Projects that seem like pet projects—that is, those that have a poor chance of success or are simple enough that the developers can act as their

---

[2] The concept of 20%, explained earlier, can help here. A common transition by an engineer from project A to project B is for that engineer to take a 20% on the new project B for a quarter and then flip the ratio to 80% on project B and 20% on their old project A for the next quarter.

own testers—must be left alone. There is no good reason from Google's perspective, our users' perspectives, or the career of the TEM in question to staff such projects.

Impact

Perhaps the one thing that sets Google apart from other software development companies is the insistence on impact. At Google, you hear the word *impact* all the time. An engineer is expected to make an impact on the team and his work should be impactful for the product. A test team as a whole is expected to be impactful. The collective work of the team should stand out and the team and product should be better off for it.

The goal for any individual engineer should be to create impact. The goal of a test team should be to create impact. The person responsible for ensuring that a test team is impactful is the TEM.

Promotion decisions revolve around the impact an employee has had on a project. During annual reviews, managers are encouraged to describe their direct reports' contribution in terms of their overall impact. As engineers progress through the higher levels of their careers, the expectation is that their impact will grow. Because TEMs manage these engineers, they are responsible for their growth and that means ensuring that they can measure their impact.

Managing impact for a team of TEs and SETs is the job of the TEM.

It's important to note that we are tasking a test team only with impact. We are specifically not asking the TEM and her team to ensure that the product is high quality. We are not asking the TEM and her team to make the product ship on time. We are not going to blame testing if the product is unsuccessful or unloved by users. At Google, no one team is responsible for these things. However, each team is responsible for understanding the project's goals and schedule and ensuring members do their part to impact all of these things positively. There is no greater compliment at Google than to be called an impactful engineer or, in the case of a TEM, to be known as someone who builds impactful teams.

Impact is a major topic during annual reviews and in promotion decisions. Junior engineers are expected to to their part of the product, more senior engineers are expected to show impact teamwide and product-wide show impact, and to get to the higher levels of the job ladder, it is important to have impact across Google (more about that later).

It is the job of the TEM to build a team capable of such impact and to ensure that every engineer is creating impact appropriate to his or her job level and skill set. Google managers are not meant to micromanage every aspect of the testing process. They are not present during every moment as an ACC is built. They are not going to review every line of code in the test infrastructure. They are going to ensure that each of these artifacts is in the hands of capable engineers who understand how to build them, that they are being used correctly, and that the development team understands their purpose and takes their results seriously. A TEM builds his team and assigns the work as he sees fit, then steps back and lets those engineers do their jobs. When the work starts, it's the job of the TEM to ensure that it is impactful.

Imagine a test team where every engineer is capable of doing impactful work. Imagine a testing process that has been streamlined to the point where every unit of work performed is purposeful and impactful. Imagine a development team that understands this body of testing work and participates in seeing it through. The job of the TEM is simply to take this imaginary world and make it real.

There is one final job of a TEM that deals with cross-team collaboration. A good TEM, especially an experienced one, is not so insular that he cannot see beyond the boundaries of his own product. Google is a company of some dozens of products all undergoing simultaneous development, testing, and use. Each of these products has one or more TEMs (depending on their size and complexity) and each tries hard to ensure its teams are impactful. As a collective, TEMs must be diligent about identifying the best practices happening in their organizations and be aggressive about communicating those practices to their peers. There is no truer way to show that a practice or tool is impactful than to see it applied successfully to multiple products.

Google is known as an innovative company and test teams at Google certainly bear that out. The number of test practices and tools that have been created and used inside Google (and many of them shipped to the outside world) shows that it is this innovative spirit that helps tie our testing teams together. TEMs don't collaborate because of some corporate mandate. They don't collaborate simply because there is a monthly meeting on their calendar. They collaborate because they don't want to miss out on the chance to adopt some awesome innovation that has emerged from another team. Who wants to be the only tester not using some impactful new tool? Who wouldn't want to work smarter?

Of course, the same can be said of the exporter of innovation. As good as it feels to have some innovation on your team work for your product, it feels even better to see another team adopt it and then another until eventually the innovation becomes part of the testing fabric of the entire company. Cross-team collaboration must be built on innovation or it will not stand the test of time.

An Interview with Gmail TEM Ankit Mehta

Ankit Mehta is a TEM who rose through the ranks as a TE doing mostly SET-oriented work. He spent his early years knee deep in code and test automation and his first big assignment as a manager was none other than Gmail.

Gmail is not an assignment for the weak at heart. It is a big product with lots of moving parts. It has integration with other Google properties including Buzz, Docs, Calendar, and so on. It also has to interoperate with mail formats from any number of well-established competitors. There is a large backend data center component; remember that Gmail is completely in the cloud and a UI served through any of the major web browsers. As if any additional complexity were necessary, Gmail has an installed base of many hundreds of millions of users who expect it to work when they fire up their browser. They expect fast, reliable, and secure service without a great deal of spam to deal with. Adding new features requires respecting the legacy and this complicates testing a great deal. When Gmail fails, the world learns of it quickly. That is a lot of egg to go on a lot of Googlers' faces and none are quite so culpable as the primary, in-the-trench test manager.

The authors sat down with Ankit to get the scoop on how Gmail is tested.

HGTS: Tell us how you approach a new testing project. What are the first tasks you perform and the first questions you ask?

Ankit: When I join a project, the first few weeks are spent listening and not talking. It's crucial to get an understanding of what's going on and to learn the architecture of the product and the dynamics of the team. I won't work with a doctor who simply prescribes me antibiotics in the first five minutes of an office visit and I don't expect a test team to work with me if I just go in with solutions straightaway. You really have to learn before you are in a position to prescribe.

HGTS: We've worked together before and don't take you for the quiet type so I imagine that once you start talking you have a lot to say!

Ankit: Oh yeah! But there is a pattern to it. Over the years, I have learned that the most powerful question you can ask is, "Why?" and that's pretty much where I go from the listening phase. Why are you running these tests? Why did you write that specific test? Why did you choose to automate this task over this other one? Why are we investing in this tool?

I think people get set in their ways and do things just because they saw someone else doing them or they test a particular feature for no other reasons than that they know how. If you don't ask them why, they won't bother questioning themselves because what they are doing has simply become a habit.

HGTS: So what answers to why do you accept as good ones?

Ankit: Two answers: 1) that it helps improve the quality of the product or 2) that it helps improve the productivity of the engineers building the product. Anything else just isn't as high a priority.

HGTS: The Gmail team is known for its focus and productivity so I guess that's where it comes from. But beyond limiting their focus to quality and productivity, what other advice do you have for test managers to build a robust work culture?

Ankit: Well, team dynamics are crucial. I sincerely believe the quality of a product is tied to the quality of the testing team. You have to have people with the right skills and the right attitude and you have to get these people doing the right things. This is especially critical for the senior people on the team as so much of the culture and momentum comes from these people. For Gmail, it took me three to six months to build the team I actually wanted, a team that was cohesive and understood each other's role. Once you get a good team, it's resistant to one or two personalities who don't quite fit.

An important part of this team dynamic is the relationship between the dev and test teams. This was not so good when I joined; the teams operated as completely separate and the value proposition of the test team was pretty much lost on the dev team. It wasn't healthy.

HGTS: Let's talk about this because it's clearly something you solved. Can you walk us through what you did to fix this culture issue?

Ankit: When I first joined Gmail, the test team was fixated on a bunch of WebDriver tests that ran with each build. They'd watch the tests run and change from green (passed) to red (failed) and made this herculean effort to fix the tests so they all ran green. The development team really didn't question this behavior too much because the tests usually found a few important problems that justified their existence. But there were weeks when a lot of code changed and the tests couldn't be fixed fast enough. The whole process was flaky and not resilient to changes to Gmail. It was an overinvestment in something that was too much work for its ultimate impact.

Because I was new to the project, I could see things that perhaps the others couldn't and it seemed to me that latency was the biggest issue for Gmail. Seriously, the primary attribute of Gmail from a customer's point of view is its speed. I figured that if we could solve this problem for the SWE team, it would earn us enough respect that we could begin to establish ourselves as equals.

It was a hard problem. We had to measure Gmail's speed across old and new versions and notice when a new build got slower. Then we'd have to sift through all the code changes in the new version to figure out which one caused the latency and then drive a fix. It was painful and time-consuming and lots of trial and error.

I worked with one of the SETs on the team to figure out a way to slow down Gmail so we could better observe and control the communication between the frontend and the data center and find regressions that affected performance. We ended up collecting a bunch of old machines from anywhere we could get them and stripping out any high-end components until we were left with a roomful of boxes with 512MB of RAM, 40-GB disks, and low-speed CPUs. We slowed Gmail down enough that we could distinguish the signal from the noise and then started long-running tests that would further stress the system. The first couple of months were tough. We had few results and some false positives. We were busy setting up the infrastructure and not producing any impact. But then the regressions started rolling in. We were able to measure the regressions on the order of milliseconds and back it up with data. SWEs were able to find latency regression in hours instead of weeks and debug them while they were still fresh as opposed to weeks later. This earned immense respect for the test team and when we embarked on the next couple of high-priority tasks (fixing end-to-end tests and getting an effective load test infrastructure running), the SWEs actually volunteered to help. The whole team saw the value of effective tests, and Gmail releases went from quarterly to weekly and then to daily releases for a subset of our production customers.

HGTS: So that's the lesson: Pick something hard and solve it to get respect. I like it. But then how do you follow up after that?

Ankit: Well, there are always hard problems to solve! But yeah, the general idea is to keep the focus on what is important. We identified the top Gmail problem and we came together and solved it. Then we went down the list and once we came together as a team, nothing was too hard. But I am a big believer in keeping things focused. Whenever I see a team trying to do too much, say working on five things and doing only 80 percent of all five, I have them step back and prioritize. Drop the number of things you are doing to two or three and nail those 100 percent. This gives the team a sense of accomplishment without unfinished work hanging over their heads and if all this works ends up impacting the quality of the product, then I can feel pretty good about it, too.

HGTS: Google managers have a notoriously high number of direct reports and are still expected to contribute technically. How do you balance this? Can you tell us about your own engineer work?

Ankit: All those directs and all that time spent coordinating others' work makes for a lot of distractions. There are really two things I have done to stay technical and contribute at the level of an engineer.

First, as I brought the SWE and SET teams together, there was always enough work to go around that I could save a chunk for myself. I was actively involved in the design phase of my vision and stayed with the project long enough to write tests myself.

Second, and really this is the crucial part, if you are going to do technical work, you have to get away from the management distractions. At first, I took a couple of days a week to work on things myself. One of my projects was to integrate Google Feedback into Gmail and this gave me a great SWE perspective on testing. Whenever I ran into a flaky test or some part of the test infrastructure that slowed me down, I understood how the full-time SWEs viewed our work. But still, whenever I was in Mountain View, people would manage to find me so I took to visiting the Gmail team in Zurich. There is a lot of peace and quiet to be found nine time zones away and as I was no one's manager there, I could blend into the engineering team without a lot of notice. I got a lot of work done in Zurich!

HGTS: Do you have any advice on staffing a testing project? What's a good developer to test ratio? What about SET versus TE?

Ankit: Well, on hiring, it's easy. Never compromise. Hiring the wrong person just to get a headcount is always worse than waiting for a better fit. Hire only the best. Period. Google doesn't release ratio numbers, but early on we were more densely populated with testers and had more than the norm. But after we solved a lot of the initial problems and got the SWE participation up, we fell back to numbers around the Google standard. In terms of the mix of skills, what worked for Gmail was about 20 percent of the testers doing exploratory testing. Any product where user experience is important must undergo exploratory testing. Another 30 percent were TEs who focused more holistically on the product and worked with the SETs to ensure maximum impact of their work, and 50 percent were SETs working on adding relevant automation and tools that would keep the codebase healthy and improve developer productivity. I can't say that will be the formula I'll use on my next Google assignment, but it worked in Gmail.

HGTS: We understand you've taken the reins for testing Google+. What are the lessons from Gmail that you're finding are the most valuable for your new product?

Ankit: Well first, don't put all your energy into the frontend. Gmail has what might be the largest distributed backend out there and there are some juicy testing problems I didn't get to. Other than that, there are a lot of lessons:

- Write tests in the same language the application is written in.

- Make sure the person writing the feature is the person responsible for ensuring the tests for that feature get executed. Tests that get ignored become a liability.

- Focus on infrastructure that makes writing tests seamless. Tests needed to be easier to write than they are to skip.

- 20 percent of the use cases account for 80 percent of the usage (give or take!). Automate the 20 percent and don't bother with the rest. Leave them for the manual test passes.

- This is Google, speed matters. If users expect one thing from us, it's speed. Make sure the product is fast. Profile it so you can prove it to everyone else.

- Collaboration with development is crucial. If you don't have it, you are nothing more than damage control and that is not a good place to be.

- Innovation is part of Google's DNA. The test team has to be seen as innovators, too, seeing important problems and devising innovative solutions.

HGTS: Have you noticed any traps that engineering teams fall into?

Ankit: Yes, assuming we know what users want and rolling out massive changes or new features without pushing them as small experiments first. What good is a bunch of great test infrastructure for a feature that is withdrawn from lack of user interest? Put out a version to a few users and get some feedback before investing in a lot of test automation.

Also, trying to build the perfect solution so that you take too long and the market moves past you. Iterate quickly and show incremental progress.

Finally, you have to find the sweet spot for testing. Write them too early and the architecture changes under you negating all your work. Wait too long and you might delay a launch for lack of proper testing. TDD is the way to go.

HGTS: And what about individuals? Have you noticed any traps that young TEs or SETs fall into on new projects?

Ankit: Yes, they get in over their head. They write lots of tests without really thinking about their full purpose or how they fit into the overall testing process. By writing them, they often don't realize they signed up to maintain them. SETs need to always remember that testing is the job of the developer and they should concentrate on getting testing into the workflow of the developer. We write tools to support this so that it is the developers who maintain the tests as they maintain the code. SETs can then focus on making the tests run faster and produce better diagnostics.

TEs sometimes fall into the same trap and act like SETs. We want TEs to take a more holistic approach. Get the entire product under control. Focus on tests from a user's perspective and help SETs and SWEs ensure that all tests and test infrastructure is actively and effectively used. Tooling and diagnostics written by TEs should impact the entire product.

HGTS: Besides the latency automation you spoke about earlier, what are some other general testing achievements that paid huge dividends for Gmail?

Ankit: JavaScript automation. We baked in an automation servlet in Gmail itself, which enabled developers to write end-to-end tests in the same language the frontend was written in. Because it used a lot of the same methods and libraries used, developers were familiar with how to write tests. No learning curve. They could easily write tests to see whether their new feature broke Gmail functionality and could also better protect their own features from being broken by any other developer. Every feature of Gmail now comes with at least one test written for this servlet. The nice part of this is that I am using this on my new job in Social. We've already seen some 20k automated tests!

Another is load testing. You simply can't get by without it at Google as all our applications are heavily used and our data centers can be busy places. We basically had to mirror a typical production setup complete with typical user traffic loads. We spent months analyzing production usage to build a representation user model. Next, we reduced variance in the data by running the load test on exactly the kind of data center machines Gmail runs on. We then launched two parallel test runs: test and control. We monitored them to watch for differences. We detected a lot of regressions and narrowed down the issue for developers.

Finally, the focus on bug prevention versus bug detection paid big dividends. We pushed automated tests early in the presubmit process and kept a lot of poor code from the build. This keeps the test team ahead of the curve and working on builds that are high enough quality to present a good challenge for our exploratory testers.

HGTS: So now that you've done this a couple times and are moving into Social, what will you look for in new hires to that test team?

Ankit: I want to find people who don't get overwhelmed with complexity and when faced with a hard problem can translate it into concrete steps that need to be solved. And then, of course, solving them! I need people who can execute and are energized by aggressive timelines rather than overwhelmed by them. I want people who can achieve the right balance between innovation and quality and have ideas beyond simply finding more bugs. And on top of all this, I want to see passion. I want people who really want to be a tester.

HGTS: And that brings us to our last question. What drives your passion for the testing space?

Ankit: I like the challenge of fast iterations and high quality, two seemingly conflicting goals of equal importance. It's a classic struggle and one that drives me to optimize them both without breaking either myself or my team! Building products is easy. Building them fast and of high quality is the grand challenge that makes my professional life challenging and fun.

An Interview with Android TEM Hung Dang

> *Hung Dang is an engineering manager at Google who was hired into his position as a manager with the express purpose to lead the Android test team. Prior to joining Google, he rose through the ranks as an engineer at Apple and Tivo.*
>
> *The strategic importance of Android is hard to overstate. In many ways, it is as big a hit as our Search and Ads business, another one of the Google collection of product home runs. As such, it gets significant executive attention and draws a lot of top-class talent. It's also a codebase that is growing fast and it's nothing for a single build to have hundreds of new code changes in a single day. It's an operating system, a platform, runs thousands upon thousands of apps, and has a thriving developer ecosystem. The number of devices that run Android is increasing quickly and includes phone handsets and tablets from any number of manufacturers. Everything from testing device compatibility, power management, and checking that the apps work falls to Hung and his team.*
>
> *The authors sat down with Hung to get the scoop on how Android is tested.*

HGTS: Tell us about the origins of Android testing. It must have been a lot easier in the early days before handset and app proliferation!

Hung: Unfortunately, that's not really the case. When I took over leadership of Android, the team was new and many of them hadn't tested an operating system much less a mobile device, and task number one was building the team and test infrastructure. I find the earliest days of a testing project the hardest. No matter how complicated and diverse a product might ultimately get, if you have the right team and the right process and infrastructure, then you make it easy. It's before all that happens that you find the hardest work!

HGTS: So let's talk about that because a lot of test managers out there struggle with this project startup and hard work right now. Can you walk us through what you did in the early days of Android?

Hung: Big challenges in those days. The first was really to get our head around the product. One thing I need all my testers to be is product experts. Everyone on my team must know every aspect of the product stack. Period. Once you get that level of knowledge, you understand what the hard testing problems are and you can start building your team around those needs. Hire people (at Google, this means drawing great talent from other teams as well) who understand the hardest problems. Android has such a deep stack from the hardware through the OS, to the framework, to the app model, and to the market. There are a lot of moving parts that demand specialized testing expertise. The first thing I do is figure that out and build a team that can take on those hard problems.

After the team is assembled, I give them simple marching orders: add value! Preferably, add value in a repeatable way. From dev to product management, testing must be seen as an enabler. Anything less and you are in the way. In the early days, adding value meant helping get the product to a successful launch. I am sure we did things back then that were out of scope for testers, but we added value and we shipped a good initial product. We enabled daily builds and got everyone on the team synchronized on the same build. No one was working at cross-purpose and the workflow was organized. Everyone was trained to report, triage, and manage bugs the same way. It really was about the right people doing the right things and working as a team.

HGTS: Okay, this is sounding pretty intense. How did the team handle it?

Hung: Well, I lost a lot of the old team, perhaps as much as 80 percent. But the cool thing is that the people who stayed became the tech leads who provided leadership for the new talent we attracted. Not everyone is fit for every project, and Google is such a big company that if Android isn't the right project, well, there is probably another one that is. Google has turned this bounty of projects into a pretty healthy testing ecosystem.

HGTS: And the positive?

Hung: The positive is definitely the focus on value. Everything we did had to have a purpose. We questioned everything. Every test case, every piece of automation, and much of what we were doing didn't stand this kind of scrutiny. If the automation didn't provide clear value, we abandoned it. Everything was value-driven and the organization was there. If I gave advice to new test managers, that's what I would tell them: Add value in everything you do and make your process for adding value repeatable.

HGTS: This is clearly not easy, even though you make it sound that way! But give us more detail about this organization you talk about. We get the bug-reporting process and workflow, but surely there is more to it here. How do you organize the work itself?

Hung: Well, I like to think about Android in terms of "pillars." I know you called them different things when you tested Chrome OS, but I like the idea of testing pillars and all my testers identify with testing one of the pillars. For Android, we've organized around four pillars: the system pillar (the kernel, media, and so on), the framework pillar, the apps pillar, and the market pillar. Ask any of my testers what they are testing and they will name one of these pillars.

HGTS: That actually makes a lot of sense. I like the way the pillars line up with the skill set of testers. You have some good at the low-level stuff and some at the high-level stuff and the pillars reflect these strengths. Very nice. So what about automation? Where does that fit into your mission?

Hung: I've learned to be skeptical of automation. Testers can get so passionate about some grand vision of automation for a product and spend months creating it only to have the product or platform change and negate everything they did. There is no greater waste of resources than writing automation that doesn't stand the test of time. In my mind, it needs to be written quickly, executed quickly, and solve a very specific problem. If I don't understand the purpose of an automated test immediately, then it is too complicated. Make it simple, contain its scope and above all, make sure it adds value. For example, we have a suite of automated tests to validate a build to see if it is good enough to move from Canary channel to Droid channel.

HGTS: Whoa, whoa, whoa! What's Droid channel?

Hung: Oh, sorry. Like I told you before we started, in Android we do things a bit different! Out channels are not the ones you use in Chrome. We have Canary, Droid-food (think dogfood except with just the Android team), Experimental, Google-food, and Street-food, which is a build we send out externally. It's the same idea as for other teams; we just call them something different.

HGTS: Okay, so you have an automated suite to identify bugs that prevent a Canary build from being qualified into the Dev channel. I get it, small in scope. Do you have dedicated SETs for this automation?

Hung: Not on your life. None of my testers specialize. Specifically, *everyone* does manual testing and I mean everyone. Exploratory testing is the best way of digging into the product and learning it well. The last thing I want is an SET to be a framework writer. I want them to be more involved with the product and know how to use it. Every tester must empathize with the user. They must be expert users and know the ins and outs of the whole product. On my team, we leave things like stability testing, power management, performance, stress, and quick checks on third-party apps to automation. For example, no human is going to find a memory leak in the camera or verify a single feature across multiple platforms—these things require automation. Things that are too repetitive for a manual test or require machine precision that humans aren't good at, that's the place you want to automate.

HGTS: So then are you staffed with more TEs than SETs?

Hung: No, just the opposite. I have about twice as many SETs than TEs. It's just that every SET is expected to act like a TE when necessary and vice versa. I don't pay much attention to titles. It's all about adding value.

HGTS: Okay, then let's talk about manual testing because you clearly take it seriously (and I admire you for that!).

Hung: I am a big believer in focused manual testing. Sitting down hacking away is unproductive. We take a close look at the daily build we'll be testing and analyze what's in it. What has changed? How many CLs have been added or modified? What new or changed functionality are we dealing with? Which developers submitted CLs? How extensive were the changes from yesterday's build? This helps us focus and instead of exploring the entire product *ad hoc*, we are able to focus on the changes from day to day and make ourselves far more productive.

This also means coordination among the team is important. Because I insist that everyone be an exploratory tester, it's important to minimize overlap. We have daily coordination meetings to identify things that are important to test and ensure someone is covering them. Manual testing, to me, is about focus and coordination. Give me those two things and I will be satisfied that the effort spent exploring is worthwhile and valuable.

HGTS: Do you create any documentation for your manual testing or is it all just exploratory?

Hung: It's exploratory *and* we create documentation. There are two cases where we document manual test cases. The first is where we have a general use case that applies to every build or is part of every major test pass. We write these down and put them in GTCM, so they are available to every tester or test vendor to pull out and use. The second case is that we document the testing guidelines on a per-feature basis. Each feature has its own unique properties, and manual testers document these as guidelines for other testers who might pick that feature as a target in some future build. So we have general, system-level use cases and feature-specific guidance that we take the time to document.

HGTS: Tell me about your demands on developers. Do you require specs? Do you make them do TDD? What about unit tests?

Hung: I suppose there is some fairytale world where every line of code is preceded by a test, which is preceded by a specification. Maybe that world exists. I don't know. But in the innovative and fast-paced world I live in, you get what you get. Spec? Great! Thank you very much, I will put it to good use. But being realistic, you have to find a way to work within the system that exists. Demanding a spec won't get you one. Insisting on unit tests won't make those unit tests valuable. Nothing a spec writer or a unit test can do (besides finding an obvious regression bug) will help us find a problem that a real user will encounter. This is my world, a tester's world. You get what you get and you use it to provide value to the product and the team.

In my experience, all engineers have good intentions. None of them want to create a buggy product. But innovation cannot be planned so precisely. Schedules and competitive pressures aren't subject to my whining about quality. I can whine or I can provide value. I choose the latter.

I live in a world where daily CLs number in the many hundreds. Yes, I said *daily*. Brilliant and innovative developers must be met with an equal amount of brilliant and innovative testers. There isn't time for demands or whining, just value.

HGTS: Hung, we are glad you are on our side! Now, a couple of quick answers if you are up for it. Given an extra day to test an Android release, what would you do?

Hung: If I had an extra day, I'd be given an extra build! There is no such thing as an extra day!

HGTS: Touche! Okay, what about regrets? Can you describe a bug that got through in a release channel that caused some user grief?

Hung: Well, first of all, every tester on the planet has experienced that. No software leaves any company without some bugs. It's the nature of the beast. But for me, all of them hurt.

HGTS: Come on, you're not getting off that easy! Name one!

Hung: Okay, there was this one active wallpaper bug a few releases ago. In certain circumstances, this wallpaper crashed on launch. The fix was easy and we pushed it quickly so that hardly any users were affected. But it still doesn't make it right. We wrote some tests for that one, believe me, we wrote some tests for that one!

An Interview with Chrome TEM Joel Hynoski

> *Joel Hynoski is a TEM who has been with Google from the early days of the Seattle-Kirkland office and has run a variety of groups over the years. He currently is in charge of all client products including Chrome and Chrome OS. Joel is known around the office as the cranky Aussie, a moniker at peace with his tester soul but at odds with his high ratings as a manager.*
>
> *The authors recently sat down with Joel for a chat about his ideas on testing and his experience on Chrome and Chrome OS.*

HGTS: Quick, tell us what kind of computer you use!

Joel: [Holding up a laptop] Chromebook baby!

HGTS: Can we search your backpack for other hardware you might be packing?

Joel: Ha! I have a cell in my pocket and a tablet around here somewhere, but I believe in using what I test and I use this Chromebook for everything and when I find something it won't do, I file a bug.

HGTS: So you are one test manager here who manages a range of products from toolbars to installers to Chrome to Chrome OS and everything else we build that runs as or on a client-operating system. That's a lot of dev teams to manage. How do you balance all these things?

Joel: Well testing itself is a balancing act. On one hand, we have to get the product out the door and test each release and do the required checks to make sure it's ready. On another hand, we need to build good automation and invest in our frameworks and infrastructure for automation. On yet another hand, we need to plan and put structure around the development-build-test-release process. On yet another hand, there are testing gurus everywhere telling the world about the newest way they have developed to get testing done and if you don't experiment with the new stuff you feel like you're stagnating.

HGTS: So are you a juggler or an octopus? Seriously, where do you stand on the ideal mix of all these things?

Joel: I try to be practical about it. I have software to ship and there are some things that have to give to make that happen. There are always tradeoffs. We may be an agile team, but we still implement a last-mile validation. We may do exploratory testing, but we still have to track the multiple release and platform streams. I don't believe in absolutes.

Truth is, there's no one model that works for any project team. Even in a single company, you get variation. Case in point: My Chrome team uses different processes than my Chrome OS team and they sit in the same building! Is one better than the other? It depends and all I can do is help the two teams communicate about what is working and what makes our job as Test more productive. Bottom line is my test team has to be ready for anything and we have to be cognizant of what's working and when something doesn't work, we have to be ready to abandon it quickly. Until I have all this totally figured out, I am going to favor a hybrid approach, a mix of developer testing, scripted testing, exploratory testing, risk-based testing, and functional automation.

HGTS: Uh, oh, it sounds like another Google testing book is on the horizon.

Joel: Yeah, give me a year and then we'll compare sales or Amazon ratings, or heck, we're Google, we'll measure relevancy!

HGTS: Okay, give us the dish on Chrome and Chrome OS testing. We went out of our way in this book to discuss the common test infrastructure Google has for web app teams, but you are in the client space and none of that applies right?

Joel: Correct, and that's what makes it such a challenge. Client is not mainstream Google. We're a web company and we know how to build and test web apps so the challenge with all my client products is to translate that expertise and tools back to the client machine. It's a real challenge when the Google infrastructure isn't there to help.

Chrome itself grew up as a small experiment; a few SWEs get together and decide they can build a better browser and they put it out for the world to use (and because it's open source, some modify it). In the early days, testing was done by the developers and a few hardcore testers who were early adopters. But with tens of millions of users, you better have a damn good test team in place.

HGTS: We know those guys; that's a good description. So now that you have a team in place, what's the biggest challenge?

Joel: The Web! Seriously, it's always changing and Chrome can't break it. There is a constant stream of add-ons, extensions, apps, HTML versions, Flash, and so on. The number of variables is mind boggling and all of them have to work. If we release a browser that won't render your favorite website or run your favorite web app, you don't have to look far for an alternative browser. Yes we have to run on a lot of operating systems, too, but they are far fewer in number and easier to test with our virtualization infrastructure here. But for my ulcers, it's the Web that I worry about.

HGTS: Yeah, variety sucks for testers. So we realize you're going to write your own book so we won't steal all your thunder, but give us two technologies or solutions that help you tame the Web.

Joel: Two? Hmm. Okay, I'll talk about application compatibility and UI automation because those have both been big wins. Everything else I will save for the next book, you know, the more relevant one?

Application compatibility is a big deal for browsers. We're trying to answer the question, "Is Chrome compatible with the applications and sites on the Web?" In other words, does Chrome render pages correctly and run web apps correctly? Obviously this is impossible to validate in its entirety because we can't possibly render every page and run every app. And even if we could, what do we compare them to? Well the way we answer this is by testing the most popular sites (we're Google, that information is easy to determine!) against reference versions of Chrome and even competing browsers. We have automation that renders thousands of sites and compares them for points of similarity. We do this for every daily build, so we catch regressions quickly. Any site that renders differently gets some human attention to figure out what is wrong.

But that's only part of it. We still have to be able to drive the sites and apps, and we do this with what we call UI Automation. Chrome has an API called the automation proxy that you can use to launch the browser, navigate to a URL, query the browser state, get tab and window information, and so on. We put a Python interface on this so you can script the browser with Python (a language a lot of testers at Google are proficient in). It makes for powerful functional automation, and we've built up a large library of "PyAuto[3]" tests written by developers and testers alike.

HGTS: Okay, so you kick butt on Chrome and because Chrome OS is just Chrome melted into a laptop, testing it is easy I would imagine?

Joel: As in I tested Sarfari so Mac OS is also tested? I tested IE so Windows is good? Yeah right! Just the fact that there is such a thing as Chrome OS means that Chrome is harder to test because I have yet another platform to add to my app compat automation!

But I'll give you this: We do own everything on this stack, which is a nice place to be. Google is in control of everything on the system, from board components all the way up to the UI. Now from the UI down, everything looks good—lots of overlap with Chrome testing. I can use PyAuto and build some really nice automation suites with significant reuse from the Chrome team. However, there's this firmware and then there's this kernel, and uh, oh yeah, a GPU, a network adapter, a wireless modem, 3G … we can fit a lot into these little boxes these days! These are all places where automation is hard to squeeze in. They are labor-intensive testing tasks that are fundamentally incompatible with the

---

[3] You can get more information about PyAuto here: http://www.chromium.org/developers/testing/pyauto.

high Google dev-to-test ratio. We were getting systems from prototype stage onward and having to mount circuit boards on cardboard boxes.

We have a system where none of our pre-existing test tools work. Chrome OS is open source and sits outside of the normal Google development systems. We've had to (almost literally) reinvent the wheel on a lot of the testing tools, redefine processes to account for the ways that the tools work, and provide these tools to external developers who are contributing code. We release the OS on up to five different platforms on three channels (dev, beta, stable) on a six-week schedule. Good thing I am Australian or I would go insane!

So we had to get creative. Where can we push back on developers to write tools? How much testing can we demand from the partners and manufacturers? How do we school our test team on how to test hardware effectively? What tools and equipment can we create that will help us reduce the manual test load? And how does that translate into running on actual devices?

HGTS: The fact that you are stating these as questions is making us worry that we are going to have to wait for your book to get answers!

Joel: Well you are going to have to wait because I don't even have all the answers yet and it's my job to get them! We are still on the first release and we've had to come up with an effective approach that marries manual testing and automation together. Autotest,[4] an open-source test tool designed initially for testing the Linux kernel, was repurposed to drive a comprehensive suite of automated tests on real Chrome OS hardware. The team working on that had to extend it a lot to deal with the issues of the platform and made a ton of contributions, which were all made open source. Autotest runs our pre-flight test queue, the smoke suite, and build verification tests for the system on both real hardware and virtual machines. And the, of course, we use PyAuto extensively to drive automation through the Chrome browser running on Chrome OS.

HGTS: You and James are well known throughout Google as the go-to guys for test hiring. You two trained our sourcers and recruiters and we know for a fact that candidates who were not sure they wanted to be testers (or testers at Google) were sent to you guys for the final sell. What's the magic here?

Joel: James and I shared an office for quite a while and we are both passionate about the testing discipline. So it is natural that we teamed up on this. But James is the loud voice, conference-speaking guy who just seems to know everyone. He succeeds because of his network. I succeed because I get people excited about the discipline. It's completely different, you know like the difference between luck and skill!

I'm kidding of course but I am really passionate about testing, and another aspect of this is about hiring the right people to be Google engineers. Chrome, specifically, has been a challenge to hire for because the tendency is to throw people at the problem. Have an issue with validating the CR-48, Samsung Chromebook, and new experimental platforms over three channels in a week? Hey, throw 30 vendors at the problem! You need to validate a Chrome S stable build in 24 hours? With 18 manual testers, that'll be a breeze!

---

[4] Information about Autotest can be found here: http://autotest.kernel.org/.

I don't want to manage a team of testers who just blindly follow test scripts. That's boring. I want to manage a team that is doing ground-breaking test development, creating new and innovative tools, and using a lot of creativity in their day-to-day work. So as we add people to the mix, I want to make sure that the technical level remains very high. This is the challenge with hiring. How do you find people with the technical skill to get into Google and help them find their inner passion for testing? Well, James knows a lot of those people, but eventually his network will run dry. I take a more comprehensive approach and dig into what makes testing a genuinely interesting and challenging problem. You'd be surprised how many people want to be developers and when they see what testing is all about, they are intrigued enough to give testing a try. Once they find out what a challenge testig is and how much fun it is, you have yourself a great tester.

HGTS: Okay, give us the pitch. Why choose a career in test?

Joel: Test is the last frontier of engineering. We've solved a lot of the problems of how to develop software effectively, but we've still have a green field of opportunity to attack the really meaty problems of testing a product, from how to organize all the technical work that must get done to how we automate effectively, and responsively, and with agility without being too reactive. It's the most interesting area of software engineering today, and the career opportunities are amazing. You're not just banging on a piece of software any more, you're testing the GPU acceleration of your HTML5 site, you're making sure that you're optimizing your CPU's cores to get the best performance, and you're ensuring that your sandbox is secure. That to me is exciting and invigorating, and why I'm really pleased that I'm in the test organization at Google and working on one of the hardest problems we have.

The Test Engineering Director

Google test engineering directors are creatures all their own. It would be difficult to write a "Life of" chapter because each one is granted full autonomy and most of them take that to heart. There are only a few things they have in common. They all report to Patrick Copeland. They use common Google infrastructure and they meet weekly to discuss their respective domains, but unlike the engineering managers from the last section (who report to directors), directors have carte blanche to guide their various products teams the way they see fit.

Directors approve hires and transfers and generally control all aspects of test staffing. They own significant budget for things like morale events, off-sites, and the buying of "schwag" (Google-branded gear, backpacks, t-shirts, jackets, and such). It's an accepted practice to compete when ordering the coolest gear for your testing troops; it's also a courtesy to order enough to share. The Google test brand is strong in the company and such schwag helps sustain that. Indeed, sometimes schwag goes viral.

Whittaker's team ordered t-shirts with the edgy logo "The Web Works (you're welcome)" on them and they were so popular that even developers were wearing them around Google campuses.

There is no attempt made with schwag or otherwise to force the teams to be in complete synchronization. There is no attempt made to minimize rework across the domains. Innovation is expected from all the teams and competition to develop automation or tools makes teams strong. However, there are special rewards in the vein of spot bonuses and peer bonuses that encourage collaboration and a tester's 20 percent time is often spent working with a completely different team under a director different than the one she reports through. In fact 20 percent time is the way most directors manage a tester who wishes to transfer to a new team: 20 percent with the new group for a few weeks followed by 20 percent with the old group for a few weeks after that.

If there is one thing about Google that preserves this collaborative and whole-company spirit despite the natural competitive human tendency, it is the open transfer process. Google engineers are encouraged to move teams every 18 months or so. Notice this is "encouraged" and not "required." Directors have to keep good relationships with other directors because we work with a shared labor pool and the ebb and flow of employees eventually favors us all.

A director's job is leadership. They must build strong teams and keep them focused on the goal of shipping high-quality, useful, and industry-changing software. They must be technical enough to gain the respect of their engineers, innovative enough to keep pace with the fast-paced Google work style, and good enough at management to keep people productive. They must be a master of Google tools and infrastructure so that no time is wasted when working through what it takes to ship every day.

What does it take to accomplish all this and be successful at Google as a test engineering director? We decided that the best way to explain it is to hear from the people who actually do it.

An Interview with Search and Geo Test Director Shelton Mar

Shelton Mar is a test director, a title equivalent to a vice president at many companies. He's also one of the longest running Google testers in the company and he pre-dates Patrick Copeland's arrival back in the days before the Engineering Productivity when the group was called Testing Services. Shelton was promoted through the ranks at Google from test manager of small teams to a directorship over search, infrastructure, and maps. Shelton is now the test executive for a product area Google calls Local and Commerce, which includes all location-based products including Google Earth and Maps.

The authors sat down with Shelton to get some of the inside scoop on Google's past and to catch up on what he has done to test Google Search.

HGTS: Shelton, you've been around Google long enough to remember the Testing Services days that Patrick wrote about in the preface. Tell us what testing was like in the early days pre-Patrick!

Shelton: Things were certainly different back then and a lot has changed in a short period of time, but one thing has always been consistent: Google has always been able to run at a very fast pace. But in the early days we were lucky. The Internet was simpler, our apps were smaller, and lots of smart people giving their best effort was good enough. We suffered a lot of last-minute fire drills, but the problem was still manageable enough that a few heroes could pull it off. Products took dependencies on the system level and end-to-end testing was both manual and scripted. The more we grew, the more those dependencies caused problems.

I am not saying anything bad about this kind of testing; it's a necessary part of validation and ensuring an integrated system works correctly, but over dependency on late cycle testing makes debugging a lot more difficult when things don't go well.

We were struggling with this problem around the time Pat appeared.

HGTS: I guess it was worse with backend systems where "end-to-end" is harder to identify.

Shelton: Exactly! We often couldn't release backend systems as fast as we would have liked because it was so hard to be sure about quality. Backend systems have to be right because they affect so many different product verticals. You get BigTable wrong, for example, and lots of apps suffer. It's the ripple effect from updating a backend system because of issues that couldn't be found using just end-to-end tests.

HGTS: So you went from an overinvestment in end-to-end validation to hard core validation of the backend server infrastructure. Tell us about the path to get there.

Shelton: Well we started by changing the composition of the team. We redefined the SET role and then focused on hiring technically strong candidates. Once we had the skill set in place, we got to work on building a better backend testing solution. We focused our work on component-level automation. Imagine a bunch of smart engineers with development and testing skills swarming our backend infrastructure and you are getting close to what happened.

HGTS: Any specific key to your success?

Shelton: Yes, it was crucial to have SWE support and buy-in. Our SETs worked closely with the development partners (notice I use the terminology "partner" as this really was a collaborative effort that test cannot assume full credit for) to build better testing practices at the developer level. Whatever we could have done on our own was amplified by this close partnership. At times, we would realize something wasn't possible at the component level and work with them to solve it at the unit level. This collaboration transformed the dynamic in the team so that the entire project team (dev + test) owned quality at the component level with test engineering focusing its time on improving process, framework, tooling, and integration testing.

HGTS: You made some pretty tough calls, such as hiring SWE quality people to test. What prompted that? Any regrets? What impact did it have on the testing culture?

Shelton: That's probably the most important transformation we've done for Google. We realized that there were three things we needed to change at Google early on:

- Push testing upstream so the entire team (dev + test) owns the quality of the deliverables.

- Test engineering is an embedded part of the project team. Thus, we need strong engineers who can understand the challenges and the technology involved.

- Apply computer science and engineering rigor to testing.

You can't accomplish these things without having smart and strong software engineers who "get" (or at least can be taught) test engineering. Once we started looking at the challenge differently, we realized we can hire and motivate the best engineers to solve difficult problems in testing. The fact that we've built up such a large team of them shows that they enjoy the work.

HGTS: During your tenure at Google, you've worked on a lot of products including Search, which is Google's mainstay. What's the hardest part of testing Search?

Shelton: Deciding on what to focus on! Often when engineers start looking at testing Search, they start talking about what Google returns from the search queries. While that's definitely an interesting area to explore, search quality requires a lot more than that. To provide consistent, reliable, and fast response to our users, we need to validate the complex and sophisticated distributed software system that actually returns results. You have to understand indexing and search algorithms. You have to understand the plumbing and how the system is built so you can validate all these actions when and where they actually occur. We focus on all this from the beginning. In reality, what we did was separate search quality from the actual plumbing of the solution. We focused on the latter and left search quality to the search quality experts on the product team. We validated the infrastructure and system that are used to handle the processing, update, and serving of Google search results, and they made sure the results Google was producing were the best results.

HGTS: When you get a new project, what is your general approach? What are the first things you usually do? From a team-building perspective? From a technical infrastructure perspective? From a testing process perspective?

Shelton: Talking in general terms, one of the first things I ask my team to evaluate is, "What's really critical for the system under test?" Performance is important for search, freshness is big for news, and comprehensiveness is critical for maps. Every app has its important attributes. Similarly for system infrastructure, data integrity is critical for storage, the ability to scale is important for networking, and utilization is key for job management systems. Once you've identified what's critical for the specific product you're testing, then focus the majority of your energy on validating that the core capabilities of the system satisfy those attributes. Worry about the easy stuff (UI tweaks and bells and whistles) only after the important stuff is right. Also focus on areas (such as design for performance) that are core attributes and difficult to change, and spend less time on things that can be updated easily. So if you start logging bugs about fonts too early, I am going to worry about your priorities.

HGTS: There is a historical tension between manual and automated testing and it seems like Google swung from lots of manual testing to lots of automated testing. Where do you stand now? What is the right split? How do you know when you have gone too far in one direction or the other?

Shelton: I feel that you automate as much as possible. We have the concept of continuous builds where manual testing just gets in the way. Validation at the component level and integration tests that execute around the clock play a role that manual testing cannot. However, automation is not resilient to change and it requires maintenance. As technology continues to evolve and change at a rapid rate, automation has to be redeveloped to keep pace.

Having said that, there are some things manual testing can do that automation cannot. An example is mobile apps where there's an explosion of hardware, displays, form factors, and device drivers that cause variance in rendering and display. In such cases, we have to resort to some level of manual testing to help in doing validation. The key is still to automate that process as much as possible. Have a machine do 90 percent of the work and apply human intelligence only to the last 10 percent ("the last mile" we call it) of the validation cycle. Automaton can do things like capture all the screens from devices, allowing us to do rapid side-by-side human inspection after our comparison algorithm filters out variance in display. Human intelligence is too valuable to waste on something a computer can do and should be applied where intelligence and human judgment is best; a repetitive task is definitely not one of those areas.

HGTS: Describe a bug that got away, one that embarrassed you after you shipped.

Shelton: Oh, you had to ask about that didn't you? Has anyone ever shipped a perfect product I wonder? Not me, unfortunately! The bugs I regret most in production were around our failure to thoroughly test data center configuration changes. In one case, a new version was pushed out into production without going through any kind of validation. That configuration change affected the quality of the search results served to end users in a negative way. We learned just how important configuration changes are to search quality. Since then, we have included configuration change as part of the qualification process and we have a set of automated tests we run before data or configuration changes are pushed to production.

HGTS: How did you define these automated configuration tests?

Shelton: By being watchful! Every time we found a configuration that negatively affected search results, we wrote tests for those configurations and any variations that might produce similarly poor results. It wasn't long before we had a good set of problematic environments added to our test suite. We then used automation to generate as diverse a set of data as we could to test those environments against. These kinds of bugs are definitely less common now because of this practice. This is definite automation that gives us a lot more confidence when we push changes into production.

An Interview with Engineering Tools Director Ashish Kumar

Google lives and dies by its tools, and the person in charge of those tools is Ashish Kumar. He is responsible for everything from the IDEs developers use to code review systems, build systems, source control, static analysis, common test infrastructure, and so on. Even Selenium and WebDriver teams report up through him.
The authors recently sat down with Ashish to get his take on this particular piece of Google magic.

HGTS: There is a general mystique about automation at Google, perpetuated by the popularity of GTAC, and you are the man behind it. Can you describe the general set of capabilities your tool set provides to Google engineers?

Ashish: My team is called the Engineering Tools team. We are responsible for building 90 percent of the tools that developers use on a day-to-day basis in order to write, build, and release quality software at Google. It's 90 percent because we don't support some of our open-source product teams yet, but we have plans in the works to support them as well.

Google is unique in that there is a significant focus on providing very capable (and scalable) infrastructure for our developers. People outside are generally familiar with technologies like MapReduce and BigTable that are used regularly by Google developers, but our developer tools infrastructure is also a significant part of that investment.

HGTS: How about some specifics?

Ashish: Okay, you asked for it! The toolset includes:

- **Source Tools:** Tools to make it easier to create workspaces, submit code changes, and enforce style guidelines. Tools to browse hundreds of millions of lines of code and easily discover code to prevent duplication. Tools to enable indexing and refactoring at scale in the cloud.

- **Development Tools:** Plugins for IDEs that allow those tools to scale to Google code and connect with services in the cloud. Tools to allow fast and high-quality reviews of code by embedding relevant signals at code review time.

- **Build Infrastructure:** This system allows us to shard builds for cross-language code across tens of thousands of CPUs and so much memory and storage that it makes my brain hurt just thinking about it! This build system works for both interactive and automated use, providing results in seconds where it should have taken hours in many cases.

- **Test Infrastructure:** Continuous integration at scale. This means running millions of test suites every day in response to every check-in by every developer. Our goal is to provide instant (or as close to instant as possible) feedback to the developer. The flip side of this scale is web testing at scale. This means running hundreds of thousands of browser sessions testing various browser-platform combinations against every Google product every day.

- **Localization Tools:** Continuous translation of strings created by developers to allow for localized versions of our products being ready at the same time as our English versions.

- **Metrics, Visibility, and Reporting:** Managing bugs for all Google products, keeping track of all development (code, test, and release) metrics for all developers in a central repository and providing actionable feedback to teams on how to improve.

HGTS: Okay, that's a lot of balls in the air. Surely it took a lot of innovation to get where you are today. But how do you balance keeping all this work going and pursuing new development at the same time? Your team isn't that big!

Ashish: We don't try to do it all is the simple answer. My team is a central Engineering Tools team that serves all of Google. Often product teams work on tools that are specific to their needs. Sometimes those tools become generally usable, and we evaluate them for a fit to making them central (and hence, allow for all of Google to use them). Other times, an engineer on my team comes up with an idea he thinks is cool. This is Google and we try our best to foster these types of organically grown startups. Our criteria for inclusion of a tool in our central team is in two parts: It has to have the potential for high impact on productivity and it has to be applicable for a large number of Google developers. After all, we are a centralized tools team so the big impact, broad audience tools are where we play. If a tool applies to only one product team, then that team should own it.

But we do start a lot of experiments as well. In order for us to get the big wins next year, there should always be a few experiments going on with one- or two-person teams working on them. Many of these start out as 20 percent efforts and I won't say no to anything done on a 20 percent basis. Individual engineers own their 20 percent time, not me. Some of these efforts fail, but the ones that succeed generally make up for all the failures put together. Dream big, fail fast, and keep trying!

Some tools' projects are enablers, so it's difficult to directly measure their impact on productivity, but all tools' projects are required to move the needle significantly in terms of productivity gains for Google.

HGTS: Is there a tool idea you thought wouldn't succeed but then did?

Ashish: Yes! Continuous integration at scale. It's such a large problem that on the surface looks completely intractable. We used to have thousands of machines running these continuous integration loops. Someone on the team suggested building infrastructure that would centralize this *for all projects at Google* and that this infrastructure would just poll source control for changes, manage a massive cross-language dependency graph for every CL in memory, and automatically build and run affected tests. I wasn't the only one voicing concern that this was too massive and that resource utilization would put our servers in the red. The skeptics were right about that; resources used are very high. But one by one our engineers overcame these technical hurdles and the system is running now and it works. We did the same thing with this project like we do with others like this. Start small, prove incremental value, and then double down as the projects begin showing value.

HGTS: Is there a tool you built that you thought would succeed but didn't?

Ashish: Yes again! Remote pair programming. Google has highly distributed development setup; many teams follow pair programming and other agile development techniques. Many times the code that you are working on might have been authored by someone in another office, and if you had a quick question, there's a delay involved that affects productivity.

One of the experiments we started was to build a "remote pair programming" plugin for our IDEs. The goal was to have tight integration with Google Talk (and video) so that as a developer has a question about modifying some code, he or she can start a chat with the author through functionality directly embedded in their development environment, The other developer would then get to see the workspace and be able to perform the edit as a pair while watching each other over video. Pair Programming without the body odor!

Unfortunately, we launched an early version (with simply the collaborative editor and no Google Talk integration), but when we didn't get the early adopter usage metrics that we hoped to see, we discontinued that experiment. Developers just didn't seem interested. Perhaps we weren't aligned with an important enough pain point for them.

HGTS: What advice would you give to a company trying to build an automation pipeline? What tools do you start with?

Ashish: Focusing on the development environment that a newbie developer would have to work with on your team is really critical. Make it dead easy to get started to check out code, edit code, test code, run code, debug code, and then deploy code. Take away the pain from each of these steps and your developers will be productive and you will produce high-quality software on time.

In order to make this happen, it is really important to define dependencies cleanly, make them explicit, and set up a continuous integration system "that just works" and provides feedback quickly to developers. If the feedback takes more than a few minutes, add more machines. CPU hours are cheaper than developer context switches and idle time. Make it as easy as typing a command to run and debug code, as well as to deploy it. If you are a web company, make it easy to launch partial deployments.

HGTS: What do you look for in an engineer for your team? It seems like just any old developer won't really cut it as a tools guy.

Ashish: Tools development requires a special love for computer science fundamentals, things like language development, compilers, systems programming, and the satisfaction of seeing your work used by other very smart developers who in turn produce greater value for the company. Really it is about finding people who want developers as their customers.

HGTS: Speaking of customers, how do you convince people to adopt your tools?

Ashish: Googlers are a unique bunch. They generally don't need a lot of selling. We hold what we call Engineering Productivity Reviews weekly and demo our tools. Engineers come, they ask questions, and if the tool solves a real problem they have, then they try it out. In general, you get good adoption for the tools that solve real problems and poor adoption for those that do not. The secret is in avoiding the latter completely or at least be willing to cancel a project that fails to show value (and do so as early as possible).

HGTS: Have you ever seen a tool that just got in the way or did more harm than good?

Ashish: Yes, but I try not to stare at them for too long. Those are projects that we very quickly disinvest in. The purpose of tooling is to automate the process and make it easier. Sometimes tool projects automate bad behavior. If developers are doing the wrong thing manually, why make it easier with a tool? The creators should have taken a step back and decided if they should be doing something else altogether rather than just automating what people were doing today.

HGTS: What's on your plate now? What are the new tools your team is cooking up?

Ashish: Well, first off, let me say that there is a lot of "keeping up" that needs to be done. The Web is changing so fast that all our tools around its technology are in constant development mode. Sometimes the changes make us do rewrites of tools and sometimes the changes allow completely new functionality. It's a constant challenge and a constant opportunity. But because a lot of what we do is internal, I can't talk about them here, but think scale, scale, and more scale and you are getting pretty close!

An Interview with Google India Test Director Sujay Sahni

An important aspect of the Google testing culture includes leveraging talent in various distributed offices by creating regional and global hubs. Hyderabad, India was the first global hub for Test Engineering established because of the talent available in India. The Googlers at this center work on key Google products that help fuel the needed change of direction and engagement from manual testers (or Testing Services) to a test engineering organization. Sujay Sahni is the test director who founded and runs the India Engineering Productivity team.

HGTS: India is a long way from Mountain View. How did Engineering Productivity get over there and evolve it into a critical path engineering office?

Sujay: Engineering Productivity teams follow a model similar to the overall Google engineering teams that place teams in centers around the world where we could find the appropriate talent. India was not a cost-based decision but solely based on the ability for us to hire exceptional talent. We placed teams in India that were big enough to have critical mass. India is actually one of a number of regional centers in which developers and testers are co-located; the others include London, New York, Kirkland, Bangalore, and some smaller offices.

We also have regional hubs that cater to a particular region like Europe. Europe's regional center was established in Zurich, Asia Pacific was Hyderabad, and the East Coast was New York. These centers worked on efforts across the region and brought together engineering efforts in the smaller Google Engineering offices in that region. This allowed for better time and talent management.

But Hyderabad is also what we refer to as a global hub as a source of talent for all of Google and engineering solutions for the testing teams. In the early years of testing at Google, Hyderabad was the biggest center for SET talent and we worked on any number of strategic projects. The Googlers at this center worked on key Google products that helped fuel the needed change of direction and engagement from Testing Services to Engineering Productivity.

HGTS: What role did India play in the evolution of testing at Google?

Sujay: The Hyderabad Center, which we abbreviate as HYD, was the first among the regional centers to be established. While we set up a center in Bangalore to be co-located with the engineering teams there, Hyderabad Center quickly became the global hub for test engineering. In the early days, the HYD center was a mix of test engineers, software engineers in Test, and a large contingency of temps and vendors. They worked on numerous important and recognizable Google products (like Search, Ads, Mobile, Gmail, and Toolbar to name a few) in various capacities and roles. Primarily, the Googlers worked on developing the critical testing infrastructure and frameworks that enabled engineering teams to automate their tests for faster releases. In 2006–2007, the HYD team constituted roughly half the SET pool at Google. One interesting anecdote: It is said that the SET role was created as a result of efforts of the first test engineer hired in HYD! Whether you give us this much credit or not, we at least indirectly paved the way from Testing Services to become Engineering Productivity.

By late 2007, we created a change in leadership with the goal to develop the team into new strategic areas, reduce fragmentation, and develop a more senior talent pool to help lead the growing number of young engineers. By early 2008, we had started establishing more leadership and regional hubs that now allowed for engineering teams to have local (or closer proximity) test teams, and this created an opportunity for HYD to focus more on areas where Google test teams had yet not ventured like advanced latency detection tools; backend. cloud performance, and stability tools; regression detection mechanisms; and client-testing tools.

Another change that began around this time was to start investing in the cloud testing and engineering tools infrastructure. This included aspects like Cloud Code Coverage infrastructure, developer IDEs, Cloud Scalable Test Infrastructure, Google Toolbox, and other experimentation efforts, most of which led to production tools. The team provided critical services and tools not only to the global engineering teams within Google, but also core infrastructure that is shared with the developers in the open-source community. Google engineers from HYD contributed to App Engine, Selenium, Eclipse, and IntelliJ plugins and various other code to the open-source community.

HGTS: These are some good and important projects. Can you give an example of one done completely in HYD?

Sujay: Yes. The Google Diagnostic Utility was developed solely out of the Hyderabad Engineering Productivity team. It allows our support teams to work with customers to diagnose issues they face with Google products by helping them identify technical specifications and configurations of their systems and computers.

There are others too. The HYD Engineering Productivity team focuses on developing engineering infrastructure, tools, and tests for all of Google. This includes developer tools like IDEs, core engineering infrastructure in the cloud for code compilation, developer testing, code complexity, code coverage, and various kinds of static analysis. For testing tools, the HYD team owns the development of test infrastructure for load and performance analysis for various Google cloud applications as well as test tools and testing for core products like Search, Enterprise, Gmail, and Ads.

HGTS: Okay, I want to follow up on some of these tools. Even the names sound interesting. Can you tell me about the code coverage tool you mentioned? Code coverage always gets a lot of attention on the Google Testing blog!

Sujay: Code coverage is a globally accepted metric to measure the effectiveness of tests for a given code base. In a traditional paradigm, each team would set up dedicated resources (engineering, hardware, and software) to measure code coverage for its project codebase. However, at Google there is a central team based in India that ensures that all Google Engineering efforts get code coverage metrics seamlessly. To get this, teams need to follow a few simple steps to enable the functionality, a one-time investment of less than five minutes. After it is set up, teams get coverage metrics for all their projects and builds with a central reporting location to view and analyze the reports.

Coverage is supported for thousands of projects, supporting all major programming languages and millions of source code files. The coverage infrastructure is tightly integrated into Google's cloud infrastructure to compile and build code and scales to the massive complexity of constant code changes (measured per minute!) and tens of thousands builds each day. It is set up to scale with a fast-growing Google codebase.

We also have supporting infrastructure that provides smart ways to provide test prioritization to detect relevant tests that need to be run based on the specific code changes. This provides targeted test coverage, better confidence in code quality, and faster feedback, saving Google a huge amount of engineering resources.

HGTS: Sounds like code coverage done right. Now tell me a little about the Diagnostic Utility you mentioned.

Sujay: The Diagnostic Utility was conceived and built through 20 percent efforts of Hyderabad's Engineering Productivity SETs. It bridges the gap between the technical knowledge of an average computer user and a Google developer's need for technical data when debugging a user issue.

To understand the reports submitted by Google users, sometimes technical data about the state of Google software is needed. This might include data as trivial as the OS, locale, and so on, to more complicated details such as application versions and configurations. Gathering this information in an easy and expedited fashion can be a challenge because the user might not be aware of such details.

The Diagnostic Utility helps simplify this. Now when Google receives an issue where additional data is needed, our support team simply creates a new configuration for this tool, outlining what specific information needs to be gathered. The users can then be contacted via email or be pointed to a unique link off of google.com and its support where they download a small (less than 300KB) Google-signed executable. This executable can diagnose a user's machine and gather only the configured data that is specific to that request and display to the user a preview of the data that he can then opt in to send to Google. Obviously the executable cleans up and deletes itself on exit, and we take extreme care to ensure user privacy is maintained and data gathered is reviewed by the users and submitted with their consent.

Internally, that data is routed to the appropriate developer to accelerate debugging and resolution. This utility is used by Google customer support and is particularly useful to teams like Google Chrome, Google Toolbar, and other client applications. Additionally, it makes getting help from Google much easier for our users.

HGTS: You mentioned performance and load testing a few times. What's the story here? I understand you guys were deeply involved in the Gmail perf testing?

Sujay: Google has a wide range of web applications, so ensuring a low latency user experience is an important goal. As such, performance testing (focusing on the speed of JavaScript execution and page rendering) is one of the key verifications done before any product release. Historically, latency issues could take days or weeks to be identified and get resolved. The India Engineering Productivity team developed Gmail's frontend performance-testing infrastructure to cover critical user actions and ensure that the things users did the most were the subjects of intensive performance testing. This is deployed and tested using instrumented server binaries, and tests are run in a controlled deployment environment that helps identify regressions while maintaining a low variance.

There are three parts to this solution:

- **Submit queues**: Allow engineers to run tests (and gather performance latency metrics) before submitting their code change. This allows faster feedback and prevention of bugs being checked into the codebase.

- **Continuous builds**: Syncs test servers to the latest code changes and runs relevant tests continuously to detect and trap any regressions. This enables the team to reduce regression detection from days or weeks down to hours or minutes.

- **Production performance latency detection**: Used to identify the particular code change that caused the production latency regression. This is done by bisecting the range of changes and running tests at various checkpoints.

This solution has helped identify many critical bugs before our products are released and has driven quality upstream as developers can easily launch these tests themselves.

HGTS: Any new innovative efforts (technical and nontechnical) that you experimented with? What did you learn from them?

Sujay: Some experiments we are working on include feedback-driven development tools that focus on gathering the right metrics and providing data to our engineering teams to improve their productivity. This also includes code visualization tools, code complexity metrics, and some other things a little more out there. Another area is advanced development environments that include improving the way engineering teams use IDEs and metrics to improve code quality and their release velocity. Other tools being developed include a Google-wide, post-mortem tool that unifies release data and makes it actionable.

HGTS: Any final words about global test engineering based on your experience working from India for a globally distributed software company?

Sujay: It's not easy, but we're proof it can work. The key lessons for me have been:

- The "follow the sun" model works well if you choose the right teams and the right projects. We have been able to work through various challenges as a globally distributed team but not without a few missteps. Having a good model for work hand-offs from one time zone to another is key. Also, pick your team and projects carefully. You have to have people who are passionate about the products you build and people who are good collaborators.

- Crowd testing is another thing that works well for us. We leverage the vast pool of talented vendors in the test community in India and take advantage of the time differences using the crowd source model, and it works well.

Hiring great talent and putting that talent to work on critical projects is the bottom line. Google didn't just go after low-cost countries because there are cheaper places than India. We tried to keep the quality of hires and opportunities that the Googlers work on extremely high. We make a big impact at Google and our TEs and SETs have fulfilling careers. We all win.

An Interview with Engineering Manager Brad Green

"Shoeless" Brad Green has been a test engineering manager for many products at Google including Gmail, Google Docs, and Google+, and he is now a development manager for Google Feedback and also experiments with Web Development Frameworks in a project called Angular. He is known around the office as the guy with big ideas and no shoes!

HGTS: We understand that you come from a development background at Apple. What made you switch to Google and why Engineering Productivity?

Brad: Linus Upson helped bring me in. He and I worked together at NeXT and he seemed really energized by Google. But somewhere in the six-month interview process, Patrick Copeland tricked me into joining Engineering Productivity. It was a good trick. I've learned so much in the role and now that I am back being a development manager again, I am the better for it. Perhaps every developer should do a tour of duty in test!

HGTS: What was the most surprising thing about the testing culture at Google when you arrived?

Brad: This was early 2007 and the transformation Patrick spoke about in the preface wasn't fully baked. I was amazed at how much testing know-how was here. Every time I met with a new group, I found some test expert who surprised me. The problem was that this expertise was so unevenly applied. In the same way that Eskimos have hundreds of words for snow,[5] Google had as many terms for styles of tests. I felt like I had to learn a new set of testing terms whenever I dug into another team's practices. Some teams had great rigor, some did not. It was clear we had to change.

HGTS: What has changed the most in testing since you arrived at Google?

Brad: Two things. First, the average developer has become much more involved in the testing process and in writing automation. They know about unit, API, integration, and full-system tests. They instinctively create more tests when they see problems that have slipped through the continuous build. Most of the time you don't even have to remind them! This has led to much higher initial quality and the ability to ship quickly. Second, we've been able to attract hundreds of top-notch engineers into test-specific roles. I like to think that the two are related. It's a culture where testing matters and doing testing is something you get appreciated for.

HGTS: Let's talk about what it is like being a manager at Google. What are the most difficult, easiest, or interesting aspects of being a manager at Google?

Brad: Google hires extraordinarily self-motivated folks. Getting things done "because I said so" might work once, but these smart folks will go off and do what they think is best after too much of that. I've been most successful by helping to guide, provide insight, and open doors for my folks to do what they're most passionate about. If I have to give a direct order, I feel that I've failed to equip them with the skills they need to make good decisions. The

---

[5] Not true as it turns out" http://en.wikipedia.org/wiki/Eskimo_words_for_snow.

word manager is in my title but I do as little of it as possible. It's really a job that requires the leadership of wicked smart and very passionate engineers. Managers beware.

HGTS: Your team has done a lot of work on metrics for developer testing. What metrics work? What data are you tracking? How has it impacted quality?

Brad: Lots of motion, little forward progress to be honest. I've been failing in this space for four years now, so I feel I've learned a lot! I say failing because we've poured tremendous work into finding magic metrics of code and test quality that teams can use as an absolute guide. But metrics are hard to generalize because context is very important. Yes, more tests are better, except when they're slow or unreliable. Yes, small tests are better than large ones, unless you really need that system test to validate how the whole thing is wired. There are useful measurements, but test implementation is nuanced and is as much an art form as the application code itself.

What I have learned is that the social aspects of testing are much harder than the computer science aspects. Everyone knows they need good tests, but for most of us, it's hard to get our teams to execute on writing them. The best tool I know is competition. You want more small tests? Compare your team against another. Hey look at Team X; they have 84 percent unit test coverage and their full test suite runs in under five minutes! How can we let them beat us? Measure everything you can, but put your trust in people. But still you have to be skeptical, no matter what testing you accomplish in-house, you still have to release it to users and there is a lot about that environment you cannot predict or replicate.

HGTS: So that explains your involvement in Google Feedback! Can you tell us a little about the purpose of Google Feedback? What problem was it built to solve?

Brad: Feedback allows users to report problems they see with Google's products. Easy, you say. Just slap a submission form on the page and let users go at it, right? Well, many teams had tried this only to find that they couldn't handle the volume of reports—in many cases, thousands per day. They also often had problems debugging issues because the information users would submit was always incomplete and sometimes inaccurate. These are the problems Feedback addresses.

HGTS: Can you tell us a bit about how Google Feedback works?

Brad: Feedback starts by gathering everything it can from a user while still protecting their privacy. Browser, operating system, plugins, and other environmental information is easy to collect and essential for debugging. The real trick is in getting a screenshot. For security reasons, browsers can't grab an image of their contents. We've re-implemented the browser's rendering engine in JavaScript in a secure way. We take the screenshot and let the user highlight the area on the page where they're experiencing problems. We then ask users to describe their problem in text. It's impossible to train users on how to submit good bug reports. These screenshots have made ambiguous descriptions clear time after time.

HGTS: But with all the users out there, don't you get the same bug reported over and over? It seems like a volume problem.

Brad: To solve the volume problem, we do automated clustering to group similar ones. If a thousand users all report the same issue, we put in a bucket. Finding these thousand issues and grouping them by hand would be an impossible task. We then rank the groups by volume to find which issues affect most users, giving a clear signal as to what we need to address most urgently.

HGTS: How big is the Google Feedback team?

Brad: The team has 12 developers and three project managers. This is a large number of project managers for a typical team at Google, but we've found it necessary with all the horizontal coordination across products.

HGTS: What was the biggest challenge, technically or otherwise, in delivering Google Feedback?

Brad: On the technical side, creating the screenshot was certainly a monumental undertaking. Many folks thought we were crazy for attempting it. It works amazingly well now. The automated issue clustering was and still is a challenge. We do pretty well on issues created in different languages, but we still have a way to go.

HGTS: What is the future of Google Feedback? Any chance it could be available for non-Google websites someday?

Brad: Our goal is to give our users a way to have a conversation with us about the issues they find in our products. Right now, the conversation is one-way. I think the future for us is in completing the conversation loop. We don't currently have plans to release this for external products, but that sounds like a good idea to me.

HGTS: What do you see as the next big leap in software testing in general?

Brad: I'd like to see a development environment with testing as a first-class feature, rather than one bolted on later. What if the language, libraries, frameworks, and tools all knew that you wanted tests with your feature code and helped you write it? That would be hot. As it is today, we have to cobble test frameworks together. Tests are hard to write, hard to maintain, and unstable when they run. I think there's a lot of value to be gained by baking in "test" at the lowest levels.

HGTS: Do you have any dirt on Dr. James Whittaker that the world should know about?

Brad: Other than the unfortunate incident in the Little Bo Peep outfit, what happens among the leadership ranks stays in the leadership ranks!

An Interview with James Whittaker

by Jason Arbon and Jeff Carollo

> *We turned the tables on James and cornered him in his office for an interview. James came to Google amidst a great deal of fanfare and is among our more recognizable test personalities. His posts dominate our blog and his appearances at GTAC bring in the crowds, and there is that whole expert witness, keynote circuit thing. His enormous personality certainly dominates the Seattle and Kirkland offices and reaches across the company like no one else, except, perhaps, Patrick Copeland. Pat might be the boss, but if Google has an intellectual leader in test, that leader is James.*

HGTS: You came to Google in 2009 from Microsoft, which you announced on your Microsoft blog without naming the company you were going to. Care to explain why? Were you just creating mystery?

James: A hard ball as the first question? Gads! You promised this would be easy!

HGTS: And you promised you'd answer our questions, so get to it!

James: Well, mostly I used the MSDN blog to broadcast my departure to the largest number of people all at once. I was being kind of a coward about quitting Microsoft and because no one was on Twitter then, I decided to quit on the mass market forum of the day. I wanted to tell as many people as I could without having to walk the halls for a bunch of face-to-face "I'm leaving" meetings. Turns out more Microsofties read my blog than bothered with my emails! It was the best way to get the word out.

The people who knew I was leaving spent a lot of time trying to talk me out of it and it's hard leaving a company that you enjoy working for. It's hard leaving the people I spent years working with. I like Microsoft and I respect the engineers who work there. It felt awful to leave and it was bad enough second-guessing myself about the decision. Truthfully, I might *have been* talked out of it if I had allowed more of those guys the opportunity to try. I really wanted to work for Google, though, and didn't want to give them the chance to stop that.

HGTS: Why? What was it about Google that drew you to us?

James: You know, it's weird. I spent my early career as a consultant professor and I founded a startup and did everything except the big company thing. When I plucked up the courage to work for a big company, I wanted big! The bigger, the better. The more sexy the work, the better. The more users I can reach with my work, the better. I wanted to see how successful I can be in industry so why not at the top companies? That's what attracted me to Microsoft long ago and it attracted me to Google later. I want big companies. I might as well work at the best big companies.

But really on top of all that was Google's emergence as the coolest testing company to work for that got me. Microsoft held that position for a long time and I credit Patrick Copeland for wresting that title from them. Google just seemed to be a cooler place to be a tester than anywhere else.

It was my interviews that sealed the deal. Patrick Copeland, Alberto Savoia, Brad Green, Shelton Mar, Mark Striebeck (and more who aren't mentioned)… all these people were on my interview loop and the conversations we had were amazing. Alberto and I filled up a whiteboard during my "interview." He even remarked afterward that he forgot to actually ask me any questions. Shelton and I actually disagreed about things we discussed, but he was so open-minded to my opinions, even though they were different, that it impressed me a lot. We agree more now than we did in the interview! And Brad? Well he's just cool. I mean he had no shoes on during the interview (in February). Even his attitude was kind of a bare feet sort of vibe. Mark spent most of the interview trying to convince me to come to Google. Ideas were flying in all these interviews. It was a rush, like a drug.

I was exhausted afterward. I remember falling into my cab and thinking I had found the best company to work for but worried I didn't have the energy to actually work there. I was really worried about being able to contribute. It was intimidating; it was outside my comfort zone. I like a challenge and the idea that my success would not come easy topped it all off. Who wants an easy job?

HGTS: And have we lived up to that reputation?

James: Well, yeah, the job is not easy at all! But I think you mean the passion part. I'll be honest, there is test passion and smart people at Microsoft too, in quantity. The difference at Google is that it is a lot easier to follow those passions. Alberto and I were never on the same team, but we could work together through 20 percent of the time and Brad and I are still collaborating on IDEs and things like automated bug reporting (Brad through Google Feedback and me through BITE). Google is good about providing outlets for such collaboration and you can actually get credit for it as part of your day job.

HGTS: We work with you in Kirkland and we've seen a big difference in morale and the pace at which the whole team here gets work done. What's your secret?

James: I will concede that Kirkland is a much better place now than before I joined, but I will stop short of taking credit for it. Part of it had to do with critical mass. My arrival preceded a massive hiring surge and we brought in some amazingly talented people. I think in the first few quarters, we more than quadrupled our testing staff. This allowed me to build bigger teams and co-locate people doing similar work even if they were working on different products. Instead of lone testers embedded with their development teams, we had groups of testers sitting together and feeding on each others' ideas. It worked wonders for productivity and morale.

The additional people also allowed me to move the veterans like you two off of your current projects and give you bigger challenges. Jeff was writing a pre-submit queue for Google Toolbar. Ga! What a mismatch in talent. Jason, you were testing Google Desktop. I tell you the secret to being a good manager is simply matching the person to the project. You get that right and your job is mostly done. The people are happier and the projects are better off. But it was critical mass that allowed me that luxury.

The other thing critical mass did is that it gave us some breathing room in terms of how we spent our 20 percent time and the fact that I had extra people to do experiments. I was able to staff some risky experimental projects. We started doing tools and experiments that had nothing to do with shipping software and more to do with following our passions. I've found that there is nothing like tool development to spur creativity and improve the morale of testers. Frankly, I think it is the most satisfying part of the job. Maybe I am more of a tools guy than I am a testing guy at heart.

HGTS: What is it that you like most about the organizational structure at Google?

James: Softball! I actually explain this to candidates when I need to sell them on Google: Testers report to testers and testers determine their own fate. These are the two things I like best about Google. Testers aren't beholden to anyone. Test has our own hiring committee, our own review committee, our own promotion committee. The U.N. recognizes Test as a separate country!

We don't have a subservient culture here. And if you want another reason, it would be scarcity of the test role. No dev team is granted testing head count without having to earn it by putting their own skin in the quality game. And testers have to be clever. We are so understaffed that we have to get good at prioritizing. We have to get good at automating. We have to get good at negotiating with developers. Scarcity is the precursor to optimization. Pat did a lot of things right, but scarcity, I think, is the one thing that forced a lot of the culture change.

HGTS: How long did it take you to acclimate to the Google culture given that you came from Microsoft, which doesn't have a centralized test organization?

James: Pat Copeland gave me two pieces of advice when I started. The first was to take some time to just learn. That was crucial. It takes a while to learn the ropes at a big company and being effective at Google was a different skill set than being effective at Microsoft. I took the first couple of months to do as Pat suggested—listen instead of speak, ask instead of try, and so on. I took him up on it. In fact, I actually think I stretched it for a couple of additional weeks!

HGTS: You said two pieces…

James: Oh yeah, sorry, got carried away. Occasionally Pat says wise things. I guess I was savoring one of them! The second I didn't like so much, but it was even better advice as it turns out. He took me aside and basically said "Look dude, I know you have a reputation outside Google, but inside, you haven't accomplished anything yet." Pat is rarely subtle; you don't have to waste a lot of time looking for nonvisual cues from him. His messages are always clear and this time, the message was that Google didn't care what I did before I got here. I had to succeed at Google as a Googler or none of the other stuff mattered. You can't get ahead at Google by walking around and proselytizing. His suggestion was that I take on something big and ship it, with some distinction if possible. I chose Chrome and Chrome OS and did just that. I was the first test manager ever for Chrome OS and after it shipped, I passed it on to one of my directs. Pat was right. It is easier to get things done after you've done something significant. My resume got me in the door, but success inside the walls of Google was crucial. The fact that I did it and contributed to a product people cared about made me someone to listen to. If I ever change jobs again, I'll reuse this formula: Learn first, build street cred second, and then start looking for ways to innovate.

HGTS: So beyond product testing, were there any other big areas Pat asked you to pick up?

James: Yeah, he asked me to own the TE discipline. The SET role had been around for a while and was pretty well understood so we knew the job ladder pretty well. We understood expectations and knew how to manage SETs for review and promotion. But for TEs, we were still trying to figure it out. Pat timed the renewal of focus on the TE role for my arrival. I think he knew he was going to use me for this even before I started. I actually suspect that he thought the pendulum had swung too far toward the SET and wanted to breathe life back into the TE role. Mind you, he never told me that, it's just my feeling.

HGTS: So what did you do for TEs?

James: Pat and I started a TE workgroup, which is actually still in existence. We met every other week, initially for two hours, and eventually down to monthly for an hour. Pat attended a few meetings and then left it to me to run it. The group was made up of about 12 TEs who were all hand-picked by Pat. I was too new to know any of them. For the first meeting, we started two lists: what rocked about the role and what sucked about it. Just making these lists was cathartic for many of the attendees. They were complaining about the same things and agreeing about what rocked. I was struck with how honest they were with Pat there. No one was sugar-coating anything! How many meetings did I attend during my career where everyone waited for the most important person in the room to talk and held their tongue because that person was there? Not at Google. No one cared what Pat thought, the meeting was about *them*, and if Pat couldn't take it, then that was his problem. It was incredibly refreshing.

That workgroup did a lot to define the TE role and rewrote the job ladder used for TE promotion guidelines. We put the new ladder to an open vote among the entire TE community and it was approved. It was cool, I spot-bonused the whole workgroup to celebrate. It was a real grass roots effort and it succeeded. We also wrote a bunch of interview guidances that were sent around to SETs and SWEs to teach them how to interview proper testers. The same information went to recruiters as well. I think it is safe to say that the TE role is as well defined as the SET role now.

HGTS: You've been at Google long enough to learn its inner workings. Can you boil Google's secret sauce down for us? What are the key ingredients to our testing magic?

James: Tester skill set (including computer science degrees), scarcity of testing resources as a forcing function to get developers to help and to get testers to optimize, automation first (so humans do only what computers aren't good at), and our ability to iterate and rapidly integrate user feedback. Any company looking to mimic what we have done should start with these four things: skill, scarcity, automation, and iterate-integrate. That's your recipe. Go cook up some Google testing stew!

HGTS: What about another book? Do you have another testing book in you?

James: I don't know. I never plan my books in advance. My first book started its life as course notes that I used at Florida Tech to teach testing to my students. I didn't plan on making it a book until I presented it at STAR and some lady came up to me and asked if I had ever considered writing a book. It was a loaded question. She was a book publisher and that's where *How to Break Software* came from. I wrote every word of that book and it was a long and cumbersome process that burned me out on book writing. My next two books both had coauthors. Hugh Thompson wrote *How to Break Software Security* and I helped. Mike Andrews wrote *How to Break Web Software* and again my role was to help. Those are really their books. I was there as a writer and thinker and manager of getting it done. I do love to write and neither Hugh nor Mike would begrudge me saying that I am better at it than they are. Would you two? I didn't think so. Neither of them would have written those books (although Hugh did go on to write another, still my conjecture holds!) if it hadn't been for me. Ultimately, whatever is going on in my professional career ends up as a book and the people around me end up as coauthors. Deny it, I dare you.

HGTS: Uh, well, readers are kind of holding the proof of what you say in their hands! We decline denial!

James: I'm not completely incapable of writing solo and the *Exploratory Testing* book was the next one I did alone. That one also came out of presentations I was giving at conferences. I did a stint of tutorials and the material built up until it was enough for a book. I am not sure I would have written this book if you two hadn't agreed to help. This was the first time the book was a total collaboration, though. I think the three of us contributed pretty equally.

HGTS: We did and we are both really happy to be involved. We may be able to code circles around you (and Jeff can code laps around you and most other people on the planet), but we'll grant you the readability in the English language! But tell us, what is your favorite part of the book?

James: All of it. This book was really fun to write. It wasn't so much about conjuring the material because the material was all there. All we had to do was document it. I guess if I had to pick, it would be the interviews. They were fun to give and fun to write up. I actually wish I had done these interviews when I first started. Hung Dang's was a real highlight. He and I spent time touring his Android lab and debated testing philosophy and the interview was intense. I hadn't taken notes that fast since I was in grad school. It was the most quality time I ever spent with him. I learned a lot about the people and processes here, much of which I really didn't know until I had to write it down. I guess that's the thing about being a journalist, you really get to know your subjects.

HGTS: What would you do if you weren't into testing?

James: Well in the technology field I'd work in developer tools and developer evangelism. I'd like to make writing software easier. Not everyone is as good at it as Jeff Carollo! I can't believe we are still hand-coding applications. The developer skills I learned back in college in the 80s are still applicable. That's crazy. The entire world of technology has changed and we're still writing in

C++. Why hasn't software development gotten any easier? Why is it that writing crappy, insecure code is still the default case? Writing good code should be easier than writing bad code. That's the problem I would work on.

The evangelism part is important too. I love public speaking and I love talking about technology to technologists. The idea that someone would hire me to interact with developers as my day job is even more exciting than testing. Let me know if you find any gig like that.

HGTS: And what if you got out of the technology field?

James: Well that's harder because I don't see my next career. I am still passionate about this one. But I think I'd like to teach management courses. You guys keep telling me I am a decent manager and one of these days I am going to sit down and think about why I don't suck at it. Maybe that will be my next book, *How Not to Suck as a Manager*. I'd also like to do work for the environment. I like this planet and think it's worth keeping nice.

Oh, and I like my beer. I very much like my beer. I can see doing the whole Norm from *Cheers* thing one of these days. I can picture it now: I walk into my local and everyone shouts "James!" and whoever is on my bar stool makes way.

Now that's what I call a job well done. I'd peer bonus Norm out of sheer respect.

CHAPTER 5
Improving How Google Tests Software

Google's testing process can be summed up quite simply: Put quality in the workflow of every engineer. When done earnestly and honestly, quality increases. Code freshly written is better. Early builds are better. Integrations are unnecessary. System testing can concentrate on real user-oriented issues. Keep the projects and all the engineers free of accumulated bug debt.

If your company has achieved this level of attention to quality, there is only one question remaining, "What's next?"

Well, what's next for Google is already beginning to take place. As we have perfected the role of testing in product development, we have created a process with more than a few obvious flaws. This chapter covers those flaws and talks about how testing is evolving, or devolving, at Google to address them. What has occurred is a decentralization of testing where the Engineering Productivity organization has been broken up and its pieces absorbed by the product teams. This, we believe, is a natural progression that occurs when a certain level of test maturity is achieved. Google is simply no longer best served by keeping development and testing separate.

Fatal Flaws in Google's Process

Testing is often seen as a surrogate for quality and if you ask a developer what he is doing about quality, "testing" is often the answer. But testing is not about quality. Quality has to be built in, not bolted on, and as such, quality is a developer task. Period. This brings us to fatal flaw number 1: Testers have become a crutch for developers. The less we make them think about testing and the easier we make testing, the less testing they will do.

Every time we sit inside on our comfortable sofas watching television while someone else mows our lawn, we see this in action. People are capable of mowing their own lawn. Worse, we are often at home doing nothing while our lawns are being mowed! Lawn services have made it easy for us, enough so that we are happy to farm this work out without thinking about it. When testing becomes a service that enables developers to not think about it, then they will not think about it. Testing should involve some pain. It should involve some concern on the part of developers. To the extent that we have made testing too easy, we have made developers too lazy.

The fact that testing is a separate organization at Google exacerbates this problem. Quality is not only someone else's problem; it is another organization's problem. Like my lawn service, the responsible party is easy to identify and easy to blame when something goes wrong.

The second fatal flaw is also related to developers and testers separated by organizational boundaries.

Testers identify with their role and not their product.

Whenever the focus is not on the product, the product suffers. After all, the ultimate purpose of software development is to build a product, not to code a product, not to test a product, not to document a product. Every role an engineer performs is in service to the overall product. The role is secondary. A sign of a healthy organization is when people say, "I work on Chrome" not whey they say, "I am a tester."

A few years ago, I saw a t-shirt at a testing conference with the phrase "I test, therefore I am" printed in Greek and English. I am sure whoever made it thought it devilishly clever, but it is a combative, anti-product slogan that puts the role of testing in an elevated light that it simply does not deserve. No role deserves it. Everyone on a team works on the product, not some part of the development process. The process itself is subservient to the product. Why else have any process except to build a better product? Users fall in love with products, not the processes that built them.

Google's separation of development and test fosters a role-based association and makes it harder for testers to align themselves with their products.

The third fatal flaw is that testers often worship test artifacts over the software itself.

The value of testing is in the activity, not the artifacts.

Every artifact generated by testers is secondary to the source code. Test cases are less important; the test plan is less important. Bug reports are less important. The activities are what go into making these artifacts that actually provide value. Unfortunately, in the celebration of these artifacts (such as counting the number of bug reports submitted by a test engineer [TE] during an annual review), we forget about the software. All testing artifacts have value to the extent that they impact the source code and therefore, the product.

A separate team of testers has a tendency to focus on the construction and maintenance of test artifacts. The product would be better served if the activities involved in testing were aimed exclusively at the source code. Testers must put the product first.

The last fatal flaw is perhaps the most insightful. How often are products released only for users to find problems that escaped even the more voracious testing process? The answer: almost always. None of us have ever been associated with a product launch that didn't suffer field issues the test team failed to identify (at Google or elsewhere). In fact, many of the best bugs in Google+, the product all three of us are working on at the time of this writing, were found by dogfooders—other Googlers outside the Google+ team trying to use the product. We were acting like users; the dog-fooders were actual users!

It doesn't matter who does the testing, only that the testing gets done.

Dogfood users, trusted testers, crowd-sourced testers, and early adopters are all in a better position to find bugs than test engineers. In fact, the less testing a TE does and the more enabling of others, the better.

So what do we do about all of this? How do we take everything that is right about Google testing and make it more product-focused and team-oriented? Now we're getting into uncharted territory and the only thing we can do is speculate. However, there are some compelling trends that this book uncovers that, we believe, form the basis for predicting the future of testing at Google and elsewhere. In fact, the software engineer in test (SET) and TE roles themselves are already migrating toward this future.

These two roles are actually diverging at Google. The SET role is becoming more and more developer-like and the TE role is going in the exact opposite direction and becoming more user-like. This is happening organically as a natural progression of a mature software development organization. Partly, the trend is due to technological innovations such as compressed development cycles and continuous availability of the latest build to developers, testers, and users alike. This gives far more opportunity to include other nonengineer stakeholders into the development process. The other part of the equation is a maturation of the idea that quality is everyone's job and not the sole domain of engineers with the word "test" in their title.

The Future of the SET

Simply put, we don't believe there is a future SET. The SET is a developer. Period. Google pays them as developers, calibrates their performance reviews against developers, and calls both roles software engineers. So many similarities can only lead to one conclusion: They are the exact same role.

As doomed as we believe the role is, the work itself cannot go away. The magic in the Google formula is the work the SET performs. SETs provide features such as testability, reliability, debugging capability, and so on. If we treat these things as features in the same sense that we treat the UI and other functional components as features, then SETs are nothing more than developers who own these features. This is the evolution of the role we think will happen at Google and other mature software shops in the near future and what better way to make test development a first-class citizen than treating it just like any other feature?

Indeed, this is the part of the process that is flawed in its current state. Every user-facing feature is managed by product managers (PMs) and built by SWEs. Code for these features is tracked, managed, and maintained by a well-defined automated workflow. However, test code is managed by TEs and built by SETs. Why? This is a relic of the history of how the roles evolved. But the evolution has peaked and it's time to treat test code as a first-class citizen: let it be managed by PMs and built by software engineers (SWEs).

Which SWEs will make the best SETs and can be trusted to own the quality features and take their work seriously? Well, at a company like Google that already has the SET role, we can simply convert all the SETs to SWEs and be done with it. But this is a subpar solution in our minds. Every SWE can benefit from having a tour of duty owning quality features;[1] however, it isn't practical (nor Googley) to simply force people in this situation. Instead, ownership of testing features should fall to new team members, particularly the more junior ones.

Here's our reasoning. Testing features cut across the entire footprint of a product. As such, the developers involved in building testing features are forced to learn the product from interfaces to APIs. What better way is there to take a deep dive into a product and learn its design and architecture quickly? Owning the test feature (either building it from scratch, modifying, or maintaining it) is the perfect starter project for any developer on any team. Arguably it is even the best starter project. As new members are on board, existing test developers move to feature development to make way for the new engineers. Everyone is fresh and engaged and over time, all developers are test savvy and take quality seriously.

Junior developers and hires fresh from college find test development the absolute best place to start. Not only do they get to learn about the entire project, but because much of the test code won't ship, they avoid the pressure and potential embarrassment of writing a user-facing bug (at least until later in their career).

The fundamental difference between this single role model and Google's existing model is that testing expertise is more evenly distributed among the SWE ranks as opposed to being concentrated in the SETs. This is an important distinction that powers greater productivity gains by removing the SET bottleneck. Additionally, because there is no difference in the titles of the engineers involved, there are no barriers or stigmas to moving from test to feature development and back: a single product, a single team, a single role.

---

[1] Google has such a program for Service Reliability Engineers (SREs) called Mission Control. SWEs who complete the six-month program in an SRE role get a significant cash reward and a leather jacket emblazoned with a Mission Control Google badge.

The Future of the TE

The need for good test engineers has never been greater. However, we believe that need has peaked and is in rapid decline. The truth is that much of the test case creation, execution, and regression testing TEs traditionally perform is available in more complete and cost-effective formats.

Much of this bounty of opportunity is due to technological improvements in the way software is delivered. Back in the days of weekly or monthly builds and painstaking integrations, it was important to have testers who could find bugs and act like users as much as possible. Bugs had to be found before shipping a product to millions of users where the issues were hard to track and the product hard to update. Not any longer. Delivering software via the Web means the ability to deliver early to a few select users, respond to their feedback, and deliver updates quickly. The barriers to developer-user communication and collaboration are gone. The life span of a bug has declined from months to minutes. It's a case of better software delivery and better user feedback so that we build, deliver (to dogfooders, trusted testers, early adopters, or actual users), fix, and redeliver faster than many users can even notice defects. Exactly where does a team of professional TEs fit into this equation? Users experience far less pain now than they did in the old days and it is time to adjust our testing resources appropriately.

Here's the bottom line. Who would you rather have testing your software: highly paid, on-site exploratory testing experts doing their best to anticipate actual usage in the hopes they find important bugs or a large army of actual users who are incentivized to find and report real bugs? Access to real users willing to report issues in exchange for early access has never been easier and with daily or hourly updates, the actual risks to these users is minimal. In this new world order, the TE role needs a complete overhaul.

Test engineering, we believe, will morph into a test design role where a small number of test designers quickly map out the testing surface, risk heat map and tours for application (see Chapter 3). Then, when dogfooders, trusted testers, early adopters, or crowd testers submit feedback, the TE can assess coverage, calculate risk impact, ensure it trends down, and adjust the testing activities accordingly. These test designers can also identify places where expertise, such as security, privacy, performance, and exploratory testing, are required and then direct that work to specialists in the crowd. There is also the work of creating or acquiring tools to collect and analyze all this incoming data. There is no test creation, no test execution, no actual testing at all. Okay, perhaps "no" is too strong a word, but certainly, this aspect of the job is minimal. It's a job that requires designing, organizing, and managing test resources that are mostly free.

TEs, we believe, will migrate to specialist roles such as security or they will become managers of testing activity that is performed by others. It is a challenging and senior role that requires a great deal of expertise. It may even be a role that pays a lot more than current TE positions, but it will be a role that requires far fewer people than it did in the past.

The Future of the Test Director and Manager

With all this change in the TE and SET roles, what does it mean for the future of test directors, managers, and even VPs at some companies? It means that there will be far fewer of them, and the more technical ones will move into more of a distinguished engineer, individual role. They will live on as thought leaders and coordinators across very loosely coupled TEs and quality-focused SWEs, but not ultimately accountable for quality or management of any specific project. Test activities should be accountable to the actual products people work on, not a centralized organization with tangential ties to shipping products and the rest of the engineering processes.

The Future of Test Infrastructure

The test infrastructure at Google is still surprisingly client-based. There are still a lot of Selenium and WebDriver tests written in Java or Python, checked into the source trees, built, and deployed to banks of dedicated virtual machines via shell scripts. These test drivers inject this Java-based test logic into the browser from code running as an application on the native operating system. This works, but our infrastructure needs an overhaul because this approach requires expensive people and machine infrastructure dedicated to test creation and execution. Testing infrastructure eventually moves entirely into the cloud. Test case repositories, test code editors, recorders, and execution will all work from within a website or from within a browser extension. Test authoring, execution, and debugging are most efficient when they occur in the same language and context as the application itself. For Google and many other projects these days, this is more often a web application. For projects that are still inherently non-Web such as native Android or iOS applications, they will be driven from the Web using adaptions of web-focused test frameworks. Native Driver[2] is a great early example of this move to Web first, native secondary.

As projects and testing needs appear and disappear more quickly in this "fail fast" environment, there will be fewer inhouse, custom test frameworks and dedicated test execution machines. Test developers will increasingly leverage and contribute to open-source projects, cobble them together, and execute them on shared cloud computing resources. Selenium and

---

[2] Google testing blog post on Native Driver: http://google-opensource.blogspot.com/2011/06/introducing-native-driver.html

WebDriver set the model for community-maintained and corporate-sponsored infrastructure development. There will be more of these projects and tighter integration between these open test frameworks, open bug and issue-tracking systems, and source control.

Sharing test data, test cases, and test infrastructure will be worth giving up imagined advantages of keeping everything secret or proprietary. Secret and proprietary testing infrastructure just means it is expensive, slow-moving, and often not reusable even within the company across projects. The future testers will share as much code, test, and bug data as possible, as the returns from the community, new forms of crowd-based testing and test creation, and user good-will will outweigh the imagined benefits of keeping everything hidden.

This more open and cloud-based approach to testing will save money, provide test infrastructure developers more visibility, and most importantly, it will enable project-level test developers to focus on the test coverage and not the infrastructure, leading to higher quality products and faster release cycles.

In Conclusion

The end of testing as we know and love it is a hard message to hear. It will be much harder for those whose careers are defined by the status quo. But there is no arguing that the software development problem has been fundamentally altered by agile development, continuous builds, early user involvement, crowd-based testing, and online software delivery. Sticking to decades-old testing dogma is a recipe for irrelevance.

This transition is already well underway at Google, although not everyone here even knows it. The engineers, managers, and directors in centralized testing are dispersing into more project-focused teams and accountabilities. This transition is forcing them to move faster and focus less on the process of testing and focus more on the product itself. As Googlers, we are seeing this transition a bit earlier than many other companies. It's likely that every tester's world will adjust to these new realities very soon. Embrace and drive these changes to remain relevant as a tester.

APPENDIX A
Chrome OS Test Plan

status: draft

(contact chromeos-te@google.com)

author: jarbon@google.com

Overview of Themes

- **Risk-based**: Chrome OS has a large test surface area, spanning a customized browser, application manager user experience (UX), firmware, hardware, networking, user data synchronization, automatic updates, and customized physical hardware from Original Equipment Manufacturers (OEMs). To tackle this testing problem in a coherent manner, the test strategy is risk-based, meaning the team will focus on the most risky areas of the system first and work its way down the list, relying heavily on thorough unit tests and code quality from the development team to form a strong foundation of overall product quality.

- **Hardware test matrix automation**: Given the variety of hardware and continual OS builds, it is important to run tests on each continuous build across the entire hardware matrix to quickly identify any regressions and to aid in isolating issues of a particular software, hardware, or environmental set of dimensions (for example, a test fails only on HP hardware in a wireless configuration on browser buildX).

- **Enable quick iteration:** Chrome OS has an aggressive schedule, so there is a premium on identifying bugs as early as possible and on isolating the specific repro conditions. All tests are runnable on the local developer's workstation to avoid bugs getting into the tree in the first place, and a large matrix of automation is executed to speed up the isolation of any regressions.

- **Open tools and tests:** Given the open source nature of ChromiumOS and the need for an OEM partner qualification, the test team makes every effort to ensure that the tools, tests, automation, and so on can be shared and executed externally.

- **Chrome OS primary browser platform**: The Chrome browser test team transitions to focusing on Chrome OS as a primary platform. Testability, automation, and so on are focused on Chrome OS first with other platforms a close second. This reflects the critical role of the Chrome browser in Chrome OS; it's the only UX and everything in the OS and hardware is there to support its functionality. The Chrome browser quality bar must be higher on Chrome OS.

- **Test delivers data**: The goal of the test team isn't, and cannot be, to ensure quality. Quality is a function of all disciplines on the project, including external OEMs, open-source projects, and so on. The test team's goals are to mitigate risk, find as many issues and bugs as possible, and provide metrics and general evaluations of functional risk to the larger team. Test, dev, Program Manager (PM), and third parties have a voice and strong influence on quality for Chrome OS.

- **Testability and the multiplier effect**: Testability, especially for the Google apps teams, external third parties, and even internally has been an issue in the past. The test team partners with the accessibility, Android, and Webdriver teams to accelerate testability and make Chrome officially supported on Chrome OS. This improves test automation productivity within the team for the Google apps teams. This also has the ultimate benefit of making Chrome the ideal platform for testing other applications for third-party web pages.

Risk Analysis

The test team drives functional risk analysis with the following goals in mind:

- Ensure that the quality risks in the product are understood.

- Ensure that the test team is always focused on the highest return on investment (ROI) activities at any given time.

- Ensure that there is a framework for evaluating any new quality or risk data that comes in as the product evolves and new data arrives.

Risk analysis simply lists the set of all known features and capabilities of the product, and the test team evaluates the absolute inherent risk for each area given its frequency of exposure and likelihood of failure combined with the severity of consequences (to the user and the business) should it fail. Then, any mitigations (such as existing test cases, automation, testing via usage, OEM testing, and so on) are deducted from this known risk. All components are then stack-ranked by the net risk, and these areas are addressed through test case development, automation, and processes.

The bottom line is to know what is at risk in the product and to always apply the resources at hand to methodically reduce the risk in the product.

Per-Build Baseline Testing

Every continual build receives the following testing in addition to dev unit tests via Buildbots.

- Smoke tests (P0 automation)
- Performance tests

Per-LKG Day Testing

Each day, the following testing occurs against the last known good (LKG) continual build:

- Manual verification of a set of functional acceptance tests (this can be limited to one type of hardware per day).
- Functional regression automation is executed.
- Continual testing of top web app tests picks up the daily rolling build (both automated and manual).
- Stress, long-running, and stability tests are conducted on a rolling basis. Re-run the tests on daily builds until no issues turn up, and then move to weekly runs.
- Continual manual exploratory testing and tour testing.
- AutoUpdate test automation.

Per-Release Testing

Every "release candidate" build for all channels.

- **Site compatibility**: The Chrome browser test team verifies the top 100 sites on Chrome OS.
- **Scenario verification**: Verify scenarios of any demos that are commonly given (maybe a maximum of two to three demos) of the Chrome OS builds to partners or at conventions.
- **P0 bug verification**: Verify all fixed P0 bugs. Verify 80 percent of all P1 bugs filed since the period of the last release.

- **Full stress and stability run**: Conduct a stress and stability run.
- **Chrome OS manual test cases**: All Chrome OS manual test cases should be run (can be divided up between testers on different hardware).

Manual Versus Automation

Manual testing is important, especially early in the project when the UX and other features evolve quickly and when testability work and automation are underway. Manual testing is also critical because a core value of Chrome OS is simplicity, and the UX needs to be pleasant and intuitive for the user. Machines still cannot test this.

Automation is key to the long-term success and efficiency of the test team and to guard against regressions. As automation is enabled in the browser, much of manual testing in priority and ROI order is also automated.

Dev Versus Test Quality Focus

The dev team is relatively large and has much more insight into component and CL-level technical details. We want dev to provide a rich set of unit and focused system tests that are added via Autotest.

The test team focuses on more end-to-end and integration test scenarios, focusing on user-exposed functionality, cross-component interaction, stability, and large-scale testing and reporting.

Release Channels

We should apply our learnings from the core Chrome browser team's success with different "channels" for users with varying degrees of tolerance for pain and willingness to provide feedback. Several channels are maintained with increasing levels of confidence in quality. This mimics "flighting" of google.com properties and allows for some level of experimentation with real-world usage before a large deployment, mitigating risk across the product.

User Input

User input for quality is critically important. You need to facilitate making it easy for users to provide actionable feedback and to organize their data.

GoogleFeedback Extension: This extension allows users to provide point-and-click feedback on any URL, and it provides a dashboard for analysis and clustering of the feedback. The test team works to support the integration of GoogleFeedback into Chrome OS and to extend its reporting into the ChromeUX.

Known Bugs Extension / HUD: For trusted users with project tasks or context, it should be easy to file a bug on the OS and see existing bugs directly in the Chrome OS browser. Longer term, this project should develop into a more general purpose "heads-up display" for project and quality data.

Support rollout to Googlers aggressively, including supporting non-standard hardware and spinup.

Test Case Repositories

- **Manual test cases**: All manual test cases are stored in TestScribe. Later, folks work on a test case repository for code.google.com.
- **Automated test cases**: All are stored in the tree in Autotest format. Everything is versioned, shared, and right next to the code under test.

Test Dashboarding

Given the large amount of data and need to disseminate it quickly, the test team invests in dedicated quality metrics dashboarding. This provides high-level, quality assessments (green and red lights), aggregates both manual and automated test execution results, and allows for deep dives into failure information.

Virtualization

It is important, especially early on, to support virtualization of the Chrome OS images. This reduces our dependence on physical hardware, speeds up imaging, supports regression testing in Selenium and WebDriver types of farms, and supports Chrome OS testing and development directly on workstations.

Performance

Generally speaking, performance is a core feature of Chrome OS, and as such, it is a large distributed project on the development team. The test team aims to aid in the execution, reporting, and trending of performance measurements in the lab, but not to focus on developing directed performance testing.

Stress, Long-Running, and Stability

The test team focuses on building long-running test cases and executing them on physical hardware in the labs. Add fault injection via the underlying platform.

Test Execution Framework (Autotest)

The test and dev teams have reached consensus that Autotest is the core test framework for test automation. Autotest is proven in the Linux community, used on several internal projects, and it is open source. Autotest also supports local and distributed execution. Autotest wraps all other functional test harnesses (such as WebDriver and other third-party test harnesses) so there is a unified interface to test execution, distribution, and reporting.

It is interesting to note that the core test tools team invests in adding Autotest support for Windows and Mac as well.

OEMs

OEMs play a key role in qualification of Chrome OS builds. The test and dev teams work to deliver the relevant manual and automated test cases for OEMs to qualify builds and hardware on their end. The test team also works closely with top-tier OEMs to include hardware variants in the daily testing to catch any OEM-specific issues or regressions as early as possible.

Hardware Lab

A hardware lab is constructed to support a wide array of netbooks and devices with common services such as power, networking (wired and wireless), health dashboards, power management, and some specialized infrastructure for directed testing of things such as wireless. The lab machines are largely managed by HIVE infrastructure.

E2E Farm Automation

The test team builds out a farm of netbooks for test execution and reporting across the large matrix of hardware and software. These farms are distributed throughout MTV, KIR, and HYD locations to provide geo-local lab access and provide near round-the-clock test execution and debugging.

Testing the Browser AppManager

The core browser on Chrome OS is the Linux version of Chrome with a Chrome OS specialized UX and features. Much of the core rendering and functionality is the same, but there are significant differences between the core browser and the Chrome OS variant (such as pinned tabs, download manager, app launcher, platform control UX, wireless, and so on).

- Chrome OS is a primary platform for core Chrome browser testing (manual and automated).

- The core browser team determines which build of the browser to integrate (based on quality and Chrome OS features).

- For each Chrome OS release candidate, the core browser team performs the usual matrix of site (app) compatibility tests (top 300 sites) on Chrome OS (currently, there is only manual testing on live sites).

- The site (app) compatability tests are partially automated via WebDriver and integrated into builbots or regular lab runs, to provide "early warning" signals for any major Chrome OS specific regressions.

- A suite of manual tests focused on Chrome OS features of the browser and App Manager is developed and executed by a team of vendors.

- As APIs are implemented, the suite of manual Chrome OS tests are automated via vendors.

- Chrome OS Chromebot should have Linux and Chrome OS variants running with Chrome OS-specific functionality and not just web apps.

- Manual exploratory testing and tours should prove valuable in finding end user-focused issues around simplicity, functionality, usability, and so on.

Browser Testability

The browser exposes many of the core UX and functional aspects of Chrome OS to the user. Much of the BrowserUX is not testable, or, it is testable only via lower-level IPC AutomationProxy interfaces that live outside of the browser. For Chrome OS, we work to unify the testing of web apps, Chrome UX, and functionality, and we work to kick off lower-level system tests. We also want to ensure that Chrome is the most testable browser for web apps, to encourage external web development teams to test first on the Chrome platform. To this end, the following is constructed:

- **Port Selenium and WebDriver to Chrome OS**: This is the core test framework driver for web apps today. The Chrome browser and OS test team are likely to pick up ownership of all Chrome-specific aspects of WebDriver moving forward to ensure a solid, testable interface for the apps teams and external testers.

- **Expose Chrome UX and functionality via JavaScript DOM**: This enables WebDriver tests to drive UX and functional aspects of Chrome as well. This functionality is exposed via the same methods as shutdown and sleep and the accessibility people (raman@) work on the ChromeViews.

- **Higher-level scripting**: Work with the WebDriver people to extend the basic WebDriver API into pure JavaScript and eventually into higher-order record/playback and parameterizable scripts (such as "Google Search <term>"). This speeds up internal and external test development, which, with WebDriver, still requires a fair amount of hunting for elements and maintenance issues when the UX changes quickly.

Hardware

Chrome OS has a set of hardware requirements and variations from many OEMs. Directed testing is needed on the core OEM platforms to ensure tight integration between the physical hardware and Chrome OS. Specifically, tests are designed for:

- **Power management**: Line and battery-powered cycles, failures, power management of hardware components, and so on.
- **Hardware malfunction**: What does Chrome OS detect and how does it recover?

Timeline

Q4 2009:

- Manual acceptance tests defined and running on continual builds
- Basic release qualification testing defined and executed for each major release
- Basic hardware labs spun up

- Complete risk analysis
- Automate E2E execution for continual builds on physical netbooks in the lab
- Hive support for virtual and physical machine imaging
- Port of WebDriver and Selenium to Chrome OS
- Some automated tests for top web apps
- Decide on test harness for dev and test
- Drive GoogleFeedback integration for Chrome OS
- Build out core test team, people, and processes
- Automated A/V tests
- Complete risk-based planning
- Manual UX testing plan

Q1 2010:

- Quality dashboard
- Automated auto update tests
- Support for automated performance testing in the lab
- Labs in HYD, KIR, and MTV all spun up and execute tests
- Chromebot for Linux and Chrome OS
- Testability support for major Chrome OS functions and UX
- Set of Chrome OS functional regression automation
- Add Chrome OS to web app regression Selenium farm
- Prototype of record and playback support for browser and UX testing
- ChromeSync E2E test case automation
- Stability and fault-injection testing
- Directed network testing
- Regular exploratory manual testing and tours to appease James J

Q2 2010:

- Risk mitigation via testing and automation

Q3 2010:

- Risk mitigation via testing and automation

Q4 2010:

- All risks are mitigated, everything is automated, there are no new issues, and there are no more UX or functional changes. The test team winds down.

Primary Test Drivers

- Test tech lead for Chrome OS platform
- Test tech lead for Chrome OS browser
- Core browser automation TechLead
- Dashboarding and metrics
- Manual acceptance test definition and execution
- Manual regression test definition and execution (and its team of vendors)
- Browser Appcompat, Core UX, and functionality (manual) and the team of vendors
- Audio and video
- Stability / fault injection
- Accessibility testing
- Hardware labs: KIR, HYD, and MTV
- Farm automation
- Hardware acceptance
- Overall direction and funding

Relevant Documents

- Risk analysis
- Hardware labs
- E2E farm automation
- Virtual and physical machine management infrastructure
- Heads-up Display (HUD)
- Manual acceptance tests
- Test results dashboard
- OEM hardware qualification tests
- Hardware usage and health dashboard
- Chrome OS manual/functional test plan

APPENDIX B
Test Tours for Chrome

The test tours include the following:

- The Shopping Tour
- The Student Tour
- The International Calling Tour
- The Landmark Tour
- The All Nighter Tour
- The Artisan's Tour
- The Bad Neighborhood Tour
- The Personalization Tour

The Shopping Tour

Description: Shopping is a favorite pastime of many people and one of the joys of traveling to somewhere new can be finding new products to buy. In some cities, the shopping is so extravagant that it serves as the primary attraction. Hong Kong has some of the largest and most elaborate malls in the world hosting more than 800 stores in a single location.

In software, commerce is nothing new, and though not every application has ways for people to spend money, a lot of them do. This is especially true as we move into an era where additional, downloadable content is the status quo. The Shopping Tour invites users to shop wherever it's possible in the software under test to validate that users can engage in commerce smoothly and effectively.

Applied: Chrome is a portal to the Internet where there's nearly an endless number of ways to spend money. Although testing every vendor isn't feasible, ensuring that the majority of retailers are accessible and that Google stores won't have any problems is. Following is a list of the top online retailers based on traffic to their sites.

- eBay (www.eBay.com)

- Amazon (www.amazon.com)

- Sears (www.sears.com)

- Staples (www.staples.com)

- OfficeMax (www.officemax.com)

- Macy's (www.macys.com)

- NewEgg (www.newegg.com)

- Best Buy (www.bestbuy.com)

The Student Tour

Description: Many students take advantage of the chance to study abroad, and while living in their new destinations, they'll use local resources to advance their knowledge of their area of expertise. This tour covers all the resources available for tourists such as libraries, archives, and museums.

Similarly, in software, many people try out a new technology and use it for research to increase their understanding of a particular topic. This tour encourages the user to do just that and to take advantage of and test all the features in the software that help gather and organize information.

Applied: Test how well Chrome can collect and organize data from a variety of sources. For example, can users take information from a half-dozen sites and bring it all together in a cloud-based document? Can offline content be uploaded and used effectively?

Suggested Areas to Test

A Student's Tour of Chrome includes

- **Copy & Paste**: Can different types of data be transferred using the Clipboard?

- **Moving offline content to the cloud**: Web pages, images, text, and so on.

- **Capacity**: Having multiple documents open at once and in different windows.

- **Transportation**: Moving data across tabs and windows and between different kinds of windows (normal and incognito).

The International Calling Tour

Description: While traveling, making calls back home can be an experience in and of itself. Dealing with international operators, currencies, and credit cards can result in some interesting things.

In software, users might want to interact with the same features (people back home) but from different platforms, privilege levels, and with different settings. This tour focuses on ensuring users get a smooth and reliable experience regardless of where they operate.

Applied: Browse to common sites and use common features, trying out Chrome on different platforms (Windows, Mac, and Linux) if available and with different connection settings in the OS.

Suggested Areas to Test

An International Calling Tour of Chrome includes

- **Operating systems**: Windows, Mac, and Linux
- **Privilege levels**: High integrity and low integrity
- **Languages**: Complex languages and right-to-left languages
- **Network options**: Proxy, Wi-Fi, wired LAN, and firewalled

The Landmark Tour

Description: "The process was simple. Use the compass to locate a landmark (a tree, rock, cliff face, and so on) in the direction you want to go, make your way to that landmark, and then locate the next landmark, and so on. As long as the landmarks were all in the same direction, you could get yourself through a patch of dense Kentucky woods. The Landmark Tour for exploratory testers is similar in that we will choose landmarks and perform the same landmark through the software that we would through a forest."

Applied: In Chrome, this tour takes a look at how easily a user can navigate from one landmark to another. Verify users can get to the landmarks, such as different browser windows, opening attachments, settings, and so on.

Suggested Landmarks in Chrome

A Landmark Tour of Chrome includes

- **Browser window**: This is the main browser window used for browsing the Web.

- **Incognito window**: The Incognito window is used for browsing under the radar; a trademark cloak-and-dagger character displays in the upper-left corner to notify the user.

- **Compact Navigation Bar**: This browser window is available from the menu; it has a search box available in the title bar of the window.

- **Download Manager**: The Download Manager displays a list of the user's downloaded content.

- **Bookmark Manager**: The Bookmark Manager is a full window that displays the user's bookmarks and it supports launching them.

- **Developer Tools**: These tools are the Task Manager, JavaScript Console, and so on.

- **Settings**: These settings are launched from the menu in the upper-right corner when you select Options.

- **Themes Page**: A page where users can personalize the appearance of Chrome OS.

The All Nighter Tour

Description: How far can you go? The All Nighter Tour challenges tourists to test their own endurance by going from attraction to attraction with little or no break in between. "Such tours are tests of the constitution. Can you last? Can you survive the all nighter?"

In software, this tour challenges the product under test to see how long it can last when its features are used over a prolonged period of time. The key is trying not to close anything and continuing one long user experience. This tour can uncover bugs that occur only after a prolonged period of time.

Applied (Chrome): Open lots of tabs, install extensions, change themes, and keep browsing in a single session for as long as feasible. Avoid closing tabs or windows when you're done with them; just keep opening up more content. If the tour extends into multiple days, keep Chrome open overnight and continue the tour the next day.

Suggested Areas to Test

An All Nighter tour of Chrome includes

- **Tabs and windows**: Open large numbers of tabs and windows.

- **Extensions**: Add a large number of extensions and keep them running.

- **Duration**: Leave **everything** open for an extended period of time.

The Artisan's Tour

Description: While some travel for pleasure, others travel for business. This tour examines how easy it is to perform business operations in a tourist's new destination. Are there local vendors? How much red tape is there to getting started?

In software, this tour looks at how easily users can develop content using the tools in the software under test. In place of local vendors and red tape, a user can take a look at how many tools the software provides in the application and how easy is it to import and export content.

Applied: Chrome has a fair number of tools for JavaScript developers and for web developers who test and run their online content. Use this tour to check out the tools, generate sample scripts, and test online content.

Tools in Chrome

An Artisan's Tour of Chrome includes

- **Developer tools**: Look at the page's elements, resources, and scripts, and enable resource tracking.

- **JavaScript Console**: Does JavaScript in the Console execute correctly?

- **Viewing source code**: Is it easy to read through the use of color coding and other help, and is it easy to get to a relevant section?

- **Task Manager**: Do processes show up correctly and is it easy to see how many resources the web page consumes?

The Bad Neighborhood Tour

Description: "Every city has bad neighborhoods and areas that a tourist is well advised to avoid. Software also has bad neighborhoods—those sections of the code populated with bugs."

Applied: The focus of Chrome is on a fast and simplified experience browsing the Web, but rich content tends to suffer. When it was first launched, it was reported that even YouTube videos didn't play correctly, and although significant progress has been made for overcoming these challenges, rich content is still an issue.

Bad Neighborhoods in Chrome OS

A Bad Neighborhood Tour of Chrome includes

- **Online video**: Hulu, YouTube, ABC, NBC, full-screen mode, and high definition.

- **Flash-based content**: Games, ads, and presentations.

- **Extensions**: Test-rich extensions.

- **Java applets**: Verify Java applets can be run successfully. Yahoo! games are popular examples of Java applets.

- **O3D**: Verify content written with Google's own O3D; for example, video calls in Gmail use O3D.

- **Multiple instances**: Attempt to run multiple instances of rich content in different tabs and windows.

The Personalization Tour

Description: The Personalization Tour shows tourists where they can go to find the largest selection of ways to personalize their experience while traveling. This can include everything from a new pair of sunglasses to rental cars, hired guides, and even clothing boutiques. In software, this tour lets users explore the various ways they can customize their experience and personalize their software to make it uniquely theirs.

Applied: Explore the various ways one can customize Chrome to a particular user's taste through the use of themes, extensions, bookmarks, settings, shortcuts, and profiles.

Ways to Customize Chrome

A Personalization Tour of Chrome includes

- **Themes**: Use themes to customize the appearance of Chrome OS.

- **Extensions**: Download and install extensions to Chrome OS to extend its functionality and appearance.

- **Chrome settings**: Customize the user's experience by changing Chrome settings.

- **Separation of profiles**: Verify that preferences for one user profile aren't able to propagate to another account.

Blog Posts on Tools and Code

001100101011011000101000

This appendix presents some of the blog posts from the Google Testing Blog.

Take a BITE out of Bugs and Redundant Labor

Wednesday, October 12, 2011 9:21 AM
http://googletesting.blogspot.com/2011/10/take-bite-out-of-bugs-and-redundant.html
By Joe Allan Muharsky
In a time when more and more of the Web is becoming streamlined, the process of filing bugs for websites remains tedious and manual. Find an issue. Switch to your bug system window. Fill out boilerplate descriptions of the problem. Switch back to the browser, take a screenshot, attach it to the issue. Type some more descriptions. The whole process is one of context switching; from the tools used to file the bug, to gather information about it, to highlight problematic areas, most of your focus as the tester is pulled away from the very application you're trying to test.

The Browser Integrated Testing Environment, or BITE, is an open source Chrome extension (http://code.google.com/chrome/extensions/index.html) that aims to fix the manual web-testing experience (see Figure C.1). To use the extension, it must be linked to a server providing information about bugs and tests in your system. BITE then provides the capability to file bugs from the context of a website, using relevant templates.

FIGURE C.1　BITE extension menu added to the Chrome Browser.

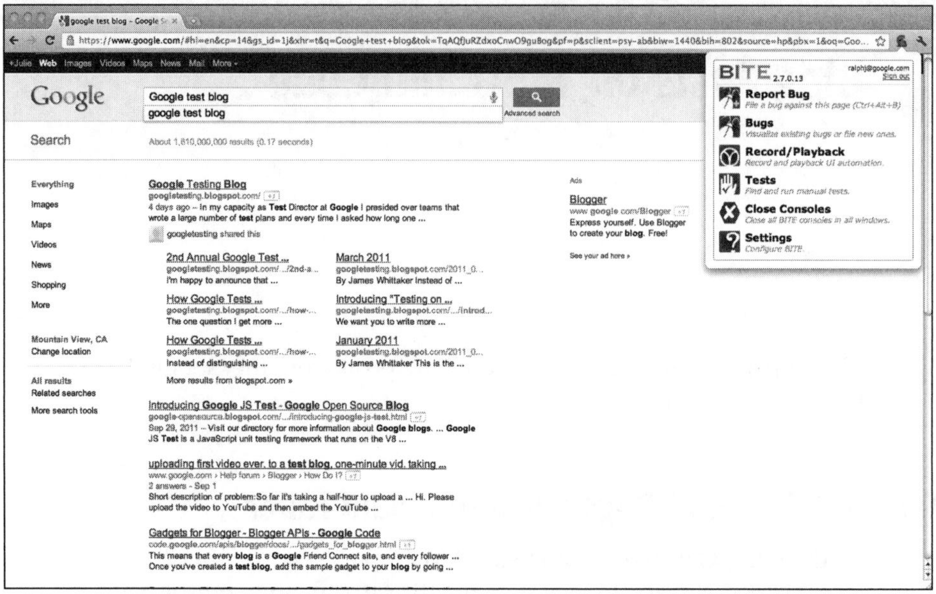

When filing a bug, BITE automatically grabs screenshots, links, and problematic UI elements, and it attaches them to the bug (see Figure C.2). This gives developers charged with investigating and/or fixing the bug a wealth of information to help them determine root causes and factors in the behavior.

FIGURE C.2　Bug Filing interface for BITE extension.

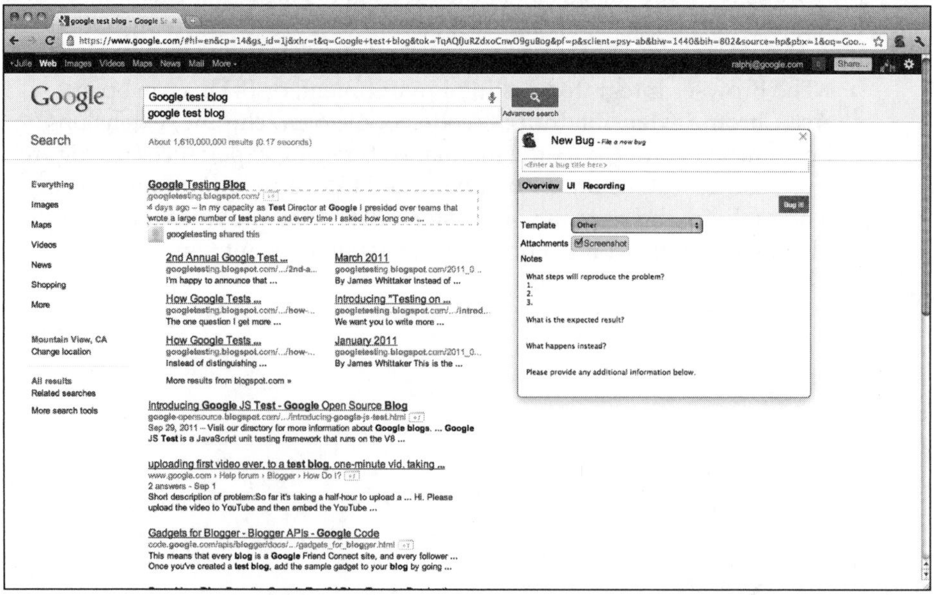

When it comes to reproducing a bug, testers will often labor to remember and accurately record the exact steps taken. With BITE, however, every action the tester takes on the page is recorded in JavaScript and can be played back later. This enables engineers to quickly determine whether the steps of a bug reproduce in a specific environment or whether a code change has resolved the issue.

Also included in BITE is a Record/Playback console to automate user actions in a manual test. Like the BITE recording experience, the RPF console will automatically author JavaScript that can be used to replay your actions at a later date. And BITE's record and playback mechanism is fault-tolerant; UI automation tests will fail from time to time, and when they do, it tends to be for test issues rather than product issues. To that end, when a BITE playback fails, the tester can fix his recording in real-time just by repeating the action on the page. There's no need to touch code or report a failing test; if your script can't find a button to click on, just click on it again, and the script will be fixed! For those times when you do have to touch the code, we've used the Ace (http://ace.ajax.org/) as an inline editor, so you can make changes to your JavaScript in real-time.

Check out the BITE project page at http://code.google.com/p/bite-project. Feedback is welcome at bite-feedback@google.com. Posted by Joe Allan Muharsky from the Web Testing Technologies Team (Jason Stredwick, Julie Ralph, Po Hu, and Richard Bustamante are the members of the team who delivered the product).

Unleash the QualityBots

Thursday, October 06, 2011 1:52 PM
http://googletesting.blogspot.com/2011/10/unleash-qualitybots.html
By Richard Bustamante
Are you a website developer who wants to know if Chrome updates will break your website before they reach the stable release channel? Have you ever wished there was an easy way to compare how your website appears in all channels of Chrome? Now you can!

QualityBots (http://code.google.com/p/qualitybots/) is a new open-source tool for web developers created by the Web Testing team at Google. It's a comparison tool that examines web pages across different Chrome channels using pixel-based DOM analysis. As new versions of Chrome are pushed, QualityBots serves as an early warning system for breakages. Additionally, it helps developers quickly and easily understand how their pages appear across Chrome channels.

QualityBots is built on top of Google AppEngine (http://code.google.com/appengine/) for the frontend and Amazon EC2 for the backend workers that crawl the web pages. Using QualityBots requires an Amazon EC2 account to run the virtual machines that will crawl public web pages with different versions of Chrome. The tool provides a web frontend where users can log on and request URLs they want to crawl, see the results from the latest run on a dashboard (see Figure C.3), and drill down to get detailed information about what elements on the page cause the trouble.

Developers and testers can use these results to identify sites that need attention due to a high amount of change and to highlight the pages that can be safely ignored when they render identically across Chrome channels (see Figure C.4). This saves time and the need for tedious compatibility testing of sites when nothing has changed.

FIGURE C.3   Example results of a QualityBot Test run. The differences in this website between versions is displayed.

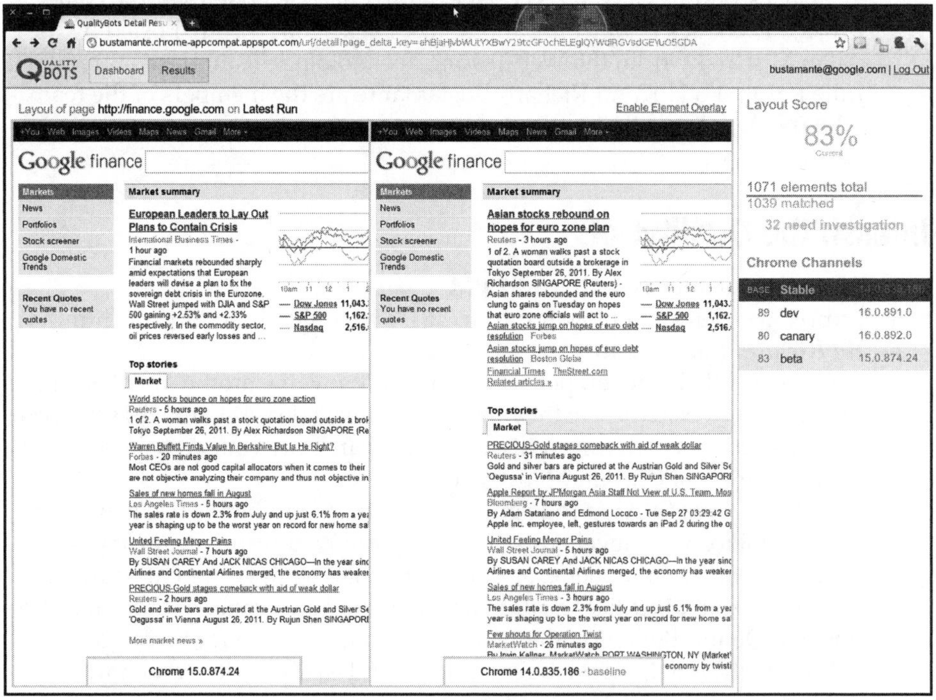

FIGURE C.4 QualityBot dashboard for Chrome across a range of websites tested across different versions of Chrome.

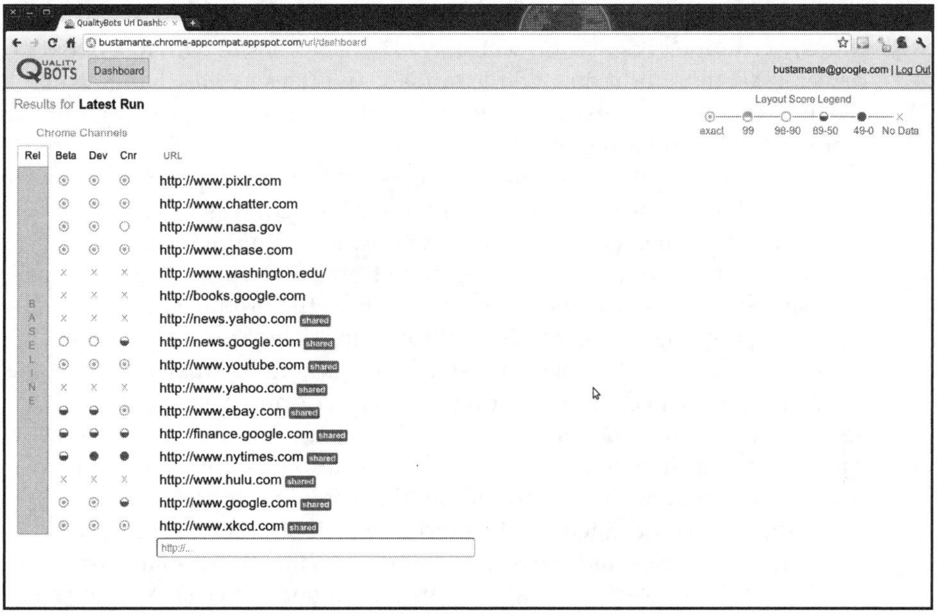

We hope that interested website developers will take a deeper look and even join the project at the QualityBots project page (http://code.google.com/p/qualitybots/). Feedback is more than welcome at qualitybots-discuss@googlegroups.com.

Posted by Ibrahim El Far, Web Testing Technologies Team (Eriel Thomas, Jason Stredwick, Richard Bustamante, and Tejas Shah are the members of the team who delivered this product).

RPF: Google's Record Playback Framework

Thursday, November 17, 2011 5:26 AM

http://googletesting.blogspot.com/2011/11/rpf-googles-record-playback-framework.html

By Jason Arbon

At GTAC (http://www.gtac.biz/), folks asked how well the Record/Playback Framework (RPF) works in the Browser Integrated Test Environment (BITE) (http://googletesting.blogspot.com/2011/10/take-bite-out-of-bugs-and-redundant.html). We were originally skeptical ourselves, but figured somebody should try. Here is some anecdotal data and some background on how we started measuring the quality of RPF.

The idea is to just let users use the application in the browser, record their actions, and save them as JavaScript to play back as a regression test or repro later. Like most test tools, especially code-generating ones, it works most of the time but it's not perfect. Po Hu had an early version working and decided to test this out on a real-world product. Po, the developer of RPF, worked with the Chrome web store team to see how an early version would work for them. Why the Chrome web store (https://chrome.google.com/webstore/)? It is a website with lots of data-driven UX, authentication, and file upload, and the site was changing all the time and breaking existing Selenium (http://seleniumhq.org/) scripts: a pretty hard web testing problem.

Before sharing with the Chrome web store test developer Wensi Liu, we invested a bit of time in doing something we thought was clever: fuzzy matching and inline updating of the test scripts. Selenium rocks, but after an initial regression suite is created, many teams end up spending a lot of time simply maintaining their Selenium tests as the products constantly change. Rather than simply fail like the existing Selenium automation would do when a certain element isn't found, and rather than require some manual DOM inspection—updating the Java code and re-deploying, re-running, and re-reviewing the test code—what if the test script just kept running and updates to the code could be as simple as point and click? We would keep track of all the attributes in the element recorded, and when executing, we would calculate the percent match between the recorded attributes and values and those found while running. If the match isn't exact, but within tolerances (say only its parent node or class attribute had changed), we would log a warning and keep executing the test case. If the next test steps appeared to be working as well, the tests would keep executing during test passes and log only warnings, or if in debug mode, they would pause and allow for a quick update of the matching rule with point and click via the BITE UI. We figured this might reduce the number of false-positive test failures and make updating them much quicker.

We were wrong, but in a good way!

We talked to the tester after a few days of leaving him alone with RPF. He'd already re-created most of his Selenium suite of tests in RPF, and the tests were already breaking because of product changes (its a tough life for a tester at Google to keep up with the developers' rate of change). He seemed happy, so we asked him how this new fuzzy matching fanciness was working, or not. Wensi was like, "Oh yeah, that? Don't know. Didn't really use it..." We started to think how our update UX could have been confusing or not discoverable, or broken. Instead, Wensi said that when a test broke, it was just far easier to re-record the script. He had to re-test the product anyway, so why not turn recording on when he manually verified things were still working, remove the old test, and save this newly recorded script for replay later?

During that first week of trying out RPF, Wensi found:

- 77 percent of the features in Webstore were testable by RPF.

- Generating regression test scripts via this early version of RPF was about eight times faster than building them via Selenium/WebDriver.

- The RPF scripts caught six functional regressions and many more intermittent server failures.

- Common setup routines such as login should be saved as modules for reuse (a crude version of this was working soon after).

- RPF worked on Chrome OS, where Selenium, by definition, could never run because it required client-side binaries. RPF worked because it was a pure cloud solution, running entirely in the browser and communicating with a backend on the Web.

- Bugs filed via BITE provided a simple link, which would install BITE on the developer's machine and re-execute the repros on their side. There was no need for manually crafted repro steps. This was cool.

- Wensi wished RPF was cross-browser. It worked only in Chrome, but people did occasionally visit the site with a non-Chrome browser.

So, we knew we were onto something interesting and continued development. In the near term, though, Chrome web store testing went back to using Selenium because that final 23 percent of features required some local Java code to handle file upload and to secure checkout scenarios. In hindsight, a little testability work on the server could have solved this with some AJAX calls from the client.

We performed a check of how RPF faired on some of the top sites of the web. This is shared on the BITE project wiki (https://docs.google.com/spreadsheet/ccc?key=0AsbIZrIYVyF0dEJGQV91WW9McW1fMjItRmhzcWkyanc#gid=6). This is now a little bit out of date with a lot more fixes, but it gives you a feel for what doesn't work. Consider it Alpha quality at this point. It works for most scenarios, but there are still some serious corner cases.

Joe Allan Muharsky drove a lot of the UX (user experience) design for BITE to turn our original and clunky developer and functional-centric UX into something intuitive. Joe's key focus was to keep the UX out of the way until it is needed and to make things as self-discoverable and findable as possible. We haven't done formal usability studies yet, but we have done several experiments with external crowd testers using these tools and with minimal instructions, as well as internal dogfooders filing bugs against Google Maps with little confusion. Some of the fancier parts of RPF have some hidden Easter eggs of awkwardness, but the basic record and playback scenarios seem to be obvious to folks.

RPF has graduated from the experimental centralized test team to a formal part of the Chrome team, and it is used regularly for regression test passes. The team also has an eye on enabling the noncoding crowd; sourced testers generate regression scripts via BITE / RPF.

Please join us in maintaining BITE / RPF (http://code.google.com/p/bite-project/), and be nice to Po Hu and Joel Hynoski who are driving this work forward at Google.

Google Test Analytics—Now in Open Source

Wednesday, October 19, 2011 1:03 PM
http://googletesting.blogspot.com/2011/10/google-test-analytics-now-in-open.html
By Jim Reardon
The test plan is dead!

Well, hopefully. At a STAR West session this past week, James Whittaker asked a group of test professionals about test plans. His first question: "How many people here write test plans?" About 80 hands shot up instantly, a vast majority of the room. "How many of you get value or refer to them again after a week?" Exactly three people raised their hands.

That's a lot of time being spent writing documents that are often long-winded and full of paragraphs of details on a project everyone already knows will get abandoned so quickly.

A group of us at Google set about creating a methodology that can replace a test plan; it needed to be comprehensive, quick, actionable, and have sustained value to a project. In the past few weeks, James has posted a few blogs about this methodology, which we've called ACC. It's a tool to break down a software product into its constituent parts, and the method by which we created "10 Minute Test Plans" (that takes only 30 minutes!).

Comprehensive

The ACC methodology creates a matrix that describes your project completely; several projects that have used it internally at Google have found coverage areas that were missing in their conventional test plans.

Quick

The ACC methodology is fast; we've created ACC breakdowns for complex projects in under half an hour. That is far faster than writing a conventional test plan.

Actionable

As part of your ACC breakdown, risk is assessed to the capabilities of your application. Using these values, you get a heat map of your project, showing the areas with the highest risk—great places to spend some quality time testing.

Sustained Value

We've built in some experimental features that bring your ACC test plan to life by importing data signals such as bugs and test coverage that quantify the risk across your project.

Today, I'm happy to announce that we're open sourcing Test Analytics (http://code.google.com/p/test-analytics/), a tool built at Google to make generating an ACC simple.

Test Analytics has two main parts; first and foremost, it's a step-by-step tool to create an ACC matrix (see Figure C.5) that's faster and much simpler than the Google Spreadsheets we used before the tool existed (see Figure C.6). It also provides visualizations of the matrix and risks associated with your ACC Capabilities that were difficult or impossible to do in a simple spreadsheet (see Figure C.7).

FIGURE C.5 Defining a project's attributes in Test Analytics.

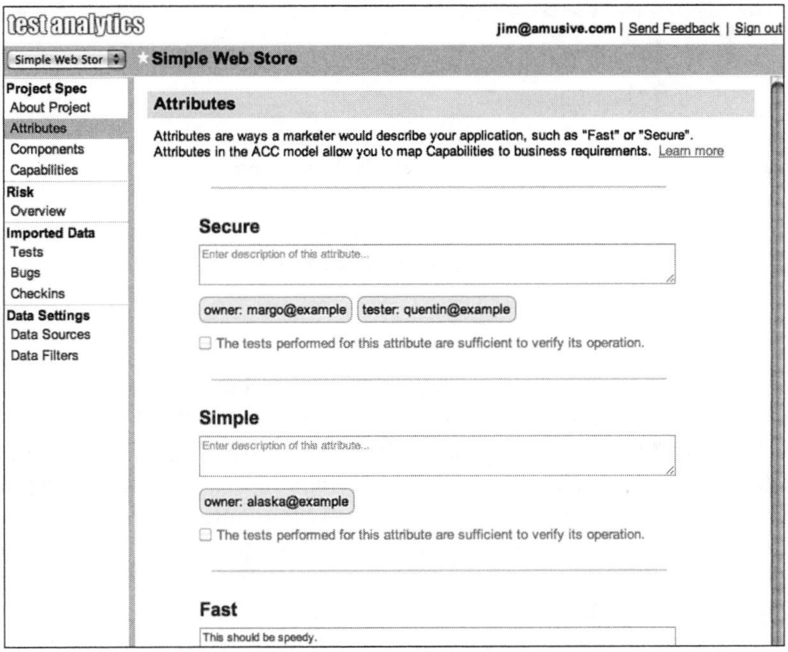

FIGURE C.6   Display of project capabilities in Test Analytics.

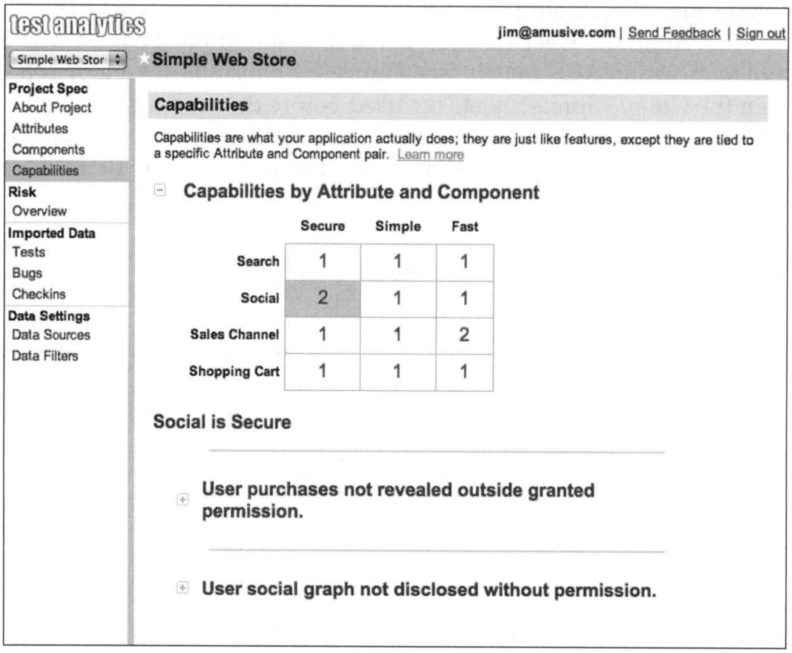

The second part is taking the ACC plan and making it a living, automatic-updating risk matrix. Test Analytics does this by importing quality signals from your project: Bugs, Test Cases, Test Results, and Code Changes. By importing this data, Test Analytics lets you visualize risk that isn't just estimated or guessed, but based on quantitative values. If a Component or Capability in your project has had a lot of code change or many bugs are still open or not verified as working, the risk in that area is higher. Test Results can provide a mitigation to those risks; if you run tests and import passing results, the risk in an area gets lower as you test.

FIGURE C.7 Displaying the risk across the matrix of attributes and components in Test Analytics.

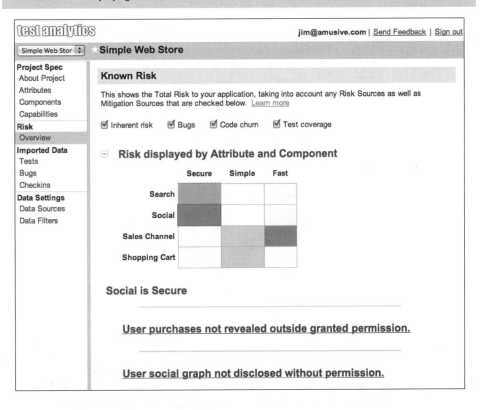

This part is still experimental; we're playing around with how we calculate risk based on these signals to best determine risk (see Figure C.8). However, we wanted to release this functionality early so we can get feedback from the testing community about how well it works for teams so we can iterate and make the tool even more useful. It'd also be great to import even more quality signals; code complexity, static code analysis, code coverage, external user feedback, and more are all ideas we've had that could add an even higher level of dynamic data to your test plan.

FIGURE C.8 Test Analytics binding to bug and test case data.

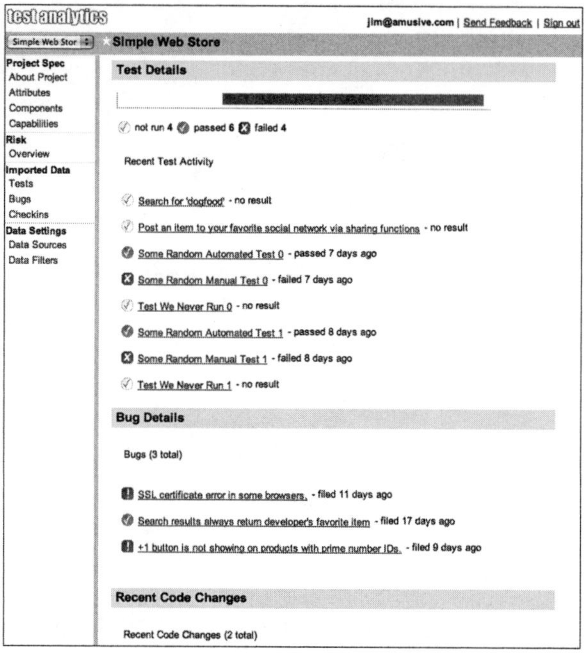

You can check out a live hosted version (http://goo.gl/Cv2QB), browse, or check out the code (http://code.google.com/p/test-analytics/) along with documentation (http://code.google.com/p/test-analytics/wiki/AccExplained), and of course, if you have any feedback, let us know. There's a Google Group set up for discussion (http://groups.google.com/group/test-analytics-discuss) where we'll be active in responding to questions and sharing our experiences with Test Analytics so far.

Long live the test plan!

Index

informIT.com
THE TRUSTED TECHNOLOGY LEARNING SOURCE

PEARSON

InformIT is a brand of Pearson and the online presence for the world's leading technology publishers. It's your source for reliable and qualified content and knowledge, providing access to the top brands, authors, and contributors from the tech community.

Addison-Wesley • Cisco Press • EXAM/CRAM • IBM Press. • que • PRENTICE HALL • SAMS • Safari Books Online

---

LearnIT at InformIT

Looking for a book, eBook, or training video on a new technology? Seeking timely and relevant information and tutorials? Looking for expert opinions, advice, and tips? **InformIT has the solution.**

- Learn about new releases and special promotions by subscribing to a wide variety of newsletters.
  Visit **informit.com/newsletters**.

- Access FREE podcasts from experts at **informit.com/podcasts**.

- Read the latest author articles and sample chapters at **informit.com/articles**.

- Access thousands of books and videos in the Safari Books Online digital library at **safari.informit.com**.

- Get tips from expert blogs at **informit.com/blogs**.

Visit **informit.com/learn** to discover all the ways you can access the hottest technology content.

Are You Part of the IT Crowd?

Connect with Pearson authors and editors via RSS feeds, Facebook, Twitter, YouTube, and more! Visit **informit.com/socialconnect**.

informIT.com
THE TRUSTED TECHNOLOGY LEARNING SOURCE

PEARSON

Addison-Wesley • Cisco Press • EXAM/CRAM • IBM Press. • que • PRENTICE HALL • SAMS • Safari Books Online

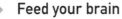

How **Google** Tests Software

Help me test like Google

Life of a TE
Life of an SET
Interviews with Googlers
more™

James Whittaker · Jason Arbon · Jeff Carollo

Safari.
Books Online

FREE
Online Edition

Your purchase of *How Google Test Software* includes access to a free online edition for 45 days through the **Safari Books Online** subscription service. Nearly every Addison-Wesley Professional book is available online through **Safari Books Online**, along with thousands of books and videos from publishers such as Cisco Press, Exam Cram, IBM Press, O'Reilly Media, Prentice Hall, Que, Sams, and VMware Press.

Safari Books Online is a digital library providing searchable, on-demand access to thousands of technology, digital media, and professional development books and videos from leading publishers. With one monthly or yearly subscription price, you get unlimited access to learning tools and information on topics including mobile app and software development, tips and tricks on using your favorite gadgets, networking, project management, graphic design, and much more.

Activate your FREE Online Edition at
informit.com/safarifree

STEP 1: Enter the coupon code: ZHPPYYG.

STEP 2: New Safari users, complete the brief registration form.
Safari subscribers, just log in.

If you have difficulty registering on Safari or accessing the online edition,
please e-mail customer-service@safaribooksonline.com